Mastering
Legal Analysis and Drafting

Carolina Academic Press Mastering Series

Russell L. Weaver, Series Editor

Mastering Bankruptcy
George W. Kuney

Mastering Civil Procedure
David Charles Hricik

Mastering Constitutional Law
John C. Knechtle, Christopher Roederer

Mastering Corporate Tax
Reginald Mombrun, Gail Levin Richmond, Felicia Branch

Mastering Corporations and Other Business Entities
Lee Harris

Mastering Criminal Law
Ellen S. Podgor, Peter J. Henning, Neil P. Cohen

Mastering Evidence
Ronald W. Eades

Mastering Family Law
Janet Leach Richards

Mastering Intellectual Property
George W. Kuney, Donna C. Looper

Mastering Legal Analysis and Communication
David T. Ritchie

Mastering Legal Analysis and Drafting
George W. Kuney, Donna C. Looper

Mastering Negotiable Instruments (UCC Articles 3 and 4) and Other Payment Systems
Michael D. Floyd

Mastering Products Liability
Ronald W. Eades

Mastering Professional Responsibility
Grace M. Giesel

Mastering Secured Transactions
Richard H. Nowka

Mastering Statutory Interpretation
Linda D. Jellum

Mastering Tort Law
Russell L. Weaver, Andrew R. Klein, Edward C. Martin, Paul J. Zwier II, Ronald W. Eades, John H. Bauman

Mastering
Legal Analysis and Drafting

George W. Kuney

W.P. Toms Distinguished Professor of Law and Director of the
James L. Clayton Center for Entrepreneurial Law
University of Tennessee College of Law

Donna C. Looper

Adjunct Professor of Law
University of Tennessee College of Law

Carolina Academic Press
Durham, North Carolina

Library of Congress Cataloging in Publication Data

Kuney, George W.
Mastering legal analysis and drafting / George W. Kuney, Donna C. Looper.
p. cm.
Includes bibliographical references.
ISBN 978-1-59460-628-1 (alk. paper)
1. Legal composition. 2. Law--United States--Language. 3. Legal research--United States. 4. Law--United States--Methodology. I. Looper, Donna C. II. Title.
KF250. K86 2009
808'.06634--dc22
2009024760

Carolina Academic Press
700 Kent Street
Durham, NC 27701
Telephone (919) 489-7486
Fax (919) 493-5668
www.cap-press.com

Printed in the United States of America
2021 Printing

To Carolyn and Don

Contents

Table of Cases

Table of Statutes, Rules, and Regulations

Series Editor's Foreword

The Carolina Academic Press Mastering Series is designed to provide you with a tool that will enable you to easily and efficiently "master" the substance and content of law school courses. Throughout the series, the focus is on quality writing that makes legal concepts understandable. As a result, the series is designed to be easy to read and is not unduly cluttered with footnotes or cites to secondary sources.

In order to facilitate student mastery of topics, the Mastering Series includes a number of pedagogical features designed to improve learning and retention. At the beginning of each chapter, you will find a "Roadmap" that tells you about the chapter and provides you with a sense of the material that you will cover. A "Checkpoint" at the end of each chapter encourages you to stop and review the key concepts, reiterating what you have learned. Throughout the book, key terms are explained and emphasized. Finally, a "Master Checklist" at the end of each book reinforces what you have learned and helps you identify any areas that need review or further study.

We hope that you will enjoy studying with, and learning from, the Mastering Series.

Russell L. Weaver
Professor of Law & Distinguished University Scholar
University of Louisville, Louis D. Brandeis School of Law

About the Authors

George W. Kuney (http://www.law.utk.edu/faculty/kuney/) is a W. P. Toms Distinguished Professor of Law and the Director of the Clayton Center for Entrepreneurial Law at the University of Tennessee College of Law in Knoxville, Tennessee. He holds a J.D. from the University of California, Hastings College of the Law, an M.B.A. from The University of San Diego, and a B.A. in economics from the University of California, Santa Cruz. Before joining the UT faculty in 2000, he was a partner in the Allen Matkins firm's San Diego office. Previously he practiced with the Howard Rice and Morrison & Foerster firms in his hometown of San Francisco, doing litigation and transactional work largely in the context of business restructuring and insolvency. During this time, he taught Legal Drafting and Advanced Legal Drafting as an adjunct professor at Hastings College of the Law and California Western School of Law.

At the University of Tennessee, he teaches business law courses including Contracts, Contract Drafting, Commercial Law, Property, Debtor-Creditor, Mergers and Acquisitions, Representing Enterprises, and Workouts and Reorganizations. Kuney writes books and articles about business, contracts, and commercial law and insolvency-related topics; advises clients nationwide regarding bankruptcy, restructuring, and reorganization; and conducts training seminars for law firm associates and summer associates regarding business law and transactional drafting. He is admitted to practice law in California and Tennessee.

Donna C. Looper is an Adjunct Professor of Law at the University of Tennessee College of Law, Knoxville, Tennessee, where she teaches Legal Process. She received her J.D. in 1989 from the University of California, Hastings College of the Law and her A.B. in 1984 from Barnard College, Columbia University. She clerked for the Chief Judge of the United States District Court for the Eastern District of Louisiana and then for the United States Court of Appeals for the Ninth Circuit. Before teaching at the University of Tennessee College of Law, Ms. Looper was a Senior Attorney for the California Court of Appeal, Fourth District, Division One and, prior to that, was in private practice in San Diego and San Francisco. She is an author of CALIFORNIA LAW OF CONTRACTS (CEB) and MASTERING INTELLECTUAL PROPERTY (Carolina Academic Press) with George Kuney. She is admitted to practice law in California and Tennessee and consults in matters nationwide.

Acknowledgments

This book would not have been possible without substantial contributions of time and effort on the part of the members of the firms and courts that we have worked for across the country. Any list of those to whom we are indebted for teaching us about legal analysis and drafting is necessarily incomplete. That said, the following individuals have contributed materially to our understanding of legal drafting and our attempts to teach that skill to law students and lawyers: Margreth Barrett, Barbara J. Cox, Peter J. Gurfein, Thomas R. Haggard, the Hon. Fredrick J. R. Hebe, Joan Heminway, Adam A. Lewis, Mark and Mary Jendrek, Robert M. Lloyd, Walter C. Machnicki, the Hon. Alex C. McDonald, the Hon. James A. McIntyre, Carol McCrehan Parker, Stacie L. Odeneal, Nancy B. Rapoport, Tina Stark, Mary Ann Darr Wegman, and our students at Hastings College of the Law, California Western School of Law, and The University of Tennessee College of Law who have helped us to better understand what should be done to begin to master legal analysis and drafting.

The works of other authors have also influenced our views and must be acknowledged. These include: M. Douglass Bellis, *Statutory Structure and Legislative Drafting Conventions: A Primer for Judges* (Federal Judicial Center, 2008); Richard K. Neuman, Jr., Sheila Simon, Legal Writing (Aspen Publishers, 2008); David T. Ritchie, Mastering Legal Analysis and Communication (Carolina Academic Press, 2008); Helene S. Shapo, Marilyn R. Walter, Elizabeth Fajans, Writing and Analysis in the Law (Foundation Press, 5th ed. 2008); Bret Rappaport, *A Shot Across the Bow: How to Write an Effective Demand Letter*, 5 Journal of the Association of Legal Writing Directors, 32 (2008); Charlotte Norris, Texas Legislative Council Drafting Manual (2008); Thomas R. Haggard, George W. Kuney, Legal Drafting in a Nutshell (Thomson/West, 2d ed. 2007); The Bluebook, A Uniform System of Citation (The Harvard Law Review Association, 18th ed. 2006); George W. Kuney, The Elements of Contract Drafting (Thompson/West 2d ed. 2006); Richard C. Wydick, Plain English for Lawyers (Carolina Academic Press, 5th ed. 2005); David E. Sullivan, Massachusetts Senate Legislative Drafting and Legal Manual (3d ed. 2003); Margaret Z. Johns, Professional Writing for Lawyers, Skills and Responsibilities (Carolina Academic Press, 1998).

Introduction

Legal drafting is different from other forms of writing. It is purposeful writing meant to inform, persuade, and memorialize events and legal analysis. Good legal drafting is marked by precision, exactitude, lack of ambiguity, and an absence of unnecessary vagueness. Many of the legal drafting books on the market are especially suited for those that have already mastered the basic skills of legal drafting and, especially, for those that seek to instruct others in that field. This book does not seek to replicate what those books and their authors have already accomplished. Rather, it is meant as a first tier, comprehensive book on legal drafting in a variety of contexts. As a result, we seek to emphasize the fundamental structures and methods of legal writing, which are grounded in a surprisingly few, elemental rules and techniques of legal analysis and presentation.

This book is unabashedly a *how to* book. It is designed to help the beginning or intermediate legal drafter identify those elemental rules and techniques and show how they are used to prepare effective legal writing in different formats, which share common elements and structures. The goal is to provide a plan of attack to produce quality work product of the type most commonly encountered in private practice and public service in the United States today. The focus is largely structural, as the structure of legal analysis drives the form and substance of all legal work product.

It is important for the legal drafter to lay aside habits that have been successful in other venues, primarily the habit of jumping to conclusions. Outside of the legal profession, being able to reach the right answer or course of action quickly, even instinctively, is rewarded. In the restaurant trade, the larger the number of meals or drinks served or dishes washed in a given time period, the better. In business, the ability to scan the market and competitors, quickly identifying your company's strengths, weaknesses, opportunities, and threats is rewarded. Although these abilities have a place in legal work, unlike these other fields, in law and legal drafting you need to *slow down and show your work*. Each step in the analysis should be explicitly stated, and no assumption beyond a common understanding of American English usage and style should be presumed. Law students frequently run up against this requirement of explicitly balanced reasoning when they receive the negative comment "conclusory" on their work product. This same sentiment, when expressed by a court, comes in the form of "motion denied—counsel has failed to make her case," and when expressed by a reviewing court as "the decision below is vacated and remanded for proceedings consistent with this opinion."

All legal analysis and writing should be concerned with explicitly identifying every link in a chain of reasoning. As was the case with long division in grade school, even if you get the right answer, you are not awarded points if you do not show your work. A court's legal opinion in support of a ruling is an obvious example. There, the court lays out the facts, lays out the applicable law as urged by the parties in their motions and briefs, and then applies that law to the facts at issue to reach a conclusion. The opinion, if it is well written, captures the whole chain of reasoning and allows an appellate court to examine each link on appeal to determine if the decision is sound.

The same can be said of motions and briefs. The goal of these documents is to persuade the court to rule a certain way and, ideally, adopt the lawyer's reasoning in the court's opinion. The audience is the court, which will examine the motion or brief and the chain of reasoning it contains to determine if it is sound. Letters to clients or opposing counsel or to an agency are no different. They seek to inform and persuade by providing a chain of reasoning to support their request, demand, or conclusion. For each, the audience expects to be able to examine the chain of reasoning.

The book begins with a discussion of legal analysis, followed by a chapter on legal drafting in general, and a chapter on citation form. These are followed by chapters on specific forms of legal drafting: letters, research memoranda, motions and supporting documents, appellate briefs, contracts and instruments, and legislation. It closes with some final thoughts on writing for the record —which is what legal analysis and drafting is all about.

The book is intended for reading and reference and is also suited for a law school legal drafting class if supplemented by appropriate problems and other assignments. The authors are happy to share past experience and discuss assignments with instructors using the book for such as class. You can contact them via email at gkuney@utk.edu.

George W. Kuney
Donna C. Looper
The University of Tennessee
Knoxville, Tennessee

Mastering
Legal Analysis and Drafting

Chapter 1

Legal Analysis

Roadmap

- This chapter examines the process of legal analysis, which involves a combination of (1) isolating and understanding individual components of the law and (2) fitting them together and explaining them as a whole.
- Statements of law are statements of what is required, permitted, forbidden, or considered in various circumstances, or what results in certain circumstances.
- Statements of law can usefully be thought of as rules or standards comprised of elements or factors.
- Tools for analyzing and interpreting statutes include using tabulation to make the statute into a checklist, analyzing the statute's structure, considering applicable case law, using the "plain meaning" rule, reviewing legislative history, looking at similar statutes in other jurisdictions, using the canons of construction, and reading law review articles and other commentary.
- When reading cases, read actively with the purpose of determining what statements of law the court used and how it applied them to the facts.
- The goal of legal analysis is to produce a synthesized understanding of the law, including statutes and case law, and how they are applied; mere sequential statutory and case analysis is insufficient.
- The basic structure for all legal analysis is IRAC (issue, rule, application/analysis, conclusion) or its advocacy-crafted cousin CRAC (conclusion, rule, application/analysis, conclusion).

Legal analysis is a system of breaking things down—be they rules, statutes, cases, etc., and then fitting the parts together into a cohesive whole. In this chapter, we explain the basic tools of legal analysis and how to use them.

A. Statements of the Law—Rules

Statements of law or rules come from a variety of sources, *e.g.*, statutes, cases, contacts, regulations, ordinances. There are several categories or types of laws. A law can be a statement of:

What is *required* in particular circumstances: "Drivers and passengers in motor vehicles must wear seat belts."

What is *permitted* in particular circumstance: "Roller skating is permitted in designated areas of the park."

What is *forbidden* in particular circumstances: "Convicted Felons are forbidden from carrying firearms."

What is the legal *result* of particular circumstances: "Unauthorized Persons who park in handicapped zones are guilty of a motor vehicle infraction and subject to a fine of $500 to $1000."

What is *considered* in determining if a result occurs or whether a law applies: "Custody determinations shall be based on the best interest of the child and shall include such considerations as: (1) The emotional bond that exists between the parent and child; (2) the ability of the parent to provide for the basic needs of the child, generally established by past practice and coinciding future ability; (3) the ability of the parent to continue the stable schedule/structure of the child; (4) the stability of the potential parent's family unit; (5) the mental/physical health of the potential parent; (6) the school/community record of the child; (7) the reasonable preference of the child 12 or older; (8) any prior abuse to the child; (9) the character of frequent guests/associates that would be around the child; and (10) the willingness of parent to nurture an ongoing and positive relationship with the other parent."

Statements of law are also set out as definitions, specific tests, or more vague standards, for example, "reasonableness." Statements of law may involve *elements*—things that are required in order for a result to occur—or *factors*—things that should be considered when deciding whether a result occurs.

Often a series of laws will apply to an issue. In other words, do not assume there will be only one applicable law or that a governing statute is *the* law.

The terms "statements of law" or "laws" include both rules, which are generally considered concrete, and standards, which are usually more flexible. Judge Richard Posner presented the distinction between rules and standards neatly in *MindGames, Inc. v. Western Publ'g Co.*, 218 F.3d 652, 656–57 (7th Cir. 2000):

> A rule singles out one or a few facts and makes it or them conclusive of legal liability; a standard permits consideration of all or at least most facts that are relevant to the standard's rationale. A speed limit is a rule; negligence is a standard. Rules have the advantage of being definite and of limiting factual inquiry but the disadvantage of being

> inflexible, even arbitrary, and thus over inclusive, or of being under inclusive and thus opening up loopholes (or of being *both* over- and under inclusive!). Standards are flexible, but vague and open-ended; they make business planning difficult, invite the sometimes unpredictable exercise of judicial discretion, and are more costly to adjudicate—and yet when based on lay intuition they may actually be more intelligible, and thus in a sense clearer and more precise, to the persons whose behavior they seek to guide than rules would be. No sensible person supposes that rules are always superior to standards, or vice versa, though some judges are drawn to the definiteness of rules and others to the flexibility of standards. But that is psychology; the important point is that some activities are better governed by rules, others by standards.

Judge Posner's categories of rules and standards are similar to the distinction drawn between elements and factors. As explained above, elements are things that must be found in order for a law to be triggered or a result to occur. Factors, on the other hand, are things that should be considered when deciding whether the law is triggered or if a result should occur.

Thus, because there can be considerable overlap among rules, standards, elements, and factors—this book uses the terms "statements of law" or "law" to encompass all. It is important in legal analysis and drafting that you be able to identify the character of the statements of law you use and confront. Below are strategies for reading and interpreting statements of law, distilling them from case law, and then explaining them to others. The discussion starts with analyzing and interpreting statutes since they are the primary source of law today.

B. Tools for Analyzing and Interpreting Statutes

1. Using Tabulation to Explode a Statute

Be alert in analyzing statutes. Statutes that are properly drafted constitute a checklist of sorts. Use a pen or pencil as you read so that you can explicitly divide the statute into elements (requirements) and factors (things to be considered), insert numbers and letters to tabulate these features, and pay close attention to words like "and" and "or" to determine how many requirements, options, and considerations there are under the statute. Reformatting a statute in tabular form on your word processor or on paper, focusing on these factors and elements, rather than looking at a large block of text, is often useful. This is your first tool for statutory interpretation.

By exploding the statute or statement of law into its constituent parts, you can identify each element or factor, and then analyze each of them in light of a given set of facts. This is much like the way engineering diagrams explode a product for which a patent is sought in order to explain the product:

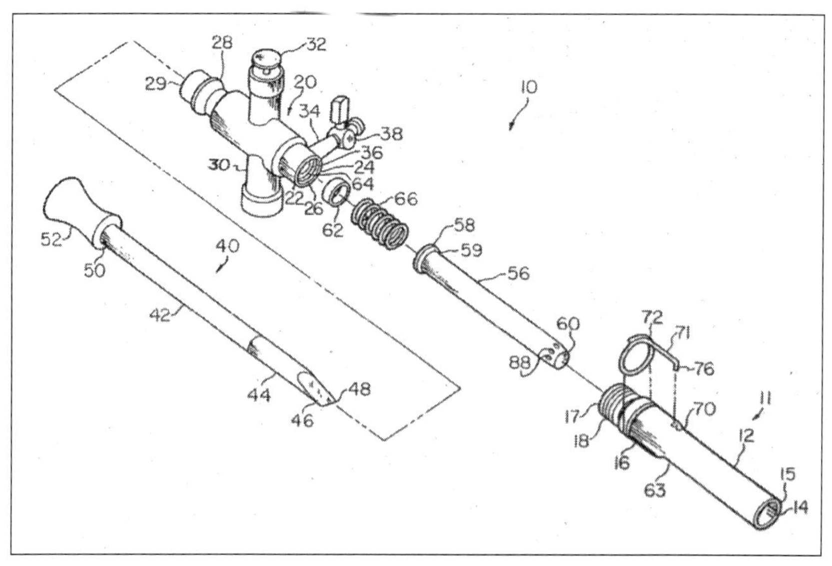

An "Exploded" Diagram.

This is the heart of legal analysis: (1) spotting the issues, (2) finding the applicable laws, (3) breaking those laws down into their constituent parts, (4) applying the parts to a set of facts to reach a conclusion.

For example, take Restatement (Second) of Contracts section 24, which operates like a statute and defines what constitutes an "offer":

> An offer is the manifestation of willingness to enter into a bargain, so made as to justify another person in understanding that his assent to that bargain is invited and will conclude it.

Even this relatively simple block of text will benefit by being reformatted in tabular form so that it resembles a checklist:

An offer is:

(a) the manifestation of

(b) willingness to enter into a bargain,

(c) so made as to justify another person in understanding that:

(i) his assent to that bargain is invited and

(ii) will conclude it.

Exploding the statute enables you to easily see each of the elements and sub-elements and allows you to then examine any particular set of facts under the standard, checklist style, to determine if each of the required elements is present.

For another example, take a sub-section of the UCC as enacted in California dealing with what additional terms in an acceptance or confirmation of an order mean. The legislature exploded the statute in the drafting process:

California Commercial Code § 2207(2)

The additional terms are to be construed as proposals for addition to the contract. Between merchants such terms become part of the contract unless:

(a) The offer expressly limits acceptance to the terms of the offer;

(b) They materially alter it; or

(c) Notification of objection to them has already been given or is given within a reasonable time after notice of them is received.

This sub-section opens with a statement that additional terms (in an acceptance or confirmation, discussed in § 2207(1)) are deemed to be merely proposals for addition to the contract. If the parties are not merchants, this is as far as the statute takes us—the additional terms are proposals, nothing more. Some additional acts of acceptance would be needed before they became part of the parties' contract.

This first sentence is followed by a second one that creates a presumption, *if the parties are merchants*, that the additional terms will be included in the contract unless one of three conditions is met. These conditions are phrased in the alternative, joined with an "or," which means that only one of them needs to be met to overcome the presumption.

Thus, the first and most important step in analyzing and interpreting statutes is to explode them into their component elements (requirements) and factors (things to be considered) creating a checklist that you can understand and explain to others.

2. Using the Structure and Other Sections of the Same Statute

Do not read a statute in a vacuum. After you explode a statute and create a comprehensible checklist, be sure to look at the entire body of related statutes to understand the structure of the whole. Often complex statutes or bodies of statutes will have logical divisions, perhaps first stating the scope of the enactment, then providing definitions of key terms, then containing positive provisions, standards, and rules; then exceptions and exemptions. All of these features can be used to understand the context of the specific statute at issue and to construe it appropriately under the circumstances. Indeed, one of the dangers of electronic research is that sections of a statute are usually displayed in isolation. Thus it is difficult not only to know how that section relates to others, but also to know whether that section is the one most germane to your issue. In order words, you may not be able to tell if there is a "better," more applicable section because you have not compared the section on the screen with others in the statutory scheme.

Moreover, there may be a section of the statute that sets out the legislative intent or policy reasons for enacting the statute or statutory scheme. For example, Chapter 2 of California's Welfare and Institutions Code provides a comprehensive scheme of juvenile court law pertaining to minor wards and delinquents. Section 202 sets forth the legislation's purposes, rules of construction, and includes definitions:

§ 202. Purpose; protective services; reunification with family; guidance for delinquents; accountability for objectives and results; punishment defined

> (a) The purpose of this chapter is to provide for the protection and safety of the public and each minor under the jurisdiction of the juvenile court and to preserve and strengthen the minor's family ties whenever possible, removing the minor from the custody of his or her parents only when necessary for his or her welfare or for the safety and protection of the public. If removal of a minor is determined by the juvenile court to be necessary, reunification of the minor with his or her family shall be a primary objective. If the minor is removed from his or her own family, it is the purpose of this chapter to secure for the minor custody, care, and discipline as nearly as possible equivalent to that which should have been given by his or her parents. This chapter shall be liberally construed to carry out these purposes.
>
> (b) Minors under the jurisdiction of the juvenile court who are in need of protective services shall receive care, treatment, and guidance consistent with their best interest and the best interest of the public. Minors under the jurisdiction of the juvenile court as a consequence of delinquent conduct shall, in conformity with the interests of public safety and protection, receive care, treatment, and guidance that is consistent with their best interest, that holds them accountable for their behavior, and that is appropriate for their circumstances. This guidance

may include punishment that is consistent with the rehabilitative objectives of this chapter. If a minor has been removed from the custody of his or her parents, family preservation and family reunification are appropriate goals for the juvenile court to consider when determining the disposition of a minor under the jurisdiction of the juvenile court as a consequence of delinquent conduct when those goals are consistent with his or her best interests and the best interests of the public. When the minor is no longer a ward of the juvenile court, the guidance he or she received should enable him or her to be a law-abiding and productive member of his or her family and the community.

(c) It is also the purpose of this chapter to reaffirm that the duty of a parent to support and maintain a minor child continues, subject to the financial ability of the parent to pay, during any period in which the minor may be declared a ward of the court and removed from the custody of the parent.

(d) Juvenile courts and other public agencies charged with enforcing, interpreting, and administering the juvenile court law shall consider the safety and protection of the public, the importance of redressing injuries to victims, and the best interests of the minor in all deliberations pursuant to this chapter. Participants in the juvenile justice system shall hold themselves accountable for its results. They shall act in conformity with a comprehensive set of objectives established to improve system performance in a vigorous and ongoing manner. In working to improve system performance, the presiding judge of the juvenile court and other juvenile court judges designated by the presiding judge of the juvenile court shall take into consideration the recommendations contained in subdivision (e) of Standard 5.40 of Title 5 of the California Standards of Judicial Administration, contained in the California Rules of Court.

(e) As used in this chapter, "punishment" means the imposition of sanctions. It does not include retribution and shall not include a court order to place a child in foster care as defined by Section 727.3. Permissible sanctions may include any of the following:

(1) Payment of a fine by the minor.

(2) Rendering of compulsory service without compensation performed for the benefit of the community by the minor.

(3) Limitations on the minor's liberty imposed as a condition of probation or parole.

> (4) Commitment of the minor to a local detention or treatment facility, such as a juvenile hall, camp, or ranch.
>
> (5) Commitment of the minor to the Division of Juvenile Facilities, Department of Corrections and Rehabilitation.
>
> (f) In addition to the actions authorized by subdivision (e), the juvenile court may, as appropriate, direct the offender to complete a victim impact class, participate in victim offender conferencing subject to the victim's consent, pay restitution to the victim or victims, and make a contribution to the victim restitution fund after all victim restitution orders and fines have been satisfied, in order to hold the offender accountable or restore the victim or community.

Thus, a lawyer analyzing other sections of California's Juvenile Court Law should do so with reference to § 202's statements of intent and purpose.

A statute or section often will not be as explicit as § 202 in indicating how terms should be interpreted. Thus, you should also examine how the same or similar words in other sections or subsections have been used. Have these words been interpreted by a court higher than the one that will hear you client's case? If so, should that interpretation also apply to the words as used in the statute that your are analyzing? There is a strong tendency in the law to give terms in similar statutes and rules the same, uniform meaning. For example, in *People v. Superior Court* (*Romero*), 917 P.2d 628 (Cal.1996), the California Supreme Court rejected the People's argument that words "prior offense" in section 667 (c)(2) of California's Three Strikes legislation meant "prior felony conviction." The court stated that this interpretation "makes no sense in context. Throughout the Three Strikes law, when the Legislature intended to refer to a previous conviction of an offense, as it did in many instances, it properly used the word 'conviction.' [citing Pen. Code] § 667, subds. (d), (d)(1), (d)(2), (d)(3), (e), (e)(1), (e)(2), (f)(1), (f)(2), (g)."

3. Using Case Law Interpreting a Statute

Often the section of the statute applicable to your matter has been interpreted by the courts. Case law interpreting a statute is your third tool of statutory construction. After you have exploded the statute and reviewed it in the context of its statutory scheme, you are ready to research and review case law dealing with the statute. Resist the urge to skip the first two steps and go directly to reading cases. Without a solid understanding of what the statute means, it will be much more difficult for you to grasp individual cases as well as synthesize them—put them together in logical order.

In dealing with statutes, courts may:

1. Determine if they are *valid*. Do they conflict with a higher authority? Does a state statute conflict with the state or federal constitution? Does a regulation or ordinance conflict with a higher ranked statute? Do rules from an appellate court case conflict with a rule or rules articulated in a Supreme Court case?
2. Determine *whether* a statute applies or *which* statute applies.
3. *Interpret* a statute—determine what its terms mean, what is required, permitted or forbidden under what circumstances.
4. *Apply* the statute to the facts before them and determine the outcome.

4. Plain Meaning—The Wording of the Statutory Section at Issue

Your fourth tool of statutory interpretation is the so-called "plain meaning" rule: Are the words of the statute clear and unambiguous? If so, then it is said that one should look no further and simply apply the terms of the statute in their plain and ordinary fashion. The plain meaning rule often comes into play when a court has not interpreted the terms at issue. Or you may conclude that a court's interpretation is contrary to the statute's plain meaning. Thus before turning to a plain meaning analysis, it is important to first explode a statute, analyze its terms in context of the whole statute, and search for case law dealing with it. Plain meaning is a useful tool, but beware. It can be too easy for courts to announce that the "meaning is plain" or that a proposed interpretation is "contrary to the plain meaning." The problem, of course, is that "plain meaning" is in the eye of the beholder.

For example, consider a procedural rule allowing enforcement of a judgment that is triggered when all *appeals* of a civil judgment are complete and opportunities for further *appeals* have been exhausted. Imagine that this rule was passed in the 19th century, when *appeals* to the United States Supreme Court were a matter of right if a federal issue had been preserved. Imagine further that it is now the 21st century and that, since the late 20th century, parties have no *appeal* of right to the United States Supreme Court. All that remains is the potential for discretionary review via a petition for a writ of certiorari. One of the parties to your client's dispute has exhausted its appeals but has petitioned for review by certiorari. Is the procedural rule triggered so that the judgment can be enforced before the petition for certiorari is ruled upon? One view is that the meaning of the rule is plain, all *appeals* are complete, so the judgment is collectable. The other view would be that events subsequent to the rule's enactment have changed matters and the meaning of the rule is not so plain. How should a court rule in the absence of any other information using the plain meaning rule? Answers may vary.

Also, it is easy to be seduced by the seeming mechanical nature of the plain meaning rule. This can lead you to embrace the fiction that, if you can convince a court that the meaning of statutory language is "plain," the court cannot look to extrinsic evidence such as legislative history to interpret the statute. Understand: If a court wants to, it will look at legislative history, no matter how plain the meaning. Whether the court will do anything with what it finds in that history is a different matter. But it takes more than a simple chant of "plain meaning" to put blinders on a court.

Raising a compelling plain meaning argument requires complete and thorough understanding of the statute, as well as any case law dealing with the statute. This should enable you to make an argument that is clear, concise and easy to grasp. Nothing is less compelling than a murky, convoluted argument that a proposed meaning is "plain."

5. Legislative History

The fifth tool of statutory interpretation is legislative history. Legislative history consists of documents and records created by the various parts of the legislature that enacted the statute. It includes statements of legislators regarding why they were in favor of a bill or why they opposed it, as well as different versions of a bill as it progressed through the legislative process. A good piece of legislative history can tip the balance in a question of how a statute should be interpreted when its meaning is less than plain and there are no judicial precedents on point.

Take care not to put too much stock in statements in legislative history, however. For every statement you find that you think supports your position, there may be just as many that support the opposite. Moreover, the statements of legislators can be written up and inserted in the Congressional Record after enactment and need never have been uttered to another person, much less made before a packed house of Congress. However, courts may give greater weight to analyses by a neutral staff professional, for example digests of bills by California's Legislative Counsel.

Legislative history also includes the various versions of the bill as it went though committees. Check to see what words were added or subtracted. This sort of analysis can bear fruit and is, perhaps, the most reliable form of legislative history that exists as it reflects the results of an actual deliberative process of the legislature.

Related to legislative history, also examine the state of the law before the statute was enacted. What was the historical context at the time of enactment? Does the section at issue codify a case? Overrule a case? Codify a case with changes? Each of these observations can be used to promote or undermine an interpretive argument regarding a statute.

6. Similar Statutes in the Same Jurisdiction

Although courts in your jurisdiction may not have addressed your statute, they may have addressed a similar statute. Examine what courts have said regarding similar words or elements, and ask if this reasoning can or should be applied by analogy to your client's case. For example, after enacting three strikes statutes, many states enacted two strikes statutes, and then even one strike statutes. In these states, case law interpreting terms and provisions in established three strikes legislation would be useful in interpreting similar terms or provisions in the new one and two strikes legislation.

7. Similar Statutes in Other States or Jurisdictions

If courts in the jurisdiction have not interpreted the same or a similar statue, determine if courts in other jurisdictions interpreted similar statutes. Especially in the case of uniform acts or restatements, often the opinions of courts in jurisdictions that were early adopters of the statute or principle can be very persuasive to courts in jurisdictions that are later adopters. Most judges would prefer not to reinvent the wheel, especially if doing so may subject them to reversal on appeal, and showing them how some other authoritative body has performed the analysis of the statute and applied it can be very persuasive.

8. Canons of Construction

The canons of construction are rules of statutory interpretation stated in the abstract. They include principles like "prefer the specific authority over the general" or the "last in time" rule which prefers more current statutes over older ones. The central, stated goal of all of these rules is to determine "the intent of the parties" although this is not a truly individualized "subjective" intent or some sort of rational "objective intent" but, rather, a sort of "collective subjective" opinion of intent based upon the reasonable interpretation of the facts of which the decision maker is allowed to take note. These canons are so general, however, that there are often more than one that might apply to a particular statute or contract provision, often in contradictory ways. As a result, it is often observed that the canons are seldom dispositive tools of legal analysis and are often used selectively to provide justification for an interpretation that has been decided upon for other reasons. Thus, although usually not dispositive, they are useful.

Some statutes contain their own rules of interpretation, such as a specification that the singular shall include the plural and the masculine gender shall include the feminine. See, for example, Title 1, Chapter 1, United States Code. Some of the other canons from the common law, which many states have codified, are listed below, with brief explanation, if necessary:

- *The Plain Meaning Rule.* If a statute's meaning is plain on its face, then one should not look beyond the four corners of the statute in interpreting it. Exceptions to this rule are found when an ambiguity can be found or when application of the rule would lead to absurd results.
- *The Rule of Strict Construction.* Often strict or narrow construction of statutes is said to be appropriate for statutes in derogation of the common law and statutes that deprive a court of jurisdiction.
- *The Rule of Liberal Construction.* Liberal or broad construction of remedial statutes is often said to be appropriate so as to give effect to their remedial intent.
- *Expressio Unis Est Exclusio Alterius.* To express one thing is to exclude another.
- *Ejusdem Generis.* When a sentence lists specific things and the list ends with phrases such as "etc.," "and the like," and "and others," the concluding general phrase should be limited by the listed specifics to things similar to those listed.
- *Noscitur a Sociis.* A word is known by its associates. In other words, interpret words in their context. This rule is particularly applicable to choosing the meaning of a homonym to be applied in a particular situation.
- *The Rule of Last Modification.* A qualifying phrase will modify only the immediately preceding word or phrase. (To avoid its application, place your qualification before any list, not after.)
- *Specific Language Trumps General Language.*
- *A Document Must Be Read as a Whole.*
- *Construe a Document Against its Drafter.*
- *Adopt a Construction that Favors Validity of a Contract or Statute.*
- *Adopt a Construction that is Consistent with Public Policy.*

9. Law Review Articles & Scholarly Commentary

Often, a student or professor or expert in the field has written a note, article, or treatise on the subject that you are working on. In these cases, it can be useful to refer to the note, article, or treatise for its suggested analysis. Often these sources, especially law review articles, are more useful for what they contain rather than for the conclusions that they reach—their footnotes collect authorities and can save you hours of research time. The article itself may be obtuse or too scholarly and removed from practice and practical reality to use directly—many are not about so much what the law *is* but what the law *should be*—but do not overlook the sources that have been collected there.

C. Reading Cases

Cases are the primary source of the interpretation, explanation, application, and determination of the validity of the law.

Legal reading, especially reading legal opinions, is not like reading a novel. Legal reading is confronting and attempting to digest the portions of a working document that are relevant to the legal inquiry at hand. This is one of the most difficult transitions for law students and new lawyers to make—developing the specific skill of *legal reading.*

Reading cases as a lawyer or as a student in a legal analysis or drafting class is different from reading cases for a traditional doctrinal law school class. The goal in reading cases for a traditional law school class is often to learn and examine legal principles and the way that they develop. Lawyers and legal drafting students read cases to solve problems and get good results. Good lawyers read cases strategically, focusing on the issues they need to address. Resist the inclination to read an opinion passively from the beginning to end. You should be just as alert in reading cases as you are in reading statutes. The focus is different, however. Often each word in a statute is important, which is why exploding a statute to identify each element or factor and their connectors is so effective. On the other hand, many times only certain parts of a judicial opinion are important or even relevant to the issues you are tackling.

Developing certain habits can increase your ability to read cases more effectively and efficiently. These habits include reading the case out of order, and focusing on the purpose of the reading. For example, one successful strategy for reading opinions is: (1) noting the date and jurisdiction first to put the case in its proper historic and procedural context, (2) finding the statement of the issue, (3) determining the ruling of the court below, (4) skipping to the end of the opinion to find out what the reviewing court does with regard to this issue, and (5) then searching in the discussion for the reasons why. Focus on the issues that are the same or similar to yours, and skim or skip discussions regarding issues that are not present in your assignment or dispute. Also, skim through the initial statement of facts, because many times the court will go over or highlight the facts that are important in its analysis and lead to its conclusion.

The order in which you read an opinion will vary based on the issues on which you are focusing and the way the opinion is written and structured. Just keep in mind that reading a case from start to finish is not always the most effective method of absorbing and understanding the pertinent material.

Attorneys hone opinion reading skills over years of practice. For newcomers to the law, these habits may seem odd or unnecessary. But developing a method to ensure time-efficient reading and digestion of legal precedent is critical to good lawyering, which is largely about absorbing, processing, mastering, and deploying large amounts of information. It is part of "working smarter, not harder."

The following subsections discuss considerations relevant to particular sections or features of judicial opinions and suggestions for approaching them in your reading.

1. Caption

The caption contains the names of the parties, the court rendering the decision, the date, and a citation or citations. Note the court from which the opinion comes, and then run through this checklist: (1) which jurisdiction does the opinion come from—is it the same as the jurisdiction your matter is in? (2) what level is the deciding court?—trial, appellate, or a supreme court or other court of last resort, (3) is the opinion designated as not for publication or otherwise restricted for precedential or citation purposes? (4) is the opinion binding and, if so, upon which courts in what jurisdiction? For discussion on binding versus nonbinding authority and the hierarchy of authority, see Chapter 3, section A(1).

The date of the opinion is important. First, you may be dealing with a statute that has been amended or recently enacted, or with a common law rule that has changed over the years. An opinion dated before a statute's or amendment's effective date, or before a change in the law will likely have little precedential value. Also, in general, the more recent an opinion, the better. If possible, one would like to be working with cases that are no more than ten years old except in special areas of law, like obscure areas of constitutional law, where precedents may be few and far between. That said, older cases can be valuable as long as one keeps in mind the context in which they were decided. Consider, for instance, a case from 1901, when automobiles were not standard means of transportation and the interstate highway system was not constructed. Such a case might have interesting things to say about the meaning of the word "vehicle" in a statute, but the context of the old case should be kept in mind when reading the case in light of the twenty-first century environment.

2. Summaries and Headnotes

These portions of a published opinion are added by the legal publisher and are not part of the court's decision. As a result, they should not be cited to or relied upon. However, they are useful tools in identifying the issues addressed and their location in the case.

A note of caution: Because summaries and headnotes are *not* part of the opinion, and were produced by the legal publisher, they may be less than accurate or may be a discussion of prior law or law that the court intended to overrule. They were not necessarily written by good lawyers or by lawyers at all.

3. Disposition

At the outset, check what the disposition was, *e.g.*, was the decision below affirmed, reversed, or vacated? This will give you perspective as you read. Courts often put things differently depending on whether they are affirming, reversing, modifying, or vacating and remanding. It is helpful to know where the court is heading before it gets there.

4. Procedural Facts

Most opinions set forth the procedural history of the case. Do not skip over this section. Instead review it strategically, noting:

(1) What type of action is being appealed, *e.g.*, a judgment after a jury verdict, default judgment, summary judgment, or evidentiary order;

(2) How the court below ruled or what the jury found;

(3) Who won, who lost, who is appealing; and

(4) On what grounds (if stated).

5. Underlying Facts

Almost every opinion contains a statement of facts, which explains the underlying story of the case and on which the opinion's legal analysis is based.

Some statements of fact can be quite lengthy. On the first reading try not to get bogged down—focus on the facts that pertain to the issues in the client's case. Attempt to categorize these facts as relevant, irrelevant, similar or different from the client's case. Often the important facts become apparent in the court's analysis or discussion section as they are used to reach conclusions. Thus, it is often best to go back and reread the statement of facts after you have finished the discussion section.

6. Issues

Look for any recitation of the issues by the court. Often, especially in more modern opinions, the court will set out the issues after its statement of the facts. Or, optimally, a court will do this at the beginning of the opinion in its introductory paragraph.

7. Statements of Law and Their Explanation

The law or rule section of an opinion may (1) determine whether particular laws are valid, (2) determine which or what laws apply; (3) interpret laws; and/or (4) explain laws, *e.g.*, how they work or why they are important.

Statements of the law can be slippery characters. Often opinions involving very specific situations contain general statements of the law that are perfectly appropriate for the case itself but are inaccurate when taken out of context and applied to different, even if analogous facts. There is rarely just one "law" or "*the* law." Think of laws as statements of what is required, permitted, or forbidden in particular circumstances, or what legally results from particular circumstances. Alternatively, think of them as listing what is required or considered in determining whether a legal result occurs, *e.g.*, whether someone is liable for a criminal or civil sanction. Statements of the law are also set out as definitions, tests or standards, with elements or factors of both. Explanations of laws often contain additional subsidiary or corollary laws.

The court may list categories or types of facts that are significant in determining if a standard has been met. These are known as *factors*—things to be considered. Factors are indicators that point to a likely result under a standard, as opposed to *elements*, which are requirements that must be met for a result to occur or a law to be triggered.

A case might have many statements of law. Try to pick out as many as you can and note their subject matter and which are based upon elements—things that are required—and which are based upon factors—things that should be considered. Also note if and how the court explains each statement of law.

Remember, in explaining the law, the court will often articulate other laws. For example, a court may state that in order for the defendant to be liable, the plaintiff must prove the defendant was negligent. Then the court may explain that proof of negligence requires a showing of (1) duty, (2) breach of the reasonable standard of care, (3) actual cause or cause in fact, (4) proximate cause, and (5) actual injury. Then for each, the court might explain the elements (requirements) and factors (things to be considered). Also be sure to check for principles of construction, *e.g.* "Criminal statutes should be narrowly construed." These will be useful in explaining the applicable law in a memorandum or brief.

8. Application of Law

When the court "applies the law," *i.e.*, discusses the facts of the case before it and why and how they meet or fail to meet the applicable laws, pay careful attention to facts the court indicates are significant. Remember that an opinion is a document drafted to support a ruling. What is included, omitted, emphasized, or downplayed is significant. Your goal is to identify the facts that are important in the court's analysis and resolution of the issues.

Not all opinions will have an application section, however. Sometimes they are not necessary, for example where a court determines that a particular law is invalid or does not apply the issue. However, other times, the court may set out the facts and the law and then announce its conclusion, without "showing its work." If that is the case, you will need to do your own application and determine which facts were significant to the court's analysis and why. Note: this sort of conclusory opinion represents suboptimal performance by a court or agency and may indicate an overburdened writing judge. Do not emulate this style.

9. Policy

In setting out or applying the law, a court may describe its reasoning in terms of the *policies* that the law is meant to promote. For example, statutes of limitations are meant to promote the timely adjudication of most disputes while memories and evidence are relatively fresh and to encourage law enforcement to promptly investigate and prosecute crimes. These goals are important for the efficient and accurate administration of justice. With particularly heinous crimes like first degree murder, this policy may be outweighed by other considerations such as the need to incarcerate, punish, or rehabilitate murderers, and, thus, there is no statute of limitations in any of the United State for first degree murder. Focus on policy discussions and evaluate how these statements might help or hurt the matter you are working on. Often policy discussions are, or are later characterized as, *dicta* (see below).

10. Holding

The holding is the court's decision on the issue along with the essential supporting facts or reasons. If the opinion has an application section, note what specific facts the court cites in coming to its conclusion. Practice setting forth holdings in citations with parentheticals—*Smith v. Jones*, ___ Rptr. ___ (Court, date) (holding that ______, when _________). Citations with parentheticals can be a very efficient and effective form of shorthand that captures the case name, citation, holding and essential facts in 2 to 3 lines of text. Considerations and methods of characterizing the holding of a case are discussed in Analyzing and Using Cases, below.

11. Dicta

Dicta, or, more fully, "*obter dicta*"—from the Latin for "something said in passing"—consist of statements included in an opinion that are not necessary to the court's holding. These statements go beyond the facts and circumstances before court and are not essential to its determination. *Dicta* can be very useful, however, in giving examples of how a rule or standard might or might not be met. To spot *dicta*, look for phrases like "for example," "such as" or "this is not a case where _______." These comments, while not binding in a technical sense as precedent, are often powerful indicators of a court's or a particular judge's attitude toward the issue discussed and how that judge might rule if faced with those facts or issues.

D. Analyzing and Using Cases

Lawyers do not read cases in the abstract. They read them with a focus on how they affect the client and the client's situation. The following sub-sections detail a checklist of things to consider when analyzing and using cases as a lawyer or as a student with a drafting assignment.

1. **Where does the case come from?** All cases are not created equal.

Is it from the same state or jurisdiction as your matter?

Which level of court decided the case—trial, appellate, or court of last resort?

When was the case decided—was it after the law(s) at issue took effect? In terms of hierarchy: the most recent case from the highest court in the pertinent jurisdiction is accorded the most weight. Then less recent cases from the highest court in the jurisdiction, assuming they are still good law and have not been overruled by later cases, or superseded by statute. Next are recent cases from appellate courts in the jurisdiction. Cases from outside the pertinent jurisdiction, other than cases from the United States Supreme Court, are not binding, although they may provide persuasive authority *if* the court chooses to consider them. See Chapter 3, section A(1) for further discussion on the hierarchy of authority.

2. **Does the case deal with the same issue as your problem or matter?** A similar issue? If so, how similar is it?

3. **What laws does the court apply or articulate?**

4. **What does the court say about those laws?** Anything to help explain them or why they are important, or to explain why they apply? Any policy statements—*e.g.* why the law is important, the purposes served? In other words, *distill the legal principles* from the cases.

5. ***What are the facts of the case?*** *Are they similar to the ones in your problem or matter? How? Are they different? How?*

6. **How does the court apply the laws to the facts?** What does the court say when it evaluates the facts based on the laws? What is its reasoning? Does it highlight certain types of facts as being important? Does it further explain any of the rules? Are there any helpful policy statements?

7. **What is the court's holding?**—The holding is the court's decision and the basis for it. How does the court decide the issue? How does the court describe the basis for its decision? Set forth the holding in a parenthetical, i.e., in one or two lines put in parentheses after the case citation. Depending on the client and their situation, it may be best to describe a holding so that it applies broadly or generally, e.g., Smith v. Jones (mandatory arbitration agreement in employment contract held unenforceable). At other times it is best to describe a holding in detail, so that it appears confined to specific facts, e.g., Smith v. Jones (mandatory arbitration agreement in employment contract held unconscionable and thus unenforceable, where it (a) lacked mutuality, (b) imposed pre-arbitration resolution procedure controlled by employer, and (c) severely limited time within which employee could request arbitration).

8. **Does the opinion contain any useful dicta?** The court may make statements that are not necessary to its holding, but that are helpful to your cause. Particularly look for when the court gives examples. Some of these can be very useful, especially when the court gives examples of how a rule or standard would or would not be met: "On the other hand, if the defendant had been carrying a knife he would have been guilty...."

E. Synthesizing Multiple Cases— Putting It All Together

There is a tendency for those new to legal analysis to engage in "sequential case analysis"—listing summaries of cases that appear relevant, leaving the reader to fit them together. Fitting cases together and making legal sense of them is the drafter's responsibility, however. Quality legal analysis is much more than just a "report" on the individual cases that deal with an issue. It should be a synthesized analysis of the laws and their application to particular facts. The drafter's job is to (1) *distill* the legal principles from multiple cases and explain what they are and how they relate to each other, *i.e.*, fit them together, and (2) *apply* those principles to the facts of the client's case and predict or advocate the outcome.

Another tendency among new legal drafters is to focus on a vague standard and repeat that standard as if this were analysis. For example, someone researching the law regarding legal restraints on alienation (transfer or sale of property) should find California Civil Code § 711, which states that restraints on alienation are valid and enforceable if they are "reasonable." Turning to the cases decided under § 711, the researcher would be met with many cases that repeat the reasonableness standard as the law. At this point the novice may conclude that the analysis is over—the answer is that the standard is "reasonableness." Reporting this result to a supervising attorney will either result in a bemused chuckle or a rebuke. The question the analysis should focus on is what factors should be considered under § 711's reasonableness standard—what types of facts, *i.e.*, factors, indicate a restraint is reasonable, or not. The list may appear to be dictated by common sense, but when it is common sense drawn from official judicial opinions, it carries greater weight and represents legal analysis that answers the question assigned.

1. Getting Started—Read the Most Recent Cases First

If more than one case appears applicable, read the cases in the order of newest to oldest. This is not typically the way that cases are assigned to first year law students in traditional law classes. In legal drafting, however, the goal is to cut through the development of the law and get to the current state of the law as efficiently as possible. It is likely that the later courts will have at least partially synthesized the cases already—meaning ideally, they will have distilled legal principles from prior cases, fit them together, and explained them. This is a starting point, and should give an indication of what the significant issues, laws, and cases are and how they evolved. Caution though: the courts might have missed things, made mistakes, or even intentionally obfuscated portions of prior cases—so read critically at all times.

2. After Reading the Cases, Write a Holding for Each

For each case, write out the holding on each issue addressed using a short parenthetical, *e.g. Smith v. Jones* (bar owner liable for employee's assault on a patron because bartender employee's duties included maintaining the peace, and thus it was foreseeable he would need to use force dealing with unruly patrons). It is important to develop your skill in setting forth specific factual holdings in connection with cases you use in your analysis. Think of these case names and holdings as building blocks and pieces that can be moved around on your analysis chart described below.

3. Sorting and Grouping

After reading the cases, newest to oldest and writing a holding for each, you should have an idea of the various issues or sub-issues involved. At this stage it is often useful to start a chart with the issues set out as categories. The next step is to sort the cases by issue. For each issue or category, note the relevant cases. Some cases may involve more than one issue and will be listed in multiple categories. Then for each issue, group the cases by result: cases that met the overall standard or requirements and those that did not. For example, if your problem involves whether a contract was formed, and the issues are (1) offer, (2) acceptance, and (3) consideration, you would first sort the cases into these three categories. Then, beginning with the first issue, offer, you would separate the cases in two groups: those holding there was an offer, and those holding there was not. The next step is to list those cases, with their holdings set out in parentheticals, on your chart (see example next page).

Notice there is a shorthand description of each case before the parenthetical containing the holding. Use this technique to help you remember and distinguish multiple cases. Also, it is best to get into the habit of *Bluebook*ing your case citations and providing a pin cite to the specific facts described in your parentheticals at the earliest opportunity. During the drafting stage you will not want to page through the cases again to find the information you need.

By sorting the cases with their holdings by issues and sub-issues and then grouping them by result, you will more easily recognize patterns, trends, and

Offer: Cases

Offer: Yes	Offer: No
Lefkowitz v. Great Minneapolis Surplus Store, 86 N.W.2d 689, 690 (Minn. 1957) (fur: offer) (Newspaper announcement stating: "Saturday, 9 AM sharp, 3 Brand New Fur Coats Worth $100.00, first come first served $1 each" was an offer).	*Leonard v. PepsiCo*, 88 F.Supp.2d 116, 117, 119 (S.D.N.Y. 1999) (Harrier jet: no offer) ("Pepsi Stuff" TV ad showing a Harrier jet with the subtitle "Harrier fighter 7,000,000 Pepsi Points" was not an offer).
Harris v. Time, Inc., 237 Cal. Rptr. 584, 586 (Cal. Ct. App. 1987) (calculator watch: offer) (Bulk mail letter picturing a calculator watch on the envelope and stating: "[Name of addressee] I'll give you this versatile new calculator watch for free just for opening this envelope before February 15, 1985" was an offer).	*Trell v. American Ass'n of Advancement of Science*, No. 04-CV-0030E(Sr.), 2007 W.L. 1500497 at *1 (W.D.N.Y. 2007) (news tips: no offer) (Internet ad on a science society's website seeking "news tips" and stating that a tip would be investigated for suitability as a news item on the website or as an article in the society's magazine was not an offer).
Johnson v. Capital City Ford Co., 85 So. 2d 75, 77 (La. Ct. App. 1956) (new model Ford: offer) (Newspaper ad stating that anyone who bought a 1954 within the remaining two weeks of September could later turn it in for the same model 1955 Ford was an offer).	*Mesaros v. United States*, 845 F.2d 1576, 1580-81 (Fed. Cir. 1988) (coin order form: no offer) (Mail advertisements sent by the United States Mint that contained an order form for the purchase of specific coins was not an offer).

factors that point to a particular result. You will also more easily recognize any commonalities between the cases.

4. Distilling and Synthesizing the Law

The essential function of synthesizing cases is distilling or extracting the laws from multiple cases and fitting them together so that you can explain the laws to your reader. To begin, review the chart you made in sorting and grouping cases—you will see what cases address the different issues and sub-issues in your matter. Then review each case separately and take down the statements of law made by the court and what the court says about them—how the court explains the laws. Statements of law come in many forms, including a list of requirements or considerations, tests, definitions, descriptions of standards, or rules of construction. Explanations of laws often contain additional statements of law.

Once you have isolated the statements of law and explanations in a case, note for each issue which of the statements of law are *elements* and which are *factors*. Elements are requirements. They must be present for a certain result to occur. Factors are indicators or considerations that may, or should, be taken into account is determining whether a standard has been met. Factors are types or categories of facts that point to a particular result, but do not mandate it. Remember not to mix up elements and factors or use the terms interchangeably. Often a court will identify factors in the law section of an opinion, e.g. "Factors include ..." Or when a court states "Important consideration are...." or "We look to whether [a description of various facts]," it is likely the court is describing factors.

After you have extracted the statements of laws on the pertinent issues from each case and determined their character, you are ready to put them together. For each issue, first look for statements of law that are repeated in the cases that overlap. These are likely your broad or overarching rules. If you detect any differences in wording or terms, review the cases and whether the differences make a difference. Did a court announce a change in the law or explain why it used the specific words it did? Did the different words yield different results? You may not be able to tell in the beginning of your analysis, but make an inquiry. Next, look for more specific or subsidiary rules that apply in more limited circumstances. These might be set out as definitions or tests or factors that further explain the broader, more general rules. Once you have assembled the statements of law for each issue and sub-issue, return to your chart and in each category write down the statements of law in order of broad/overarching ones to more narrow specific ones, along with the case(s) from which the statements came. Sometimes the statements of law will nest together easily, with broad statements of the general law, then lists of elements with specific tests and or factors for each. Other times, there will be "holes" of little or no statements of law on certain sub-issues. You will also find that statements of law may appear to contradict each other and cannot be neatly reconciled. That is all part of legal analysis and drafting. Your goal is to set forth and explain the law in a way your reader will easily understand—even if it is complicated.

When a case contains a list of factors, the court has helped synthesize them already. Other times you will have to synthesize factors yourself. To do this, for each case, note the type of facts the court considered significant in coming to its conclusion. Check first in the application section, where the court discusses whether the facts meet the rules, test or standards it had set out and explained. If the opinion does not have an application section—in other words, the court simply announces its decision after setting out the rules—reread the statement of facts in the opinion and sort out the facts that appear most significant to you. This is also where your sorting and grouping chart of case names and holdings is useful—review it and look for trends and similarities and differences in the facts of the cases that met the tests or standards and those that did not.

This process may seem tedious in the beginning, but with time it should become second nature. It is important that you go through the process so that your reader does not have to.

As an example, under the issue "offer" in the example above, after you have charted the cases and their holdings, the next section of the chart might contain these statements of law:

Offer: Laws

"Whether an advertisement is an offer rather than an invitation to make an offer depends on the legal intention of the parties and the surrounding circumstances." *Lefkowitz*, 86 N.W.2d at 691 (fur: offer)

"Whether an offer has been made depends on the objective reasonableness of the alleged offeree's belief that the advertisements or solicitation was intended as an offer." *Leonard v. PepsiCo* (harrier jet: no offer) .

The general rule is that advertisements do not constitute offers. *Leonard v. PepsiCo*, 85 F.Supp.2d at 122 (Harrier jet: no offer); *Trell*, 2007 W.L. 1500497 at *6(news tips: no offer); *Harris v. Time, Inc.*, 237 Cal. Rptr. at 587 (calculator watch: offer)

An exception is where the advertisement is "'clear, definite, and explicit, and leaves nothing open for negotiation.'" *Leonard v. PepsiCo*, 88 F.Supp.2d 124 (Harrier jet: no offer) (quoting *Lefkowitz*, 86 N.W.2d at 691);

> "There is, however, a fundamental exception to this rule: an advertisement can constitute an offer, and form the basis of a unilateral contract, if it calls for performance of a specific act without further communication and leaves nothing for further negotiation." *Harris v. Time, Inc.*, 237 Cal. Rptr. at 587 (calculator watch: offer) (citing but not quoting *Lefkowitz*, 86 N.W.2d at 691).

Note that there are two iterations of the exception to the general rule in the last two entries; these may or may not be significant, depending on the facts of your problem.

When making extracting statements of law from the cases and putting them in your chart, take the time to make sure the case citations are in proper *Bluebook* form and provide pin cites to the specific pages where those statements of law can be found. This will make the drafting process much smoother.

You likely will not use all the statements of law contained in your chart in your memorandum or brief, and you will probably be paraphrasing and/or combining various statements. However, you want to list the statements of law that appear relevant to the issue so that you can consider and evaluate them in the analysis and drafting processes.

F. Organizing Legal Analysis—the IRAC

In organizing and presenting legal analysis, two formats predominate:

IRAC: Issue, Rule, Application/Analysis, Conclusion

CRAC: Conclusion, Rule, Application/Analysis, Conclusion

The IRAC or CRAC format will form the basis of discussion on issues and subissues in memoranda, briefs, opinions, and almost any other form of legal drafting that predicts, advocates or defends an outcome. The two are variants of each other. IRAC is used for more neutral sounding analysis while CRAC is used for analysis with more of an advocacy slant.

The simple IRAC is the best strategy for tackling the traditional law exam essay question. First, identify all the issues a fact pattern presents, then for each issue state the applicable rule or law, or the majority and minority rules. Then apply the rule(s) or law(s) by discussing whether the facts in the problem meet or fail to meet those rule(s) or law(s), then state your conclusion, and move on to the next IRAC. In legal analysis and drafting, you will use a more complex variation of the basic IRAC—because this structure is usually the best way to deliver information in a way your reader can most easily understand. In office memoranda and supporting memoranda and briefs to courts, in addition to setting forth the statements of law, you will also need to *explain* them, *e.g.*, their purpose, how they operate, what factors are considered, and *illustrate* them by including specific factual examples from cases you have used in your analysis.

I. Identify the issues: A "legal issue" arises when there is a question as to whether the facts of the situation satisfy or trigger a governing law. In a legal analysis or drafting class, especially in the beginning, the issues presented in the problem may be identified for you, or made easier to identify if the problem quotes or cites to the applicable statute or other law. In the real world the client will often come with a description of events and ask "Can they do that?" or "Do I have a case?" The lawyer must then identify the issues based on her knowledge of the law.

To identify the issues that must be resolved to address your client's matter, you must identify:

1. The elements or factors of the applicable law, and
2. The facts that tend to prove or disprove each element and all relevant factors of the standard.

To select the issues that will merit detailed discussion:

- Focus on questions within the scope of your set of facts.
- Identify all relevant legal questions—outline the applicable laws and their relevant elements or factors.
- Exclude "givens" from detailed discussion. For example, if you are dealing with a statute that applies only within the city limits, and your client's property is squarely within these limits, you need only note this fact—you do not need an IRAC on this issue.
- Determine which elements or factors are present in your set of facts.
- Set forth issues/sub-issues in a "whether, when" format. For example: Whether there was an effective offer, when the customer asked the seller, "would you take $100 for that printer?"

Remember, an issue may have sub-issues. For each issue/sub-issue that merits discussion, construct an IRAC or a CRAC. Nest them in a hierarchy and provide introductory and conclusion paragraphs to transition the reader through the hierarchy.

R. Identify, Explain and Illustrate the Rules—the Law: Laws come from many sources—statutes, cases, contracts, ordinances, policies, *e.g.*, "No shoes, no shirt, no service." Sometimes you will need to address or define an ambiguity in the law. For example, does "No shirt, no shoes, no service" mean only those with no shirt *and* no shoes will be denied service, or that those with no shirt *or* no shoes will be denied service?

In identifying the applicable laws, start with the most general, then move to the specific. Often a law will be derived from a series of cases—since cases and holdings often build on each other. Sometimes you will identify a majority approach and a minority or contrary approach.

In addition to identifying the laws, you should explain them and illustrate them—to give your reader a clear understanding not only of what they are, but "how they work." Often in explaining law, you will set forth additional laws. For example, you may set forth the general law, "An employer is liable for the acts of its employee that are within the course and scope of employment." You will then explain what is meant by "course and scope of employment" setting out tests or standards for each with elements or factors. In other words, you will explain a general law with more narrow specific laws. The discussion will seem merely theoretical unless you illustrate the laws by setting forth factual examples for the cases showing when employees considered to be working within the course and scope of their employment and when they were not.

Use the charts you made in distilling and synthesizing the law to develop the Rule/Law section. Review and evaluate the statements of law you have listed. Are there ones that set out a law so clearly and distinctly that you should quote them? Are there legally significant terms or terms of art that should be quoted? Often times you will be able to state a law more clearly in your own words. Short statements of law that relate to each other might also be paraphrased and combined.

Where two or more statements appear similar, evaluate if they are articulating the same law or law-explanation just in slightly different ways, or if the differences in wording are significant. If the former, you will likely paraphrase the law or law explanation, unless one of the statements is so clear and precise you cannot say it better yourself. If the latter, you will need to explain the differences and why they are or might be significant.

The goal is to transform the statements of law from your chart into a logical and easy to follow discussion that sets out and explains the laws applicable to the issue. Resist the urge simply to transfer the statements of law from the chart to the Rule/Law section verbatim. Doing so will result in a string of quotes from cases that will appear disjointed.

To help you illustrate the laws, review the chart of cases with their holdings in parentheticals that you made when sorting and grouping the cases. Use these case holdings to help illustrate the laws—they provide specific factual examples of when a law or standard was met and when it was not.

Finally, do not discuss the client's facts in the rule section. Early drafters often have a hard time with this. They want to apply the laws as they go. For the reader, however, this results in piecemeal analysis that is much harder to follow. Thus, set forth, explain, and illustrate all the applicable laws first, then when you are done, apply them.

A. Apply the Law: This is where you analyze for each issue and sub-issue whether the facts and circumstances meet or fail to meet the laws you set out, cx plained and illustrated in the law or rule section. To do this, use both logic and analogy.

> **Logic:** Logic is useful for clear "black and white" requirements—think of it as a matching game. For example, if the law is "No shoes, no shirt, no service," ask: whether the client is wearing a shirt. Is he wearing shoes? If the answer is no to both questions, service will be denied. If he is wearing a shirt, but not shoes, or vice versa, the answer will depend on whether the rule is interpreted to be conjunctive or disjunctive—("No shirt *and* no shoes no service" vs. "No shirt *or* no shoes, no service").

> **Analogy/Distinction** Many laws will not be so definite. For example, what if the law is "no dew rags" and the client is wearing a hippie-style bandana? A Hell's Angel style bandana? An East-L.A. style bandana? This is when you use reasoning by analogy. That is to say, answer the question: how is your situation, your facts, alike or different from the facts of a case or cases that have already been decided? Carefully read how courts dealing with the same or similar rule have applied the law; note how the courts treat the various elements or factors, what they say about them and how important they are. What did the courts decide? What facts were significant for the courts in making their decision? How were the facts in those cases similar to or different from the facts in your case? Why? How?

Begin the application section with your overall conclusion of whether the facts meet or fail to meet the basic law regarding the issue or sub-issue. Then tell why and show how your conclusion is sound and well supported. Readers want to know "the answer" from the beginning, and they will be better able to follow your analysis if you tell them up front the point you are making. Think of *telling* as making assertions or predictions regarding whether a law (be it a definition, a test, a standard, or rule) is satisfied or not, followed by citation to supporting authority. *Showing* involves applying logic, or more likely, comparing and contrasting the client's facts with those of the cases you have used to illustrate the laws.

For research memoranda and when preparing to draft a brief, be sure to analyze both sides—pro your client and con. This is critical. As an advisor, you do your client or supervising attorney a disservice by not advising her as to both sides of the issue, the pros and the cons, the authorities for and against her position. As an advocate, you undermine your authority by leaving out counter arguments. You must raise them and then tear them down with reasoned analysis in order to be an effective advocate. Distinguishing, diminishing, and/or assailing contrary authority are essential skills to master as a legal drafter. As a judge or other decision maker, your decision will be labeled "conclusory" or "result oriented" and subject to reversal by a higher authority if you do not present and weigh both sides of each argument before reaching a sound, reasoned conclusion.

Finally, remember that any statement of law, explanation, or case that you use in the application section must first be set out in the rule of law section. This is not merely an arbitrary requirement. If a law, explanation or case is important enough to use or refer to the application section, it is essential to familiarize the reader with it in the law or rule section.

C. Conclusion: If the issue or sub-issue is complicated or presents several counter arguments, wrap up your analysis by restating your conclusion. Otherwise, you may eliminate this step, since you have set forth the conclusion in the first sentence of the application section. You do not want to waste space and the reader's time by tacking on a "canned" conclusion at the end of your analysis.

IRAC/CRAC Check List

Rules/Laws

1. Make sure that all the laws for the particular issue are set out, explained and illustrated using case examples in one section.

2. No discussion of any facts particular to the current client or matter in the rule/law section

3. Each rules/laws section should begin with a topic sentence setting out the basic rule/law

4. Laws, explanations, and illustrations should be accompanied by a citation to supporting authority.

5. For each issue and sub-issue, are the applicable laws set out, explained and illustrated in logical order, importance, broad to narrow, general to specific? Are they easy to follow and understand?

6. Have you made good use of examples from the cases so that the various rules are easy to grasp?

7. Are any laws or explanations missing?

Application/Analysis

1. The application/analysis section should discuss whether the facts particular to the current client or matter meet or fail to meet the laws set out in the rule/law section.

2. Each application/analysis section should begin with a topic sentence setting forth your overall conclusion on the issue or sub-issue, with a supporting citation.

3. Assertions, conclusions, or predictions should be accompanied by a supporting cite; case comparisons or contrasts should be accompanied by case cite(s).

4. No new laws, law explanations, or cases in the application/analysis section. They must first be set out in the rule/law section of that IRAC or in the summary that discusses the overarching rules.

5. After you have set out your overall conclusion on the issue or sub-issue with a supporting cite, how well do you show that your conclusion is correct and well supported? Have you addressed all the facts that are relevant in deciding the issue? Have you addressed the facts in a logical sequence—*e.g.* most important to "also-rans?" Have you drawn useful comparisons and contrasts with the cases? Watch for application sections that appear too conclusory, not supported enough.

6. Counter arguments: Have you addressed facts or rules the other side is likely rely on? Do respond to the counter arguments effectively by pointing out essential problems or weaknesses, as opposed to simply asserting the analysis in your main discussion is "better."

Checkpoints

- Legal analysis is a process that entails a combination of (1) isolating and examining individual components of the law, and (2) fitting them together and explaining them as a cohesive whole.
- Statements of law, sometimes called rules, come from a variety of sources, including statutes, cases, contracts, regulations, or ordinances.
- A law can be a statement of:
  - o What is *required* in particular circumstances;
  - o What is *permitted* in particular circumstances;
  - o What is *forbidden* in particular circumstances;
  - o What *legally results* in particular circumstances;
  - o What is *considered* in determining if a result occurs or whether a law applies.
- Statements of law are also set out as definitions, specific tests, or more vague standards.
- Statements of law may involve:
  - o *elements* – things that are required in order for a result to occur, and/or
  - o *factors* – things that are considered when deciding whether a result occurs.
- Often a series of laws will apply to an issue. Thus do not assume that there will be only one applicable law of that a governing statute is *the* law.
- Statutes are the primary source of law today.
- It is essential to develop your skill in reading and understanding statutes. First and foremost, be alert in reading a statute, as every word and their placement may be important.
- Tools for analyzing and interpreting statutes include:
  - o 1. Using tabulation to explode a statute into its constituent parts so that you can identify each element and factor and how they relate.
  - o 2. Viewing the section at issue using the structure and other sections of the same statute. In other words do not read and analyze the section in isolation.
  - o 3. Case law interpreting the statute. Often the applicable statute has been interpreted by the courts. Cases may (a) determine if a statute is *valid*, (b) determine *whether* a statute applies or *which* statute applies, (c) *interpret* a statute, or (d) *apply* a statute. Resist the urge, however, to go directly to reading cases, skipping the first two steps of statutory interpretation and go directly to reading the cases. Have a solid understanding of the statute and what it means first.

Checkpoints *continued*

- o 4. The plain meaning rule—the wording of the statute at issue. Beware of the plain meaning rule, however, because whether a meaning is plain or what meaning is plain is usually subject to debate.
- o 5. Legislative history—documents and records created by the various parts of the legislature that enacted the statute. It includes statements of legislators, different versions of the bill as it progressed through the legislative process, and analyses by committees and legislative staff professionals.
- o 6. Similar statutes in the same jurisdiction that have been addressed by the courts. If courts have not addressed the section at issue, they may have addressed similar ones.
- o 7. Similar statutes in different jurisdictions that have been addressed by those courts.
- o 8. Canons of construction—rules of interpretation stated in the abstract. Remember, more than one may apply with conflicting results.
- o 9. Law review articles and scholarly commentary. Court may use comments from experts in a field to aid in interpreting statutes. Law review articles are also useful for the authorities collected in their footnotes.

- While statutes are the primary source of the law, cases are the primary source of interpretation, explanation, application, and determination of the validity of the law.
- Be just as alert in reading cases as in reading statutes. However, rather than focusing on every word of a case, read cases strategically, focusing on the issues you need to address and the law and facts that relate to them. This may involve reading the components of a cases out of order, *i.e.*, other than from start to finish, or skirmish certain portions and coming back to them.
- Cases often contain (1) a caption, (2) a summary and headnotes, (3) the disposition, (4) procedural facts, (5) underlying facts, (6) an indication of the issues being addressed, (7) statements of the law and their explanation, (8) an application of the law, and (9) the holding, which is the court's decision on the issue along with the essential supporting facts or reasons.
- Cases may also contain statements of policies that the law is meant to promote, and *dicta*—statements included in the opinion that are not necessary to the court's holding. Look for statements of *dicta* that give examples or how a rule or standard might or might not be met.
- In reading a case strategically for how it affects the client and the client's situation use this checklist:
  - o Where does the case come from and what level of court decided it?
  - o Does the case deal with the same or similar issue as your problem or matter?
  - o What laws does the court apply or articulate?

Checkpoints *continued*

- o What does it say about those laws?
- o What are the facts of the case?
- o How does the court apply the laws to the facts?
- o What is the court's holding? Depending on the client's situation, is it better to describe the holding so that it applies broadly or narrowly?
- o Does the case contain any useful dicta?

- In legal analysis you will need to (1) *distill* the legal principles from multiple cases and explain what they are and how they relate to each other, and (2) *apply* those principles to the facts of your client's situation and predict or advocate the outcome.
- In dealing with multiple cases use this process:

  o Read the cases in the order of most recent, to oldest. It is likely that later courts will have synthesized (at least partially) the cases for you—meaning they will have distilled the legal principles from prior cases, fit them together, and explained them.

  o For each case, write out its holding on each issue in a short parenthetical.

  o Sort and group the cases. Create a chart with that sets out the issues as categories, then sort the cases based on which issue(s) they address. Then for each issue/category group the cases by result: those that met the overall standard or requirements and those that did not. Once your chart is complete look for patterns, trends or factors that point to a result.

  o Distill and synthesize the legal principles from the cases. Once you have sorted, grouped and charted the cases, reread them individually and take down the statements of law and what the court says about them for each issue. Then determine which of the statements of law are elements, and which are factors. Then for each issue fit the statements of law from each case together is as logical and cohesive whole as possible. This usually means going from general statements of law to more specific statements and from broad statements of law to more narrow statements.

- Organize and present you legal analysis using the IRAC (Issue, Rule/Law, Application, Conclusion) or CRAC (Conclusion, Rule/Law, Application, Conclusion) formats. These formats organize and deliver information in a way that is thorough, comprehensive, and easy for the reader to understand.
- Use the IRAC Cheat Sheet below to create the building blocks for the analysis and discussion sections of memoranda and briefs, modifying it to CRAC if needed:

I: Issue

Set out the issue you will address. Issues are questions that must be answered in order to solve a legal problem.

Checkpoints *continued*

To identify the issues that you must resolve, you need to identify: (1) the elements or factors of the applicable law, and (2) the facts that tend to prove or disprove each element of the standard. In the beginning, it is helpful to use the "Whether [a particular element is met], when [set out the essential facts]" format. More advanced drafters may wish to modify this rather rigid format, but master it first as it is an excellent default format.

R: Rules/Laws

Set forth and explain the applicable laws in order of broad to specific/general to narrow. Illustrate your rules and explanations with examples from the cases. This will require you to DISTILL and SYNTHESIZE laws and explanations from all the applicable cases. Often, detailed or narrow laws are used to explain broader laws.

Think of this section as one comprised of three components: Law, Law-Explanation, and Law-Illustration.

A: Application/Analysis

Begin with the conclusion regarding whether the facts in your case or matter meet or fail to meet the basic law you have laid out in the prior section, with a cite to your strongest case(s). This is the topic sentence. Then in order of broad to narrow, strongest to weakest:

(1) *Tell* the reader why the facts meet or fail to meet the laws that have been set out and explained, with citations to supporting cases (these are your "assertions"), and

(2) *Show* the reader how the facts meet or fail to meet the laws that have been set out and explained by comparing and contrasting them to the facts in the cases cited in the rule/law section—be sure to pinpoint cite to these cases as you discuss them and your client's facts.

In a separate paragraph address any arguments, laws, or cases the other side is likely to rely on (*i.e.*, address counter arguments). Think of the application as the "tell and show" section. The goal is to show that your conclusions and assertions are sound and well supported.

Do not introduce or refer to any new laws, explanations, factors, cases or facts in the Application section. They must first be set out in the rule/law Section or the Statement of Facts.

C: Conclusion

If the issue or sub-issue is complicated or involves several counter arguments, briefly restate the conclusion, its principal justification, and include a citation to your essential case(s). Often you may eliminate this step because the topic sentence of the application clearly sets out your conclusion on the issue or sub-issue.

Chapter 2

Legal Drafting, Generally

Roadmap

- The key to good legal drafting is ensuring that the audience can easily understand and follow it.
- There are three key strategies for organizing legal drafting:

  (1) establishing context before details,

  (2) placing familiar information before new information, and

  (3) making your structure explicit.
- Paragraphs are essential building blocks of most legal drafting. Paragraphs begin with a topic sentence that identifies the subject or point of the paragraph. Then each sentence must be related to the topic sentence and to the sentences around it.
- Sentences in legal drafting should be as clear, direct, and concise as possible. The goal is for your readers to quickly and easily understand them.
- The drafting process is a multistep process involving:

  (1) organizing your preliminary materials into a workable outline,

  (2) writing the first draft,

  (3) revising and rewriting,

  (4) editing, and

  (5) proofreading.
- Do not expect to produce a quality document in one draft or the night before it is due.

A. Three Strategies for Organizing Legal Drafting

Your goal in legal drafting is to organize complex information so that your readers can understand it as easily and clearly as possible. Knowing the law and how it applies are not enough; you must make it easy for the reader to see and understand your analysis and agree with your conclusion. Most legal drafting has the following sections, in the following order, although they may be named differently depending upon the form of document being produced.

A. Introduction;

B. Issues;

C. Facts;

D. Law;

E. Analysis; and

F. Conclusion

Later chapters of this book explore the permutations of this structure in various specific forms of legal drafting.

There are three basic strategies for organizing complex information within this structure:

(1) Establish the context before adding the details,

(2) Place familiar information before new information, and

(3) Make your structure explicit.

1. Establish the Context before Adding the Details

Be sure to give readers enough context or background information to easily understand the various details you supply—including how those details fit and why they are important. By the time you are ready to draft a document you will have analyzed all of the facts and issues and become thoroughly familiar with them. Remember that your reader is not as familiar with these facts and issues. Thus, for example, before you discuss specific facts in a memo, explain the client's problem or goals, and before you explain the specific prongs of a test, set out the basic law for which the test was designed. Otherwise, your reader will not easily understand the specifics and why you are discussing them.

To ensure your reader has enough background and context to understand the details remember these drafting principles:

(1) state the general before the specific;

(2) state the broad before the narrow; and

(3) state the rule before the exception.

Background or context begins with the title and the introduction or summary in a memo or brief, and the title and recitals in contracts and legislation. In the statement of facts section of a memo, the first paragraph should identify the parties, players, and general situation—the client's problems and goals. The same is true for contracts and the first sections of a statute or regulation.

When discussing the applicable law, make sure the reader knows the broad legal principles first, and then give the rationale, elements, factors, tests, and other details. When applying the law, make sure the reader is already familiar with the rules, standards, and cases you use, and remind them as necessary.

When making or developing a point, make sure your readers know from the beginning what the point is, why it is important, and how it fits into the analysis. You are familiar with the material, but they are not. You know what points you are making; be sure your readers will also—without any work on their part. Using the IRAC or CRAC structure for memos and briefs will help you accomplish this. It is especially important to begin your application section with your overall conclusion on the issue or sub-issue and then explain or, tell why and show how, that conclusion is sound and well supported. "Tell" by making assertions or predictions supported by authority; and "show" by comparing and contrasting your facts with the facts of the cases you have used in the law section. Adhering to this method will help you ensure that the points you make are explicit to the reader.

Similarly, do not make or expect your readers to connect the dots, add 2 and 2 together, or complete the analysis for you. Many beginning drafters assume that if they "lay the information out there" it "will be obvious" or readers will "make the connection" or come to the same conclusion as the drafter. Not so. Assume that your readers will not only be unfamiliar with what you are writing about, but also will be skimming the document. You need to clearly state the issue, give your conclusion, and do the analysis—telling and showing them why and how your conclusion is sound and well supported. Imagine yourself holding a mallet when you draft and revise—you should be hammering points home for the readers.

2. Place Familiar Information before New Information

Placing familiar information before new information is similar in purpose to providing context before details—ensuring easy comprehension by the reader.

The first step is to first make sure you familiarize your reader with important information you will use and build on later in the document. Thus, in drafting memos and briefs, adhere to the IRAC or CRAC structure. Any law, law-explanation, or case you use or refer to in the application section must first be set forth in the rule/law section. Similarly, any fact you use or refer to an application section should first be set forth in the statements of facts. If a law, law-explanation, case, or fact is important enough to use in your analysis, the reader should already be familiar with it. Also, do not allude to a law, rule, or standard that you have not yet addressed. The English literature practice of foreshadowing has no place in legal drafting.

Second, make sure the reader understands how a piece of new information—be it a fact, a law, a standard, an element, a factor, an explanation, a reason, or a policy—emerges from and connects with the information the reader has already consumed. You may assume it is obvious or that the reader will see the connection or relationship. Do not. Show the reader how the new information connects with the old. Use transition words, *e.g.*, "similarly," "moreover," "conversely," as well as sentences that explicitly guide the reader: "Even if Mary ran the stop sign, this did not cause the accident."

Some useful transitional words:

To add or build on material:
Moreover
Furthermore
Also
In addition
Similarly
Likewise

To indicate or introduce alternatives or differences:
Conversely
On the other hand
However
But
Yet
Still
Although
Though

To indicate a result:
Thus
Therefore
Hence
Accordingly
As a result

3. Make the Structure Explicit

An explicit, easy-to-follow structure is essential in legal drafting. This is why you should learn and embrace the IRAC and CRAC structures from the beginning. Do not organize as you go. Have a clear idea of how you need to deliver the information so that the reader can easily understand it. Make sure your thoughts and points do not appear scattered or random. *Do not just retrace the path you took when you were initially thinking about or analyzing the issue.* Often in these initial stages you will begin with the details and experiment and fit them together to build to a conclusion. In preparing or revising your first draft of a legal document, however, put your conclusion first and then explain why and how that conclusion is sound and well supported. In other words, "turn your analysis on its head." Also be sure to eliminate stray wanderings, recursive loops, and paths that resulted in dead ends. Readers are not interested in the writer's musings on the issue or the amount of thought the writer put into producing the document. They want conclusions or predictions, set forth explicitly, then well explained and supported.

In memos and briefs, the statement of facts might be logically organized chronologically, by issue or subject, or by witness. Rule sections should be organized from general to specific laws, from broad to narrow laws. Application sections should begin with a topic sentence stating the overall conclusion, followed by supporting reasons in order of strongest to weakest. Avoid producing work product that makes your analysis sound like: "and another thing, and another, one more, oh here's another point...." This may be difficult in the beginning because you may not be sure which of your reasons are strongest, or which points are most important, but it is important that you make a concerted effort to order your analysis.

Chapter 8 regarding transaction documents contains suggested formats and organizing tips for transactional documents.

Finally, in all legal drafting make your organization explicit by making good use of clear and informative titles, headings, topic and transitional sentences.

B. Paragraphs

The well-written and organized paragraph is key to legal drafting of all sorts. Paragraphs are the essential building blocks of legal writing. Think back to what you learned in grade school and middle school about paragraphs—and what you may have forgotten or underutilized since then.

Paragraphs have three essential requirements:

> *1. Paragraphs must begin with a topic or transitional sentence that clearly identifies the point, the main idea, the subject of the paragraph.*

The paragraph's first sentence must clearly inform the reader what that paragraph is about. In memos and briefs the topic sentences of paragraphs in the statement of facts should indicate the type of facts addressed, *e.g.*, "Mr. Jones suffered serious injuries in the accident." Paragraphs regarding the law should begin with the basic law regarding the issue or sub-issue, *e.g.*, "Generally, minors' contracts are voidable at the election of the minor." In applying the law, the topic sentence should contain your overall conclusion on the issue or sub-issue, *e.g.*, "Steven probably will be able to void the contract he entered into when he was fifteen." Many times writers will build up to a conclusion that they put at the end of the paragraph. This is backwards. Do not bury your lead. Make the conclusion your topic sentence and then show why and how it is correct and well supported. The same is true in transactional drafting: sections and subsections should be arranged in a self-supporting hierarchy. See Chapter 8.

2. Every sentence in the paragraph must relate to the topic or transitional sentence—to the subject or point you identified there.
In reviewing your paragraphs, check each sentence against your topic sentence. If you have written sentences that do not relate to the topic or transitional sentence, it may be that you should break the paragraph up into two or more paragraphs, or perhaps you should revise your topic or transitional sentence. The same is true in transactional drafting. Beware of the section that tries to do too much—break it up with subsections, defined terms, information schedules, and the like.

3. Every sentence in the paragraph must relate to the sentences around it.
This is accomplished by (1) arranging the sentences in a logical sequence, for example chronological order; general to specific; broad to narrow; order of importance—most important, to supporting, to "also-rans"; and (2) using transition words that signal how the sentence relates, *e.g.*, similarly, likewise, moreover, conversely, however, on the other hand.

Finally, check your paragraphs for length. Save the one or two sentence paragraph for the rare occasion when it can be used for effect or flourish. Check to see if the sentences should be combined with or folded into other paragraphs, or if the very short paragraph should be developed more. Also check for paragraphs that are longer than ¾ of a page. Ask if these should be broken into more than one paragraph connected by transitional sentences. As with sections in transactional documents, beware of the paragraph that tries to do too much or contains more information than the reader can easily assimilate.

C. Sentences and Word Choice

Sentences in legal writing should be as clear, direct, and concise as possible. Always look for ways to use fewer words and to eliminate unnecessary words. The following are tools to accomplish this goal:

1. *Make the Subject Concrete and Put the Action in the Predicate.* Where possible, always make your subject a person or entity—something that acts—rather than a concept. For example "The jury [entity as subject] is not likely to convict Ms. Philips" rather than "The possibility of the jury's convicting Ms. Philips [concept as subject] is remote. Beginning legal drafters must make a conscious effort to do this—because the law, especially in law school, is often discussed in terms of concepts. However, at the root of these concepts are people. For example, adverse possession is a legal concept, but in order to acquire title by adverse possession a person must *do* certain things and *act* in certain ways. Negligence is a legal concept, but in order to be liable for negligence a person must *act* or *fail to act* in particular circumstances.

Generally, avoid the passive voice as it obscures the action and sounds weak and uncertain. The exception to this rule is when one is seeking to conceal an actor's identity or it is unknown.

> Generally yes: *Officer Pitcain made mistakes while investigating the crime by ___.*
>
> Generally no: *Mistakes were made in the investigation.*

On the other hand, if you are representing Officer Pitcain, you would likely want to obscure the subject and would use passive voice. Thus, if you use the passive voice, make it a conscious choice.

2. *Stamp Out Narration.* Eliminate any words or sentences that simply narrate the process of your analysis, *e.g.*, "This issue was addressed by the Illinois Supreme Court" or "Guidance is found in the case law." Instead, state the rule, requirement, test or standard and cite the case(s). The citation supports—or holds up—the preceding statement.

3. *Avoid Nominalizations.* Unbury your verbs. For example: "We represented Ms. Philips" rather than "We provided representation to Ms. Philips." "I fixed the flat tire and flushed the radiator" rather than "I performed repair services on the vehicle."

4. *Use Plain Language.* Avoid legalese—lawyer sounds—and words or phrases you would normally not use. This sounds easy enough, but beginning

legal drafters have a tendency to use words that they think sound "legal" or sophisticated but merely sound pompous or obtuse. Also, if you use a word you would not use normally, you run the risk of misusing it or getting it wrong—even slightly—which will make you look like a fool. Even if you have a large, sophisticated vocabulary, resist the urge to use an uncommon or complicated word if simpler word will do. A primary goal in legal drafting is to ensure that readers easily understand the words. On the other hand, do use legal terms of art—those that communicate a concept particular to the law—where appropriate. For example "The defendant moved for *summary judgment*" versus "The defendant opposed the lawsuit." In avoiding legalese, be sure not to use slang or overly casual terms, *e.g.* "Bob slapped a lawsuit on him." Finally, you should not use contractions, *e.g.*, write "you are" instead of "you're." Some readers will think contractions are fine, but others will see them as errors and a sign of poor drafting. You are drafting to please a wide audience.

5. *Use Fewer Words.* In legal drafting, you are competing for the reader's time and attention; therefore, do not use more words than necessary to clearly and accurately communicate the information. The first four tools listed above, will help you to use fewer words. In addition, you should check your sentences specifically for unnecessary words or "chaff" and delete them. For example, "in the event that" should be replaced with "if; " "for the reason that" should be replaced with "because."

6. *Avoid Intrusive Phrases or Clauses.* Do not interrupt yourself with subordinate dependent clauses (the descriptions that are set off by commas in the middle of the sentence). Either make them into their own sentence, move them to the beginning or end of the sentence, or eliminate them entirely. In other words, subjects should be close to verbs, and verbs close to objects.

7. *Choose the Right Word.* Make sure you use the right word. For instance, courts *rule, hold,* or *conclude*, but they do not *feel* or *argue*. Also make sure the word you use is a word, *e.g.*, "irregardless" is not a word. If you are unsure if you are using the correct word in the correct way, *look it up*.

8. *Put yourself in the position of the distracted, unfamiliar reader.* Are any of your sentences too long or hard to follow? Three lines on the page is stretching the limit. Take a hard look at sentences over two and a half lines, and sentences under two-thirds of a line (for choppiness). In reviewing long sentences, ask if you can use fewer words and clearly communicate the same idea; if you can, do so. If not it is likely you have packed too much content into one sentence and should break it up into more than one sentence. Also, use enumeration—(1), (2), (3) for example—to aid the reader in keeping

track of requirements in a legal rule, even if you do not use fully tabulated (exploded) format to present it. In reviewing short sentences check for tone —do they appear abrupt or choppy?—and see if they should be combined with sentences around them. If you think a reader might have to read a sentence more than once to fully understand what it means, the sentence should be revised.

Sometimes beginning drafters resist these tools because they think they should not have to "dumb down" their writing for the reader. They need to abandon this attitude at the outset. Legal drafters should do everything needed to make their documents easy to follow and readily accessible to readers.

9. *Use the past tense when describing events that have already occurred.* This includes underlying facts and facts and rulings in cases: In *Smith v. Jones* the court *held* ..." Mr. Black *stated* in his interview.... Use the present tense, however, for events or circumstances that are ongoing "He exercises five times a week."

10. *Remember to Keep it Simple.* Use short words found in everyday speech (but avoid slang) that best express your intended meaning. Avoid Latin and other forms of legalese, which are opaque and pompous. Some key rules about word choice are listed below:

- Avoid elegant variation—using a word and its synonyms—use one word for each concept and use the same word each and every time you refer to that concept.
- Beware of pronouns. Use them only if their antecedent (the thing they refer to) is unmistakable. Cure unclear pronoun references by using the noun itself.
- Do not use "aforesaid," "hereinabove," and similar ancient-sounding words.
- As much as possible, use "the," "this," or "that" rather than "said" or "such."
- Do not use "he/she." Rather, attempt to use gender-neutral terms.

D. The Drafting Process

Legal drafting is a multistep process: (1) organizing your preliminary materials into a workable outline; (2) writing the first draft, (3) revising and rewriting, (4) editing, and (5) proofreading. You will need to build in time for each step as well as time away from the document. The days of waiting until the night before the due date and spinning straw into gold are over.

1. Organizing Preliminary Materials into an Outline—Creating an Explicit Structure

Before you begin drafting any legal document, you must organize your materials into a workable outline. The form and complexity of the outline will depend on the document and your working, thinking, and drafting styles. In all cases, though, you should put your preliminary materials in order and create an explicit structure for the document. The structure may change as you draft and revise, but you should begin with one. Once you have organized your thoughts and created a structure—the framework for your document—you need to start drafting. Do not get bogged down in the organizing step of the process or use it to put off actually writing.

2. The First Draft

The first draft is where you get your thoughts and ideas down and where you test them. In the first draft a significant amount of legal analysis occurs as you write and think through the issues. Writing forces you to think critically. Conclusions or assumptions you may have made in the research or preparation stage may not write up when it comes time to explaining or defending them, or in drafting you may come to different conclusions. You may also discover gaps in your preparation or analysis. Thus it is important to begin the first draft early in the process and well before the document's due date. The most important part of the process of the first draft is to get it done. The first draft will not be a masterpiece and you should not try to make it one. At this stage do not overly concern yourself with sentence structure, word choice, or even paragraph structure, all of which you can fix later. Just write.

You do not need to start with the beginning of a document. You might start with a section or issue that seems easiest, then, as you get warmed up, you can tackle other sections. If you find yourself getting bogged down or frustrated with a section, step back and examine why. It could be that some of your preliminary analysis or conclusions are faulty or do not make good sense when put down on paper. You may need to think through issues again. That is part of the first draft process. If you have tested your assumptions and analysis, but are still bogged down in a section, move to another part of the document. Sometimes all you need is time away to regain perspective. Remember, your goal with the first draft is not perfection; it is getting it done so that you can start revising and rewriting, the most critical stage of the process.

3. Revising and Rewriting

After you finish your first draft, put it away for at least a day if possible. Although you will have revised and rewritten as you produced the first draft, you did so from the perspective of the writer organizing and putting thoughts down on the page. You need fresh eyes for the revising and rewriting stage of the drafting process, which is where you turn your draft into a quality document. A mistake made by beginning drafters is becoming attached to their drafts. In the revising and rewriting stage you must detach yourself and approach the document from the perspective of the reader—the client, a court, the assigning attorney, etc.

First assess the document's structure and content—does it address all issues and sub-issues involved in a logical way? A good way of testing this in memos and briefs is to create a heading and topic sentence outline, explained in Chapter 5, section D (memos) and Chapter 6, section G (trial briefs). After you have made any revisions needed to ensure that the document logically addresses all issues and sub-issues, set it aside for a day, if possible. The next step is assessing how *well* they are addressed. At this stage, test paragraphs and individual provisions: are they logically arranged and easy to follow? Do they follow the three requirements discussed above for effective paragraphs? After paragraphs, move to sentence structure and word choice; use the 10 tools described in section C to test and revise your sentences so they are clear, direct, and easy to understand. Revising and rewriting is a critical multi-step process. It will take longer than you think to be thorough and objective, especially in the beginning. That is why you should start the first draft as early as possible, and block out more time than you think you will need to revise and rewrite.

4. Editing

After you are satisfied with your revisions of the document, set it aside again. The next step is editing—reviewing the documents from the reader's perspective for flow and easy understanding. Revising and rewriting can be an arduous process; editing should not be. Think of it as touching-up versus making full scale repairs. Check your sentences and words to make sure they are as clear and concise as possible and that they are logically arranged. Ask yourself, "Can I say this in fewer words?" A good technique is to read the documents aloud, which forces you to put yourself in the place of the reader. Poor phrasing or confusing sentences that seem fine on screen or paper often reveal themselves when read aloud. Editing is an important stage in making sure the document is easily accessible to the reader. However, be sure not to get bogged down in this stage, *e.g.*, rewriting the same sentence over and over, changing a word, then changing it back, and so on. It is possible to overwork a document and lose perspective.

5. Proofreading

When you are satisfied you have a high quality, thorough, and easy to follow document, put it away for at least a day. In the final proofing stage, *print out the document* and examine it strictly for errors—punctuation, grammar, capitalization, missing words that were dropped in the revising or editing process, incorrect words that spell check did not recognize, *e.g.*, "trial" versus "trail." Proofreading and editing should be kept as separate steps. While editing you will miss proofing errors or even create them, because your focus is different. Some proofreading techniques are reading the document aloud, reading with a straightedge so that you only see one line at a time, and reading the document backwards, from the end to the beginning. Beginning drafters may underestimate the importance of the proofreading stage and not leave enough time to do a thorough job. This is a big mistake. Documents with proofing errors look shoddy and tell the reader that you do not care, even if you do.

Checkpoints

- The key to good legal drafting is ensuring that the audience can easily understand and follow it.
- The three key strategies to organizing legal drafting are:
    - o establish the context before discussing the details;
    - o place familiar information before new information and show how new information emerges from or relates to familiar information;
    - o make the structure explicit.
- The well-written and organized paragraph is the building block of all good writing, legal or otherwise.
- Paragraphs have three essential requirements:
    - o Paragraphs begin with a topic or transition sentence that identifies the point, main idea or subject of the paragraph.
    - o Every sentence in the paragraph must relate to the topic or transitional sentence.
    - o Every sentence in the paragraph must relate to the sentences around it. This is accomplished by arranging the sentences in a logical sequence, and by using transition words that signal how the sentences relate, *e.g.*, similarly, moreover, however.

Checkpoints *continued*

- Sentences in legal drafting should be clear, direct, and concise, and quick and easy to understand. Some tools for accomplishing this:
  - o Make the subject concrete and put the action in the predicate. Where possible, always make your subject a person or entity that can *act* rather than a concept.
  - o Stamp out narration—eliminate words or sentences that narrate the process of your analysis, *e.g.* "Guidance is found in several cases."
  - o Avoid nominalizations—unbury your verbs, *e.g.*, write "We represented Ms. Jones" rather than "We provided representation to Ms. Jones."
  - o Use plain language—avoid legalese and words that might not be quickly and easily understood by the average reader.
  - o Use fewer words—no more than necessary to clearly and accurately deliver the information or convey your point.
  - o Avoid intrusive phrases or clauses—do not interrupt the main point of your sentences. Subjects should go close to verbs and verbs close to objects.
  - o Chose the right word—the one that is correct and most accurate.
  - o Put yourself in the position of the distracted, unfamiliar reader and check if any of your sentences are too long or not easy to follow. Ideally sentences should be between three quarters of a line and two and a half lines.
  - o Use the past tense for events that have already occurred.
  - o Keep it as simple as possible.
- Legal drafting is a multi step process involving these steps:
  - o Organizing your materials into and outline. Before beginning to draft, organize your thoughts and materials into an explicit structure. The structure may change as you draft and revise the document, but it is important to begin with one.
  - o Writing the first draft. The first draft is where you get your thoughts and ideas down and where you test them. Writing forces you to think critically. The most important things about the first draft are to just write and get it done.
  - o Revising and rewriting. This stage involves distancing yourself from the draft and approaching it as a *reader.* Assess the document's structure and content—does it address all issues and sub issues in a logical way? Then assess how *well* you have addressed the issues and sub issues. This involves critically reviewing any IRACs, CRACs, paragraphs, clauses, provisions, or sentences and rewriting them as necessary, with the unfamiliar reader in mind.

Checkpoints *continued*

- Editing. After your have revised your draft, the editing process involves fine tuning the document for flow and ease of understanding so that it is easily accessible to readers.
- Proofreading. Once you are satisfied that you have a high quality documents, put it aside. Then print it a go over it with a fine tooth comb ensuring that there *no errors*. Do not combine the editing and proofing steps. Suggested techniques are reading the document aloud and reading with straight edge so that you see only one line at a time. Proofing errors make a document look shoddy and the drafter look bad.

Chapter 3

Citation and Quotation: Why, When, and How

Roadmap

- Citations in legal documents are used to identify and attribute the sources used by drafters in preparing the document and show those readers where to find those sources.
- Quotations are used when communicating the exact words of the original source, should be accompanied by a citation, and should be used sparingly.
- Every statement, explanation, and illustration of the law in a memorandum or brief should be accompanied by a citation to the statute, case, or other legal authority on which it is based.
- Every statement of fact, description of fact, or allusion to fact in a brief or memorandum to the court should be accompanied by a record citation to evidence that establishes that fact.
- Whenever you use a source's exact words, you must put quotations marks around those words and provide a citation to that source.
- Your legal drafting and analysis will be judged in part by the quality and correctness of your citation form.

A. Purpose, Audience, and Goals

The purposes of citations in legal documents are to:

(1) identify and attribute the sources used by drafters in preparing the documents, and

(2) show readers where to find those sources.

Quotations are used when communicating the exact words of original sources, and are accompanied by citations to those sources. The audience for citations includes lawyers in the same firm as the drafter, opposing counsel, judges, law clerks, and court attorneys.

1. Citations to Legal Authority

Citations to legal authority are used to support statements, explanations, and illustrations of the law and to identify the sources from which they come so that the readers can find and review that authority for themselves. Citations to legal authority are also used in the application sections of the IRAC and CRAC formats in supporting predictions and assertions and in comparing and contrasting the facts in the client's case with those in the cases used in describing the law. Your goal is to show readers that your legal analyses and discussions are sound and well supported.

Legal authority includes primary authority such as constitutions, statutes, cases, rules of procedure, administrative regulations, and ordinances. Primary authority are *sources* of law. Legal authority also includes secondary authority such as treatises, legal periodicals, encyclopedias, and dictionaries, law review articles, and websites containing reports and statistical data. Secondary authority comments on the law, but is not a source of the law. Sometimes considered "in between" these primary and secondary sources is legislative history, including legislative counsel' digests, legislative committee reports, and statements of legislator's comments in the legislative record. Remember that legislative history is not dispositive as to the meaning of legislation—legislative history is what was *not* enacted, after all, and due to legislative rules allowing after-the-fact augmentation of the record, the statements of legislators in the legislative history may not have even been made or heard prior to enactment of the statutes themselves.

Thus, legal authority is not created equally. There is a *hierarchy*. Within primary authority, there is *binding* (also called mandatory) authority and *optional* (also called persuasive) authority. Binding authority must be followed by the court hearing your case.

Binding primary authority includes the United States Constitution, the constitution and statutes of the state or jurisdiction in which court is situated, and case law rendered by the United States Supreme Court, and higher courts in that state or jurisdiction than the court at issue. For example, a state trial court in California would be bound by cases decided by the United State Supreme Court, the California Supreme Court and California appellate courts. A federal district (trial) court in California would be bound by cases decided by the United State Supreme Court, the United States Court of Appeals for the Ninth Circuit, and for questions of state law, by the California Supreme Court.

Optional primary authority is just that—optional. A court may choose to consider it, or not. Optional primary authority comes from a state or jurisdiction other than one in which the court is situated, *i.e.*, constitutions, statutes or and cases from another state or, on the federal side, cases law from another circuit. Additionally, cases from courts of the same or a lower level within the jurisdiction are optional authority. For example an intermediate appellate court in one part of the state is usually not bound by a decision of an intermediate appellate court in another part of the state. Such decisions by equal level courts are likely to be quite persuasive, however.

Secondary authority such as legal treatises and law review articles is optional. Its persuasiveness depends on the quality and reputation of the sources and their authors or editors. When a secondary authority is relied on in a judicial opinion, its status is elevated. For example, if a court defines a term in a case using a quotation from Black's law Dictionary, that particular definition, as incorporated into the judicial opinion, become primary authority on that matter.

Legislative History is secondary authority in that it is not a source of the law. However it often does more than comment on the law—it can provide insight and evidence regarding what the law means, its purpose, how it should be interpreted and the like. Thus, although it is optional authority, courts can be persuaded highly by legislative history. See Chapter 1, section B(5) for further discussion regarding legislative history.

Primary Authority

(Sources of Law)

Binding Primary Authority

- Constitution
- Statutes
- Regulations
- Court rules
- Case law from a higher court

In the state or jurisdiction in which the court as issue is situated.

Optional Primary Authority

- Constitutions
- Statutes
- Regulations, rules
- Case law

In a state or jurisdiction other than the one in which the court at issue is situated, or

Case law from an equivalent level or lower court in the same jurisdiction as the court at issue.

Secondary Authority—Always Optional

- Legal Treatises,
- Legal Encyclopedias,
- Legal Dictionaries,
- Law review Articles and the like.

Legislative History—Optional but Often Persuasive

Documents and records created by the various parts the legislature that enacted the statute, including:

- Statements of legislators regarding why they were in favor of a bill or why they opposed it;
- Different versions of a bill as it progressed through the legislative process; or
- Reports and analyses by committees and staff members such a legislative counsel.

2. Citations to the Record and to Exhibits

Citations to the record and exhibits are used to support statements of procedural history and statements of fact in memoranda to the trial court and appellate briefs. These record citations allow readers to review and verify the facts that are stated. Your goal is to show that your description of procedure and description of the facts are accurate and found either in the trial court record, exhibits provided to the trial court, or the record on appeal.

Factual sources include trial and depositions transcripts containing testimony, as well as contracts, letters, and other statements memorialized in documents that have been authenticated and provided to the court. Procedural sources include pleadings, motion papers, court orders, and minute orders setting hearings, case management conferences, and the like.

3. Quotations

Quotations are used when it is important to communicate the exact words of a source. For example, the particular wording of a statute, or a controlling standard or definition set forth in a case, or the exact statement of a party or witness if it is important to your position or analysis. Quotations are always accompanied by a citation to their source—whether legal authority, or factual authority found in the record or an exhibit.

B. When to Cite or Quote

1. Legal Authority

Beginning drafters often feel like they are citing all the time and that the flow of the legal discussion and analysis is being constantly interrupted by cites. Experienced readers, however, expect citation to legal authorities in memoranda and briefs and for drafters to identify, with particularity, the legal authority on which their positions and analyses are based. These readers skip over the citations when verification of the statement is not important to them and hone in on them when it is. A missing citation makes these readers wonder if there is any support for the proposition stated other than the author's voice. In other words, beginning drafters should become comfortable with citation—or citing—as soon as possible.

Every statement, explanation, and illustration of the law should be accompanied by a citation to the statute, case, or other legal authority on which it is based. Beginning drafters usually have little difficulty with this concept in when dealing with statements of the law that are expressly articulated in a particular statute or case. For example, when drafters state a definition or a particular test that has been clearly set forth in a case, they will cite that case. Similarly, when using the facts and holding of a case to illustrate the law, drafters will provide a citation to that case.

But when beginning drafters have synthesized cases and developed a statement or explanation of the law, they may leave out citation to the legal authority on which the statement or explanation of the law is based, thinking "I came up with that on my own." The reality is, no, they did not—not entirely. Rather, their statement or explanation was based on legal authority they read and analyzed and the reader needs to be told what legal authority it was. Similarly, when beginning drafters read a convoluted or complicated case and then come up with a way to explain a law in their own words that is easier to understand, they must be sure to cite the case on which their explanation is based. Readers of memoranda and briefs are usually not interested in a drafter's own ideas independent of legal authority, so be sure to show what authority supports your statements and explanations.

Also cite to legal authority to support any predictions, assertions, or conclusions you make in memoranda or briefs. This includes the application/analysis portions of any IRAC or CRAC used the discussion, as well as in any executive summaries, preliminary statements, statements of the case, or final conclusions. These citations show that any prediction, assertion, or conclusion you make is legally supported and identify the authority so the readers can locate and review it themselves.

Many beginning drafters resist citing to legal authority in the application/analysis portion of an IRAC or CRAC because they have recently cited the same authority in the rule/law portion. However, if drafters do include cites to support their predictions, assertions, or conclusions in the application/analysis, readers are forced to refer back and attempt to find the supporting authority themselves.

Finally, when discussing the facts of your case in the application/analysis portion of any IRAC or CRAC, link these facts specifically with the facts of the cases you have used in the rule/law portion to illustrate the law. Thus, you compare and contrast the facts of your case with the facts in those cases and cite to those cases. This shows the readers how and why the particular client facts are legally significant. For example:

> Mr. Smith's use of the southwest portion of his neighbor's property was open and notorious, satisfying the first requirement for acquiring a prescriptive easement. *Tanner*, 131 N.E.2d at 52. A reasonable landowner would have been put on notice of Mr. Smith's use. *Machnicki*, 148 N.E.2d at 4. Similar to the claimant in *Machnicki*, Mr. Smith planted a vegetable garden, installed a fountain, and built a gazebo—all extending onto his neighbor's property. *Id.* at 3.

In the above paragraph the reader is not forced to go back to the rule/law section to figure out which authority supports the drafter's two assertions. The reader also does not have to go back to remind herself what happened in the *Machnicki* case to understand why the facts discussed by the drafter are legally significant.

2. Cites to the Record and to Exhibits

a. Memoranda to the Trial Court

Cite to the record in describing the relevant prior procedure and the relevant facts in support of or opposition to motions to the trial court. Thus, when describing the procedural history leading up to the motion, provide a record cite for every pleading, order, or other document in the trial court's file that you refer to or that reflects the actions you describe. This demonstrates that your description of the proceedings is accurate and supported by the particular documents in the trial court's file, and allows the judges, law clerks, or court attorneys to locate and review those documents for themselves. Documents in the court's file will usually be numbered consecutively and, increasingly, a list of the documents in the file and the number assigned to them found on line through PACER and other services. Moreover, unless the record cites are voluminous, it is usually a good idea to attach the documents cited as exhibits in support of your memorandum. This makes it easy for the judge or court attorney working on the motion to be able to review those documents.

In the statement of facts drafters need to identify the source for any fact that is set forth, described or alluded to, and provide a document supporting that fact if a supporting document is not already in the court's file. Drafters provide these documents by attaching them as exhibits to their memoranda. Examples of sources for facts in the statement of facts are (1) witness testimony contained in prior hearings or in depositions, (2) pleadings containing allegations alleged by plaintiffs and denials and defenses asserted by defendants, (3) contracts or other documents evidencing agreements between the parties, (4) discovery such as answers to interrogatories, (5) letters between parties, counsel or other relevant persons. In other words drafters must cite to *evidence* that supports the facts described in the statement of facts, and provide that evidence if it is not already in the court's file. For the sake of the reader's convenience, drafters may choose to also attach documents in the court's file as exhibits.

b. Appellate Briefs

The record on appeal consists of the documents from the proceedings below that the parties have designated to be in the record—that they consider relevant for deciding the issues on appeal. Procedures for designating the record are described in Chapter 7, section F(3)(b). Citations to the record are contained in both the statement of the case and the statement of facts section of an appellate brief.

An appeal's pertinent procedural history is generally set forth in the Statement of the Case—the purpose of which is to tell the appellate court what is being appealed and to describe the nature of the action, the parties, and how and why the matter has come before the court. Thus, every procedural act and document described should be followed by a cite to the appellate record so that the judge, law clerk, or court attorney working up the case can easily locate the pleading or other document detailing the action. For an example of a statement of the case with citations to the record see Chapter 7, section F(2).

Absent exceptional circumstances, the statement of facts in an appellate brief may contain only the facts and evidence that were presented to the court or jury below. Thus, any fact set forth or described must be accompanied by citations to the appellate record that enable the persons working up the appeal to look up and review the original the source. Citations to the record enable the reader to confirm that the facts described were actually presented to the trial court or jury, and to verify the drafter's accuracy in describing those facts.

3. Quotations

Drafters should use quotations sparingly to communicate a source's exact words. It is often important to quote the exact words of the controlling statute or, if a particular test or standard is described clearly and concisely in a case, it is a good idea to quote that specific test or standard. The same holds true with clear definitions articulated by courts. Also, there will be times when it is best to quote a person's specific words in the statement of facts if they are important in your analysis, for example whether a person's statements amounted to an offer or an acceptance. Also, at times a person's exact words will create a more powerful impression than a paraphrase. For example:

> *The defendant told police "Yeah, I shot him—right between the eyes. So what?"*
>
> as opposed to
>
> *The defendant acknowledged shooting the victim.*

Drafters should avoid drafting statements of facts that are a series of quotes because this often leads to long, repetitive text that readers will tend to skim or skip over. Drafters should also avoid discussions of the law that are essentially a series of quotes from the cases strung together. This is often an indication that the drafter has not done sufficient synthesis and analysis. Also, long strings of quotes often appear disjointed and are cumbersome for readers to wade through.

If you have tried to paraphrase a source but your words are still quite close to the original, you should instead quote the source's words and note any omissions or changes you have made using ellipses and brackets (described below). A very close paraphrase erroneously implies that another person's words are yours and is misleading.

Beginning drafters will sometimes repeat verbatim the words used in a headnote that are not actually found in the case itself. Headnotes, however, are not part of the opinion and should not be quoted. Doing so followed by a citation to the case containing the headnote implies these are words of the court, which is inaccurate. On the other hand, it is also misleading to repeat the exact words of a headnote without quotation marks and thus pass the words off as yours. The solution is to come up with different and ideally, better, words to use.

Some beginning drafters also put quotation marks around their own words in an attempt to emphasize them. This stems in part from the spoken practice of pantomiming quotation marks when making a sarcastic or euphemistic reference. Do not do this in legal drafting. When you feel that you must emphasize a word for this or another purpose, use italics; and, above all, resist the urge to over emphasize—effective prose communicates its message well without the technique.

Finally, use quotation marks to define terms that you will use throughout your document and for which you want a short, standardized term, *i.e.*, the defendant, Peter Jones ("Jones") or the Asset Purchase Agreement between Melody Partners LLC and Roncho Promotions, Inc. dated June 7, 2010 (the "APA").

C. How to Cite

1. Legal Authority

In most jurisdictions court rules specify acceptable cite forms for memoranda and briefs—usually *The Bluebook: A Uniform System of Citation* and occasionally a style manual particular to the state, *e.g.*, the *California Style Manual.* In law school you will probably be assigned the *Bluebook* or the *Association of Legal Writing Directors (ALWD) Citation Manual* through which to learn the most common rules of citation. Following either will result in citations that look substantially the same. Learning proper citation form and the rules of citation is like learning a new language—it takes practice and the more you use it, the easier it becomes. In the beginning, drafters will need to use the index of the *Bluebook* or *ALWD Citation Manual* often to find out how to cite a particular source.

Two things to keep in mind as you work on mastering citation: (1) your legal drafting and analysis will be judged in part by the quality and correctness of your cite form, and (2) the goal in citation to legal authority is to clearly convey enough information concisely so that readers can easily identify the source and look it up themselves.

Some of the basic rules in citing legal authority, particularly cases, are discussed below.

a. Information Contained in a Case Citation

A case citation contains a number of components that convey information to the reader, primarily:

1. the case name;

2. the reporter(s) containing the case and well as the reporter's volume number, the first page of the case, and the particular page(s) that contain the information the drafter has referred to (often call a "pin cite" or "pinpoint citation").

3. The court that decided the case; and

4. The year of the decision.

For example:

1 2 3 4
Siedle v. Putnam Invs. Inc., 147 F.3d 7, 10 (1st Cir. 1998).

The reporter is the Federal Reporter, Third Series, volume 147. The case begins on page 7 and page 10 contains the pertinent information referred to by the drafter, *e.g.*, the holding, a test, or a set of facts. This information allows the reader to look up the case either in hard copy or on-line. The deciding court was the United States Court of Appeals for the First Circuit, and the year the case was decided was 1998. This information tells the reader about the weight of authority—the level of the deciding court, its geographic jurisdiction, and how recent the case is.

Readers will know the citation language shorthand and will grasp all this information quickly. For example, readers will know that the numbers 7 and 10 refer to page numbers, thus it is not necessary and, indeed, incorrect to write "p. 7." Beginning drafters will need to look up the rules regarding abbreviation of case names, which reporters to cite and their abbreviations, the abbreviations for courts, etc., in the index of the *Bluebook* or the *ALWD Citation Manual.* The *Bluebook* has tables and the *ALWD Citation Manual* has appendices that explain how to abbreviate and that contain various abbreviations to use.

Note: The case name is set forth in italics. Although the examples from the *Bluebook's* "blue pages"—also called "practitioner style pages"—underline case names, drafters in the 21st century, armed with a personal computer, laser printer, and a word processor, should use italics. Previously, case names were underlined in memoranda and briefs because most typewriters could not produce italics. That is not the case now with computers. Also, using italics makes for a cleaner, more professional looking document.

b. Citation Sentences and Clauses

Generally, a citation or citations are set forth in a separate citation sentence following the sentence of text. For example:

> Adequate notice lies at the heart of due process. *Mullane v. Central Hanover Bank & Trust Co.*, 339 U.S. 306, 314, 70 S. Ct. 652, 94 L.Ed. 865 (1950).

There is a period after the word "process" and then two spaces and a new sentence containing the citation to *Mullane*.

Sometimes citations are contained in clauses that are inserted in to the textual sentence. For example, if a sentence contains two propositions and one case supports one proposition and a different case supports the other:

> This motion is made on the grounds that (1) the Asset Purchase Agreement between the Debtor and the Successor, by its terms, does not apply to products liability claims arising after the sale, *In re Eagle-Pitcher Indus., Inc.*, 255 B.R. 700, 704 (Bankr. S.D. Ohio 2000), and (2) as a matter of law, sales under section 363(f) of the Bankruptcy Code do not extinguish causes of action for personal injuries that occur after the sale, *Hexcel Corporation v. Stepman Co.*, 239 B.R. 564, 570 (N.D. Cal. 1999).

In the above example, each citation clause is inserted right after the portion of the text it supports, preceded by a comma. The problem with using citations clauses like this is that is often results on long and cluttered sentence. It would be best to break up this example into two sentences, each supported by separate citation sentence:

> This motion is made on two grounds. First, the Asset Purchase Agreement between the Debtor and the Successor, by its terms, does not apply to products liability claims arising after the sale. *In re Eagle-Pitcher Indus., Inc.*, 255 BR 700, 704 (Bankr. S.D. Ohio 2000). Second, as a matter of law, sales under section 363(f) of the Bankruptcy Code do not extinguish causes of action for personal injuries that occur after the sale. *In re Hexcel Corp.*, 239 B.R. 564, 570 (N.D. Cal. 1999).

c. The Sequence of Multiple Cases in One Citation Sentence

At times the drafter will want to show that more than one case supports the proposition or other information contained in the textual sentence. The rules regarding the order in which to list those cases reflect the hierarchy of authority discussed in section 1, supra, and in Chapter 1, section D. This order is based on the court that decided the case and the date of the decision. Cases from the pertinent jurisdiction come before cases from outside the jurisdiction and secondary authorities (law review articles, etc.). Then, within the pertinent jurisdiction, cases from courts of last resort come before cases from intermediate appellate courts, which come before cases from trial courts. Within each court level, cases are arranged from newest to oldest.

Thus, the most recent case from the highest court would come first in the citation sentence. An older Supreme Court case would come before a more recent appellate court case:

> *Mullane v. Central Hanover Bank & Trust Co.*, 339 U.S. 306, 314 70 S. Ct. 652, 94 L.Ed. 865 (1950); *Jones v. Chemetron Corp.*, 212 F.3d 199, 209–210 (3rd Cir. 2000).

Sometimes drafters will have good reason to list multiple cases in a different order than called for in the *Bluebook*. This would be so, for example, if an appellate court case is more on point, while the cases from the court of last resort supports the more general proposition. They may do this, but they must insert the signal "*see also*" before the higher ranked case in order to continue to comply with the rules of citation:

> *Jones v. Chemetron Corp.*, 212 F.3d 199, 209–210 (3rd Cir. 2000); *see also Mullane v. Central Hanover Bank & Trust Co.*, 339 U.S. 306, 314, 70 S. Ct. 652, 94 L.Ed. 865 (1950).

Note: Multiple authorities within citation sentences are separated by semi colons as if they were closely-related independent clauses.

d. Short Citation Forms

Beginning drafters should become familiar with the basic short forms of citations. Short form citations are not required, but they save space in the document. For example:

Full citation:

> *Siedle v. Putnam Invs., Inc.*, 147 F.3d 7, 10 (1st Cir. 1998).

Partial case name and reporter short form:

> *Siedle*, 147 F.3d at 10.

A textual reference using the partial case name and reporter short form:

> In *Siedle,* the court rejected this argument. 147 F.3d at 10.

When citing to the same case previously cited with no intervening cites:

> *Id.*—When citing to the same page as that pin cited in the previous cite.

Id. at 11.—When citing to a different page than the one pin cited in the previous cite.

The period in "*Id.*" is italicized.

The full cite contains the most information, followed by the partial name and reporter short form. Each of these cite forms gives the reader the information needed to look up the case. Using the short form *Id.* requires the reader to refer back in the document to find this information. This is not a problem if they do not have to look to very long or hard. However, if the readers would have to go back to another section or turn the page to find the information necessary to look up the case, it is best to use the partial name and reporter short form.

There must be no ambiguity regarding which case *Id.* refers to. For example, if the previous citation sentence contains more than one case, many readers will not be sure which case the drafter meant in using the *Id.* short form.

Finally using a partial name followed by just a page number, *e.g.*, *Siedle* at 11, is not a proper short form citation, and, for many readers, this will mark the drafter as a hack.

When drafting, never convert citations to short forms until the last draft. The danger in doing so is that the authorities may be deleted or reordered during the revision process and what was once a perfectly proper short form is now inappropriate in that no earlier full citation is present or a lonely *Id.* remains referring back to where a primary authority is no longer present.

e. Citations to Other Sources

The *Bluebook* and the *ALWD Citation Manual* also contain detailed rules and explanations regarding citations to myriad other sources including constitutions, statutes, federal rules, legislative history, treatises, law review articles, and electronic databases. Drafters should consult the index of either of these manuals before citing to any of these sources. The indexes are detailed and may contain the exact source you intend to cite.

2. Cites to the Record and to Exhibits

There are not uniform detailed rules for citing to the record and to exhibits. The local rules of court in various jurisdictions may state requirements regarding citing to the record and exhibits, and counsel should always check these rules before preparing memoranda to the trial court or appellate briefs. What is key is for drafters to clearly (1) identify the source supporting each procedural act or fact they describe, (2) show where to locate that source, and

(3) adopt a consistent citation form throughout the document. Often this means longer descriptions in the beginning followed by abbreviations and defined terms.

An example from a motion to a bankruptcy court:

> GWII was incorporated on September 12, 2001. Two days later, on September 14, GWII and the Debtor entered into an Asset Purchase Agreement (the "APA") whereby GWII agreed to purchase substantially all of the Debtor's assets. (A true and accurate copy of the APA is attached hereto as Exhibit "A", APA, at p. 1). Three days later, on September 17, 2001, the Debtor instituted voluntary Chapter 11 proceedings in this Court. The sale of Debtor's assets to GWII was approved by this Court on November 14, 2001, with the Order approving same being filed on November 15. (A true and accurate copy of the Sale Order is attached hereto as Exhibit "B", Sale Order at pp. 1–3, 10).
>
> The Sale Order's list of interested parties did not include persons or entities who might possess claims in the future, nor did the Sale Order note any attempt by the Debtor to notice them. (Exhibit B, Sale Order, at p. 5.) Nowhere did the Sale Order provide that GWII not be deemed to be a successor to the Debtor, to have merged with or into the Debtor, or to be a continuation or substantial continuation of the Debtor or the Debtor's enterprise—even though these findings were a condition to closing in the Sale Order. (See Exhibit "A", APA at p. 43).

Notice that, unlike citations to legal authorities, the citations to the documents and exhibits are set off in parenthesis. A reason for this is to clearly distinguish cites to exhibits from the text. Since citations to legal authorities often include italics, this rather than parentheses distinguishes them from the text. Also, the abbreviation "p." is used to denote page numbers in the documents. Often cites to documents in the record or attached as exhibits will include abbreviations for pages "p.", clauses "cl.", paragraphs "¶" to clearly identify portions of the document cited.

An example from an appellate brief:

> Kuney served the motions to intervene and dissolve or modify the Stipulated Protective Order on all parties to *Baystate Technologies, Inc. v. Bowers*, No. 91-40079, and the appeal, *Bowers v. Baystate Tech., Inc.*, 320 F.3d 1317 (Fed. Cir. 2003), as well their successors and all attorneys involved. (Docket No. 551, Notice of Motion and Motion filed February 21, 2007, Appendix, Tab 2, p. 10.) Robert Bean (Bean), who

> is not party to the stipulated protective order, filed the only opposition to the motion. (Docket No. 555, Bean's Opposition filed March 21, 2007, Appendix, Tab 8, p. 129.) Thereafter, Kuney and Bean entered into a settlement providing that Kuney could use the jury exhibits and the confidential and nonconfidential appeal appendixes filed in *Bowers v. Baystate Tech., Inc.*, 320 F.3d 1317 (Fed. Cir. 2003), Case No. 01-1108-11109. (Docket No. 557, proposed stipulated order signed by Kuney and Bean's counsel, Appendix, Tab 10, p. 140.) The terms of this settlement are set forth in a proposed stipulated order filed with the District Court on April 2, 2007. (Docket No. 557, Appendix, Tab 10, p. 140.) No action was taken by the District Court regarding Kuney and Bean's settlement and the proposed stipulated order, however.

For more examples of citing to the record and to exhibits see Chapter 6, section C(2)(d), and Chapter 7, sections F(2), (3)(b).

D. How to Quote

The *Bluebook* and the *ALWD Citation Manual* also contain rules regarding quotations. We have included some of the basics.

1. Using Quotation Marks

In general, when you use the exact words of another source, put quotation marks " " around those words and put punctuation marks inside the quotation marks:

> "Under fundamental notions of procedural due process, a claimant who has no appropriate notice of a bankruptcy reorganization cannot have his claim extinguished in a settlement pursuant thereto." *Chemetron II*, 212 F.3d at 209–10.

If you need to quote within a quote, put single quotation marks around the internal quote:

> "The purpose behind requiring notice to creditors is to provide them the 'opportunity to be heard' which is 'the fundamental requisite of due process of law.'" *In re Chance Indus., Inc.*, 367 B.R. 689, 708 (Bankr. D. Kan. 2006) (quoting *Mullane v. Central Hanover Bank & Trust Co.*, 339 U.S. 306, 314, 70 S. Ct. 652, 94 L.Ed. 865 (1950)).

However, if the quote is fifty words or more, the words are set out in a single spaced, indented block quotation, and quotation marks are omitted:

> The court in *Chance Indus., Inc.* further explained the constitutional inadequacy of notice by publication to potential future claimants:
>
> > Some of the future claimants may not be living persons at the time the notice is given, so they are not necessarily capable of seeing it. If they are alive and actually see the notice, they could not recognize themselves as affected in any way by the bankruptcy case and will, therefore, take no action to ensure their interests are represented. The purpose behind requiring notice to creditors is to provide them the 'opportunity to be heard' which is 'the fundamental requisite of due process of law.' Such a notice by publication is an exercise in futility as applied to creditors who are not only unknown to the debtor, but are also unknown to themselves. It cannot possibly define the requirements of the Due Process Clause.
>
> > 367 B.R. at 708 (quoting *Mullane v. Central Hanover Bank & Trust Co.*, 339 U.S. 306, 314, 70 S. Ct. 652, 94 L.Ed. 865 (1950)).

Use block quotes sparingly, since many readers tend to skip or skip over them. If you do block quote, introduce or follow it with a sentence that explains the point or substance of the quote.

2. Indicating Omissions or Alterations in a Quote: Ellipses and Brackets

If you alter a quote from what appears exactly in the source document, you need to indicate omissions with ellipses and any changes to words or letters with brackets.

Three ellipses (dots) separated by a space in between each indicate that you have omitted a word or words from the quote (" . . ."). There should be a space before the first ellipses and after the third: "The defendant shot . . . him in the hip." If you omit the last words of a sentence you need four dots—three represent the ellipses, and the fourth is the period at the end of the sentence: "But Franklin, the defendant, shot James Cook in the hip. . . ."

If you omit an entire paragraph, indicate this omission by putting a three dot ellipses centered on a separate line in between the quoted paragraphs.

When you make changes to words of a quote, by adding or changing words, letters, or case (*e.g.*, upper case to lower case) you indicate those changes by putting your version inside brackets. Examples:

> "[T]he defendant shot [the victim] in the hip."

This indicates that the drafter left out the first part of the sentence in the original quote and thus had to capitalize the "T" in "the." Also, the drafter changed the original sentence to replace "James Cook" (see above) with "the victim."

3. Citing Original Sources and Indicating Emphasis

Every quotation must be followed by a pin citation to its source. If the quote contains an internal quotation, the source for that quotation must also be pin cited in an explanatory parenthetical :

> *In re Chance Indus., Inc.*, 367 B.R. 689, 708 (Bankr. D. Kan. 2006) (quoting *Mullane v. Central Hanover Bank & Trust Co.*, 339 U.S. 306, 314, 70 S. Ct. 652, 94 L.Ed. 865 (1950)).

You would not need an explanatory parenthetical if the court in *Chance* had merely cited to *Mullane* as opposed to having quoted language from that case.

You may emphasize words in quotations that were not emphasized in the original source, but you must note this added emphasis in an explanatory parenthetical:

> "Under fundamental notions of procedural due process, a claimant who has no appropriate notice of a bankruptcy reorganization *cannot* have his claim extinguished in a settlement pursuant thereto." *Chemetron II*, 212 F.3d at 209–10 (emphasis added).

If the original source has emphasized words in a sentence or sentences that you quote, you do not have to explain that the emphasis was in the original source, but many drafters often do to make this clear—adding the explanatory parenthetical: "(emphasis in original)."

E. Conclusion

This chapter has summarized the basics of why, when, and how to cite to the record and to authorities. These rules may seem technical and small minded, but they are fundamental to legal drafting. Failure to follow them will mark you as a disorganized novice and will increase the workload of those reviewing your documents, never a good thing whether the reviewing party is your employer, the court, or a decision maker to whom you are appealing. Your practice should be to cite, correctly, as you draft. Leaving citation or *Bluebook*ing to the last minute means creation of extra work and a frantic attempt to complete the task before a deadline. Citing correctly as you go provides an audit trail for your work and analysis and produces better documents in less time (and, thus, for less money). For beginning drafters, this may mean *Bluebook*ing the cases they intend to use in correct form *before* they start to draft.

Checkpoints

- Citations in legal documents are used to:
  - o identify and attribute the sources used by drafters in preparing the document, and
  - o show those readers where to find those sources.
- Quotations are:
  - o used when communicating the exact words of the original source,
  - o should be accompanied by a citation, and
  - o should be used sparingly.
- Citations to legal authority are used to support all statements, explanations, and illustrations of the law and to identify the sources from which they come so that readers can look up those sources for themselves.
- Citations to legal authority are also used in the application portion of the IRAC and CRAC formats in:
  - o supporting any predictions or assertions, and
  - o comparing and contrasting facts in the client's case with those in the cases used in describing the law.
- A key goal in citing legal authority is to show that your legal analyses, discussions, predictions, and assertions are sound and well supported.
- Legal authority is not created equally. There is a hierarchy.
- First there is primary authority, such as constitutions, statutes and cases. Primary authorities are sources of law.
- Within primary authority there is:
  - o Binding (sometimes called mandatory) primary authority, which must be followed by the court your case is in. Binding primary authority includes the United State's Constitution, the constitution and statutes of the jurisdiction or state in which the court is situated, and case law rendered by the United State Supreme Court, and higher courts in that state or jurisdiction.

Checkpoints *continued*

- o Optional (sometimes called persuasive) primary authority, which the court may chose to consider or not. Optional primary authority comes from a state or jurisdiction other than the one in which the court at issue is situated. It also includes cases law within the same jurisdiction or state rendered from a courts on the same or a lower level as the court at issue.
- Then there is secondary authority—authorities that are not a source of the law but which comment on and/or describe the law. Secondary authority is always optional, and its persuasiveness depends on the quality and reputation of the source.
- Secondary authority includes:
  - o Treatises, legal periodicals, encyclopedias, and dictionaries, and law reviews.
  - o Legislative history.
- In most jurisdictions court rules will specify acceptable cite forms legal authority; often the default format is the *Bluebook*.
- Learning citation form is like learning a new language. It may be slow going in the beginning, and drafters will need to resort often to index of the *Bluebook*, or the *ALWD citation Manual*. The goal in citation to legal authority is to clearly and concisely provide enough information so that readers can easily identify and look up the source.
- Citations to the record and exhibits are used to support statements of procedural history and statements of fact in trial and appellate court briefs.
- Record and exhibit citations allow readers to identify, review and verify any procedural or factual event described in the brief.
- In trial briefs, drafters should cite to documents in the court's file that support any description of procedural or underlying facts. If the documents supporting a stated fact is not in the court's file, the drafter should identify the document and provide it as an exhibit attached to the brief.
- The record on appeal consists of documents from the proceedings below that the parties have designated to be in the record, including transcripts from hearings and trial.
- Absent exceptional circumstances, the statement of facts in an appellate brief may contain only facts and evidence that were presented to the court or jury below.
- When using another source's words, put quotation marks around those words.
- If you have tried to paraphrase a source, but your words are very close to the original, you should quote the source's words and put any changes in brackets, and note omitted words with ellipses.

Checkpoints *continued*

- Do not put quotation marks around your own words.
- Your legal drafting and analysis will be judged in part by the quality and correctness of your citation form.

Chapter 4

Letters

Roadmap

- Letters are used in the legal profession to inform, persuade, create a legal consequence, or to make a request or demand.
- Although usually less formal than a memorandum, pleading, or brief, keep in mind that letters are not just intended for their recipient to read; they may become exhibits to later motions or briefs. Therefore, the same care must be exercised when drafting a letter as when drafting a motion or brief.
- Letters have a standard structure that it is best to internalize and follow automatically, customizing it to fit particular needs like those of a confirming letter or a demand letter.
- Keeping in mind the potential audiences for each letter and the specific purpose that you hope to achieve will keep your legal letter drafting focused, professional, and appropriate to the task at hand.

A. Purpose, Audience, and Goals of a Letter

The purpose of a letter, like that of other forms of legal drafting, is to inform, persuade, create a legal consequence, or to make a request or demand. Letters are generally less formal than memoranda, pleadings, briefs, or other forms of legal drafting.

This chapter focuses on three basic letter forms: the confirming letter, the demand letter, and the transmittal (sometimes called enclosure) letter. A confirming letter confirms an event or agreement arrived at in a conversation. A demand letter requests or demands that the recipient or the recipient's client do something or stop doing something, and includes the grounds for the request and the consequences of failure to comply. A transmittal letter is enclosed with documents sent to the recipient. It describes those documents and may include requests, instructions, or other information relating to them.

As with all correspondence, *draft these letters to serve your client's and your interests no matter who reads them.* The fact that a letter is addressed to a particular person and stamped "confidential" or "privileged" does not mean it will not be more widely disseminated or end up the subject of litigation, attached as an exhibit to a motion, complaint, or indictment directed at either your client or you, personally. Thus it is safest to assume the letter will be read by a third party at some point and to draft accordingly. In drafting letters follow the writing principles discussed in Chapter 2. Your goal is to be direct, concise, and easily understood. With most letters, the writing process will be quicker and less involved than with memoranda, briefs, or transactional documents. However, it is important to take time to thoroughly proofread any letter that goes out over your signature. Do not leave this to an assistant or other staff. Administrative staff is likely just as pressed for time as you will be and will not have your vested interest in the letter. You also do not want to develop a reputation for sloppy work product either inside or outside your office.

B. Letter Components and Structure

Confirming, demand, and transmittal letters have similar structures and components. They are single spaced, with a single blank line between each paragraph, and contain these parts:

1. Inside Address

The inside address is that of the recipient. It should, of course, be accurate. Included above the inside address is information indicating the means of transmission if other than U.S. Mail, which is assumed if none is specified, e.g., Via Fax (888) 555–1212.

2. The "Re: Line"

Under the address of the recipient, the subject matter of the letter should be concisely set forth after the abbreviation "Re:" (short for regarding), optimally in just one or two lines of text. If the letter involves a court action, the case name, docket number and court should be included. The Re: line is the first indication of the letter's subject matter and should not be overlooked. It is used for filing and retrieval purposes in manual filing systems and for coding purposes in automatic ones.

3. Salutation

Generally, the salutation should be business-like no matter what your relationship is with the recipient, unless you specifically want it to appear otherwise. By using the Mr./Ms. format consistently, *e.g.*, Dear Mr. Luskin, Dear Ms. Rapoport, no unintended inference should be drawn from the salutation.

Casual or familiar sounding salutations such as "Dear Nancy," "Dear Michael," or even "Dear Mike," may result in unintended inferences from the recipient and other persons who read the letter. The recipient may find the salutation condescending or sexist. Even if you have known and worked with the recipient for 20 years, consider the impression a familiar salutation may have on another person reading the letter. Your client will likely get a copy of a confirming or demand letter, and may think you sound awfully cozy with the opposing counsel or party. Or a judge or law clerk may review a series of your letters as part of a case file and wonder why you have consistently addressed female counsel as "Nancy" and male counsel as "Mr. Luskin." The reason could be you have known and worked with Nancy for 20 years and have never met Mr. Luskin in person. However, you may have left an unintended impression of sexism or favoritism with the judge, jury, or law clerk who later reads the letter.

Thus, think carefully about the impression you want to, or may, create and, as a default, use the formal Mr./Ms. format unless you have a specific purpose like introducing an air of informality or familiarity.

4. First Introductory Paragraph

The purpose of this paragraph is to identify your role, the dispute or matter (incorporating the Re: line), and the parties. The first paragraph provides further context for the letter. Even if you have written several letters to the recipient, include this information both as a reminder and for the benefit of other persons who may later read the letter. An exception may be made for short transmittal letters to the client.

5. The Next Paragraph(s), The Body

The first sentence of the body of the letter should state the letter's purpose: specifically what you are confirming, demanding or transmitting. Then elaborate and provide support as necessary, laying out the pertinent facts and any relevant authorities. Be clear, concise, and accurate. Do not embellish, exaggerate, or use more words than necessary.

6. Penultimate Paragraph

The penultimate or second-to-last paragraph of a confirming letter sets out your request for a response if the confirmation is inaccurate. In a demand letter, the second-to-last paragraph reminds the recipient of your specific demand or request. In a transmittal letter, it asks the recipient for any questions or comments regarding the documents transmitted, any instructions given, or requests you have made.

7. The Closing Paragraph

The closing paragraph is just that—it ends the letter in a succinct, professional manner. "Thank you for your time and attention to this matter" or the like is typical.

In the case of a demand letter, always hold out an olive-branch for discussions of an appropriate and truly out-of-court resolution, even if convinced it is hopeless. You are projecting your good-faith attempts to be reasonable that should inure to your benefit if the other side does not respond appropriately and the dispute is later heard by a third-party decision-maker. Also, remember that rational clients do not really want to win lawsuits, they want to (or should want to) avoid them, and your client is likely to receive a copy of the letter at some time.

8. Signature Block

"Very truly yours" and "Sincerely" or "Sincerely yours" are the most common phrases used and are placed directly above your signature.

9. Carbon and Blind Copies

You have two ways to indicate who is receiving copies of the letter directly from you at the time of transmission to the other side: "cc's" and "bc's". Carbon copies —the term is a throwback to office practices before the photocopier when carbon paper was used to make copies—"cc's," are shown on the signature page so that the addressees can see them and are on notice that the communication has been sent to them. Blind copies, or "bc's," are shown on a separate sheet attached only to your copies of the letter. Good candidates for receipt of bc's of letters to opposing counsel are your clients—by doing so, you are keeping them informed of events in their cases or other matters, and it is no business of opposing counsel that you are communicating with your clients. If transmission to cc's or bc's is by methods other than U.S. Mail, it is customary to indicate those methods and the addresses to which they were sent.

C. The Confirming Letter

A confirming letter is meant to be just that, a letter confirming something—an event, appointment, or agreement reached in some other manner, usually in conversation. For example, if you represent the defendant in a lawsuit and, based upon the timing of the plaintiff's filing and service of the complaint, your client's answer is due during a week when you are scheduled to be in trial or on vacation, you might telephone opposing counsel to request an extension of time in which to file a responsive pleading, perhaps thirty days. (We have used the term responsive pleading, because after reviewing the complaint you may choose to file a motion to dismiss or demurer rather than an answer). Assuming plaintiff's counsel agrees, it would be normal practice for you to draft and bear the expense of preparing a confirming letter to memorialize this agreement (and take any other actions necessary to notify the court of the extension if required to do so by local rules).

In drafting a confirming letter, it is important to stick to the facts of the agreement. There is no reason to present any more background or justification for the agreement than is necessary to preserve the agreement in writing. Attempts to include additional, surplus facts, allegations, and characterizations will undermine your credibility and your relationship with opposing counsel and will likely trigger a counter letter or letters, leading to a costly and wasteful exchange. Absolute accuracy is important in establishing your credibility as a professional. Thus, for example, if a response would otherwise be due on December 15 and opposing counsel granted you a thirty day extension, you should *not* suggest in your confirming letter that the response is now due on January 15, which might be the case if the agreement had been for a one-month extension. December has 31 days, meaning that the response with a 30-day extension would be due on January 14. The confirming letter should either state the correct date, January 14, or state that a thirty-day extension was granted.

A confirming letter should be as short as possible and include in the second to last paragraph an affirmative request for a reply from opposing counsel if there is any disagreement with statements in your letter. A single statement of: "If anything in this letter does not accurately reflect our agreement, please inform me as soon as possible as, otherwise, I will rely upon our agreement as reflected above." Note how this statement sets up the grounds for estoppel: It is a statement made with a request for correction if it is inaccurate and notice of intent to rely upon the agreement as stated in the absence of timely notice of disagreement.

A brief appreciative yet professional closing is appropriate. For example, "Thank you for your consideration."

The most prudent course of action during litigation and heated or multi-party negotiations is to document all interim or incremental agreements, whether procedural or substantive, and to cc all parties that may be affected by the agreement, directly or indirectly. A bc to your client is an easy way to satisfy your ethical duty to keep your client informed of progress in the case.

A Sample Confirming Letter

Kuney & Looper, Attorneys at Law
1401 Laurel Avenue
Knoxville, Tennessee 37916

Michael Luskin, Esq. December 1, 2011
Luskin, Stein & Eisler, LLP
300 Madison Avenue, Suite 3400
New York, New York 10017

Re: Alan v. Bates Knife Co. et al, Case no. 5372-011-RRB, S.D.N.Y.;
Extension of time to respond

Dear Mr. Luskin:

This firm represents defendant Bates Knife Co. in the above-referenced matter in which your firm represents the plaintiff Ms. Alan.

I write to confirm our agreement regarding the deadline for my client to respond to your client's complaint. Earlier today, I requested and you agreed to a 30-day extension of time for my client to file an answer or other responsive pleading to your client's complaint. The original deadline for the answer was December 15, 2011, which, in keeping with our agreement, has now been extended to January 14, 2011.

If the above terms do not accurately represent our agreement in this matter, please let me know. Otherwise I will rely upon its terms as stated above.

Thank you for your consideration.

Very truly yours,
/s/
George W. Kuney

[bc: Loraine Pedowitz, Esq., Bates Knife Co.]

D. The Demand Letter

The demand letter is a form of letter sent to opposing counsel or sent to an opposing party if the identity of counsel is not known. It can be a pre-suit demand letter, informally seeking a remedy for a wrong that will be the subject of a complaint if redress is not forthcoming, or it can be used after suit is filed to seek performance of a duty owed by law or by agreement as a prelude to a motion to compel or similar proceeding. Thus, demand letters may have two different purposes:

(1) to actually persuade the recipient to comply with the demand, or

(2) to make a record if a lawsuit or motion is filed.

In either case, although the name "demand letter" is accurate, the best demand letters are *not* demanding or obnoxious in tone. They feature fewer adjectives and characterizations than the complaint or motion that will follow if the demand or request is not complied with. For further discussion regarding writing for the record see Chapter 10.

There are several reasons for this. First, if you want the recipients to comply with your request or demand, you need to *persuade* them—show them why and how complying is in their best interests. Berating recipients in an obnoxious tone will only put them on the defensive and make them want to fight you and your client, rather than work with you.

Part of persuading the recipient is explaining the consequences of not complying—which often includes a legal action against them. Litigation is usually the least efficient or effective way of solving a problem, however. Thus, you must thoroughly discuss with your client the benefits and expenses involved in litigating the matter before you draft a demand letter threatening suit. Many clients may come to you adamant about filing suit—not just to recover a remedy, but to "obtain justice" or "teach a lesson." These are rarely the outcome of any litigation. Some recipients will respond only to a lawsuit, but your goal in a persuading demand letter is to solve the problem without one. Thus, in a professional manner, you want to clearly and succinctly show the recipient the strength of your positions and the risks, burdens, and costs associated with a lawsuit. You do not want to trigger a heated response, *e.g.*, "Oh, yeah [expletive]? See you in court!"

Moreover, if the matter does end up in litigation, the demand letter may become an exhibit reviewed by a jury or court with whom you want to leave a reasonable and favorable impression. Thus, even if the intent of the demand letter is to actually persuade, rather than create a record, drafters are well advised to craft their letters with both the recipient and third-party decision-makers in mind, as discussed below.

When drafting a make-a-record type of demand letter, your audience is more the third-party decision-maker than the recipient, whom you have probably already contacted informally. It is written to be used as an exhibit to a motion requesting relief from a judge, arbitrator, or the like. As a result, the demand letter must contain enough detail to set the context for this third party audience but avoid unnecessary characterizations, details, or items that are subject to reasonable dispute.

Once a judge or other decision-maker has been faced with one of your letters as an exhibit to a motion and found that the letter is an unreliable document, much of your credibility for the rest of the action will be negatively affected. Reputations of counsel for fair play, honesty, and professionalism are hard to earn and even harder to maintain. With jaded decision-makers, it takes many instances of honorable, professional conduct to build a good reputation and often only one instance of attempted over-reaching or mischaracterization to lose it.

Demand letters should contain a brief but complete statement of whom you represent, a clear statement of the request or demand, and the underlying facts and law or agreement that you purport justify your request. A reasonable time limit for response should be given, generally 15 to 30 days absent exigent circumstances. Do not make any specific threats of action to be pursued unless you are willing to be boxed into that course of action. Better, generally, is to remain flexible by concluding with a statement to the effect that "we will pursue all appropriate courses of action if this request is not complied with." Your demand letters should not be perceived as empty threats—as they will if you promise action or retaliation that you do not later pursue. They should be seen as promises of a course of future action. So, keep them general, allowing yourself the ability to choose the most appropriate course of action when the time comes to do so.

It is best to close with a professional invitation for discussion of the matter such as, "if you wish to discuss this matter and its resolution, please contact me at your earliest convenience." The "earliest convenience" language sets the tone of a demand for action. The word "demand" need never appear at all. Remember, the goal of the demand letter is to present your request less formally than by complaint or motion, but strongly and accurately. Your audience, as noted above, is not limited to opposing counsel or their client. It includes other parties to the dispute, their counsel, a future decision-maker, and perhaps the press and public at large.

Sample Demand Letters

In the first example that follows, the clients have come to the attorney at wit's end because for the past year the house next door has been rented to a series of college students who have been making your clients' lives miserable with their odd hours and loud parties that frequently spill out of the house into the front yard. The owner of the house inherited the property from her mother and lives out of state. Your clients have contacted the property manager/rental agent several times, but he has ignored them. They came to you expecting to file a lawsuit, but in meeting with them you learned that their goal was to have a normal quiet life again, as soon as possible. They think the property manager is the problem—that the absentee owner is happy with the rental income, which is higher on a per bedroom basis when renting to students, but is otherwise oblivious. You have decided to write to the rental agent and cc the owner, and draft with both readers in mind.

Kuney & Looper, Attorneys at Law
1401 Laurel Avenue
Knoxville, Tennessee 37991

Roger Spuck October 20, 2011
Buena Vista Properties, Inc.
1327 Fourth Street
San Diego, California 92030

Re: 12 Sea Avenue

Dear Mr. Spuck:

I represent Marc and Catherine Jolley, who own and live in the home at 16 Sea Avenue next door to 12 Sea Avenue, which you manage and lease on behalf of Sarah Thompson.

I write to request that you stop renting 12 Sea Avenue to tenants who interfere with the Jolleys' use and enjoyment of their property. For the past year 12 Sea Avenue has been rented to a series of students who have regularly disrupted the Jolleys' lives and those of other neighbors. On both weekdays and weekends, the tenants have frequent large parties that spill over into the Jolleys' yard. These parties are noisy, and party guests throw trash, including beer bottles, cans, and cigarette butts, onto the Jolley property and block their driveway with cars. The Jolleys' flowers and shrubs have been destroyed. The police have come out many times to break up the parties, and Mr. Jolley has called and written you to complain, but unfortunately this conduct continued.

Because of the conduct of the tenants and their guests, 12 Sea Avenue has become a nuisance under California Civil Code § 3479, which includes "Anything which is offensive to the senses, or an obstruction to the free use of property, so as to interfere with the comfortable enjoyment of life or property ..." But just as critical, as currently rented, 12 Sea Avenue jeopardizes the property value of homes in its quiet, upscale residential neighborhood—particularly its own value and the value of the Jolleys' home next door.

If the noise, parties, trespass, and other disruptions do not cease within 30 days, the Jolleys will pursue all appropriate courses of action to regain the full use and enjoyment of their home and to protect its value. I write to you because I believe it is within your power and ability to fix the problems caused by the current rental of 12 Sea Avenue.

If you would like to discuss this matter and its timely resolution, please contact me at your earliest convenience.

Very truly yours,
/s/
George W. Kuney

/

cc.: Marc and Catherine Jolley
Sarah Thompson

The next sample is written to an opposing counsel who has not complied with a request for production of documents and not responded to follow-up phone calls and emails. It is a make-a-record demand letter.

Kuney & Looper, Attorneys at Law
1401 Laurel Avenue
Knoxville, Tennessee 37916

VIA E-MAIL AND U.S. MAIL

Nancy B. Rapoport, Esq. October 10, 2010
Rapoport & Neal, P.C.
4505 S. Maryland Parkway
Las Vegas, Nevada 89154

Re: LBS II, Inc. v. Ruxpin Entertainment, Inc., Case no. 07684-FS
United States District Court, N.D. Cal.

Dear Ms. Rapoport:

As you know, this firm represents LBS II, Inc., the plaintiff in this action, against your client Ruxpin Entertainment, Inc.

I write to request compliance with, and a response to, our first set of requests for production of documents, served upon you July 13, 2010. By the original terms of these requests for production, response to this discovery was due August 12, 2010. Fed. R. Civ. P. 34; Local Rule 7034. At your request, however, we extended the time for your client's response by mutual agreement to October 1, 2010.

As of the date of this letter, we have not received any response to our request for production of documents, now 9 days overdue. Further, you have not responded to two prior telephone calls and e-mails to you regarding this matter. If your client does not respond fully to this discovery request within 15 days, we will take appropriate action to enforce and protect our client's rights.

If you wish to discuss this matter and its timely resolution, please contact me at your earliest convenience.

Very truly yours,
/s/
Donna C. Looper

bc: Stacie Odeneal, Esq., LBS II, Inc.

E. The Transmittal Letter

A transmittal or enclosure letter is enclosed when sending a document or series of documents to the recipient. Generally, it explains what the documents are and may include requests, instructions, or other information regarding those documents. They are among the simpler letters to write, but we include them because they can easily be neglected or given short shrift, since the drafter has often just finished drafting the more complicated documents being sent. This is a mistake, as the transmittal letter creates the first impression regarding those documents. Transmitted letters with proofing errors or that appear slap-dash or abrupt create a bad impression that will linger with the recipients as they review the documents you have sent.

Transmittal letters usually are written to clients or to other attorneys who are working on a transaction. In the second instance, different versions of the documents are often emailed back and forth with changes and comments noted using a track changes word processing function. This raises document control and metadata issues discussed in Chapter 10.

Sample Transmittal Letter

Kuney & Looper, Attorneys at Law
1301 Laurel Avenue
Knoxville, Tennessee 37996

Lynne Tietjen
1822 Via Lago
Rancho Santa Fe, California 92067

December 20, 2011

Re: Pacific Kinematics, LLC; Sale Documents

Dear Ms. Tietjen:

Enclosed are copies of the final, fully executed documents governing the sale of substantially all the assets of your business, Pacific Kinematics. The master asset purchase agreement is the main document, supported by the purchaser's promissory note and security agreement granting you a security interest in the assets sold. As you know, payment for the business is deferred over a 10-year period, with monthly payments of principal and 10% interest totaling $4,050 being due. The purchaser's president, Jayne Vandaloo, has indicated that, if the business remains profitable, she may be interested in discussing an early discounted payoff. For now, however, the documents provide for a 5% prepayment penalty.

Also enclosed is a copy of the UCC-1 financing statement filed with the Office of the Secretary of State to perfect your security interest in the business's equipment, inventory, and accounts receivable. *This UCC-1 statement is valid and effective for a period of 5 years and must then be renewed in order to remain effective. Renewal is a simple matter of filing a continuation statement, and that can be done any time in the 6-month period before the initial UCC-1 expires.* Additionally, note that the security agreement requires the purchaser to keep the business's assets, your collateral, at their present location unless you consent to their relocation. They must also maintain adequate insurance covering your collateral.

Finally, also enclosed is the original of the lease of the lot and warehouse in which the business is located. Monthly rent is $2,500. The term is 4 years and the purchaser has two 3-year extension options, to be exercised within four months of the lease term's expiration. Rent under the extensions is based upon the original rental adjusted upward by the difference in the consumer price index over the prior term.

If you have any questions regarding this matter or any of the enclosed documents, or should you need further legal services, please call me.

It has been a pleasure working with you on this transaction, and we are pleased to see this deal come together so easily.

Very truly yours,
/s/
Donna C. Looper

Note the italicized language. It is important to define the scope of the continuing relationship with the client, if any, to avoid the potential for later malpractice claims. *See, e.g., Barnes v. Turner*, 606 S.E.2d 849 (Ga. 2004) (attorney that failed to inform client of renewal requirement for UCC-1 financing statement held to have undertaken a duty to renew the security interest himself).

F. Conclusion—Confirmation, Demand, and Transmittal Letters

Confirming, demand, and transmittal letters are some of the most basic letters of a lawyer's trade. Yet there are quite a few important considerations that must be taken into account. In this age of informal e-mails, instant messaging, and the like, less and less attention is being paid to the impressions that correspondence may create in audiences other than the initial addressee. It is critical in drafting legal correspondence to reverse this trend. Every letter (or e-mail, or instant message, etc.) may end up as an exhibit to a complaint or motion against your client or you. Keep that in mind as you draft and create the effect that you desire for all potential audiences.

Simple as these tasks sound, they are both complex and important. You are making a record whenever you draft legal documents. Make it one you can live with and stand on.

Checkpoints

- Letters are used in the legal profession to inform, persuade, create a legal consequence, or to make a request or demand.
- Although usually less formal than a memorandum, pleading, or brief, keep in mind that letters are not just intended for their recipient to read; they may become exhibits to later motions or briefs. Therefore, the same care in legal drafting must be exercised when drafting a letter as when drafting a motion or brief.
- Letters have a standard structure that it is best to internalize and follow automatically, customizing it to fit particular needs like those of a confirming letter or a demand letter.
- Confirming letters confirm an event, appointments, agreement, etc. that was reached in a conversation. Confirming letters should be succinct and accurate — sticking to the facts agreed to in the conversation. They should include a request for a reply if the recipient does agree with statements in the letter.
- A demand letter is a letter sent to opposing counsel or an opposing party or potential opposing party if counsel is unknown that not requests or demands that the recipient do or stop doing something.
- Demand letters may have two different purposes:
  - o to actually persuade the recipient to comply with the request or demand, or
  - o to make a record if a lawsuit or motion is filed.
- Demand letters should be professional not obnoxious in tone. Obnoxious, combative, or berating demand letters will (1) fail to persuade the recipient to comply, and (2) leave a negative impression of the drafter if the letter becomes an exhibit in litigation.
- A transmittal or enclosure letter is used when sending a document or series of documents to the recipient. It explains the documents and may include requests, instructions, or other information regarding them.
- The biggest risk with transmittal letters is that drafters may give them short shrift because they have just finished drafting the documents being sent. This is a mistake. Poorly drafted or proofread transmittal letters reflect poorly on the drafter and the documents being sent.

Chapter 5

Research Memoranda

Roadmap

- Research memoranda are used to make a record of your legal reasoning and predictions and to show that they are well supported by research and analysis.
- The goals in drafting a research memo are to solve a problem, be thorough, and be concise.
- It is important to analyze both sides of a problem in a research memo and present both the good news and the bad news, the pros and the cons, the strengths and weaknesses of a client's matter.
- Memorandum formats are formal structures within which to organize the materials and parts of a memorandum; they should be learned, internalized, and followed as they represent a traditional, familiar format that readers expect.
- Organization of the discussion section of the memorandum requires you to present your analysis in IRAC format, using nested sets of IRACs, one for each issue and sub-issues.
- Memoranda should be prepared with the thought that they will be shared and read more widely than by just the assigning attorney.

A. Purpose, Audience, and Goals of Research Memoranda

The purposes of research memoranda are to make a record of your legal reasoning and predictions and to show they are sound and well supported by your research and analysis. You may be asked to predict whether a cause of action or defense is likely to succeed or whether a transaction is feasible. Or you may be asked to predict advisable strategy, *e.g.*, which causes of actions or defenses are the strongest, or what ways a transaction can be structured and which are most advantageous.

The immediate audience of the research memorandum is the assigning attorney—the one who asked for the research. Assume this person is busy and pressed for time; they will want your predictions to be clear and the memo to be direct and easy to follow. They will expect the memo to come to an actual conclusion, even if it is qualified—as long as your qualifications are well explained. Assigning attorneys are not interested in an academic research paper reporting on the state or evolution of the law on an issue. They want an answer. They will hope your prediction is good news for them or the client, but that cannot always be the case. The assigning attorney will need to be apprised of "the good, the bad, and the ugly" in order to make informed decisions and advise the client. However, it must be clear in your memo that you are aware of and concerned about the clients' interests. Thus, do not appear cavalier or disinterested in delivering bad news and understand that bad news is usually scrutinized more than good news.

It is likely others will read the memo as well. The assigning attorney will probably share it with other attorneys in the firm who are working on the case, and possibly attorneys outside the firm who are working on the same side. The client may be sent a copy of the memo. Also, the next audience for your memo may be a judge or court attorney since research memoranda are often turned into memoranda supporting or opposing motions. Your audience may also be the case file or a research bank, which means the memo will be read months or even years later when the issue in the case is ripe or reappears in another matter. Thus do not assume your reader (even the assigning attorney) will be familiar with the matter or will know of any detail or material you have not expressly set out in the memo.

Your goals in drafting a research or prediction memo are (1) to solve a problem, (2) be thorough, and (3) be concise. Problem solving is the main goal. Memos address practical, real life problems and situations. In memos you need to give the answer clearly and directly, whereas in college essays you may have simply described the problem. It is not enough just to give the answer, however. Just like in elementary school math: You must show your work. In addition to stating your conclusion, you need to show how and why it is sound and well supported. The memo must be thorough and the analysis must deal with all sides of a problem, including those that may hurt the client's position. Your goal is *not* to adopt and defend a view. Thus, do not make the mistake of ignoring bad news. To make an accurate prediction of how a court will rule, or what a jury will find, you need to examine arguments on both sides. Even if you believe the client's position is strong, do not fall into the trap of being conclusory—explain why and how the facts and law support the position.

Memos must be *both* thorough and concise. Doing both is often challenging for beginning drafters, but this is an essential skill to develop. You are competing for the time and attention of your readers—even if they assigned you the problem in the first place. No one wants to read a 10 page memo if 5 pages will do. Since you cannot sacrifice thoroughness for concision, you need to search for and delete sentences and words that do not contribute to solving the problem at hand. Every sentence and word in a memo should be part of showing how and why your predictions are sound and well supported. Look for places where you have lapsed into college-paper-like description, or where you have simply narrated your research process. Delete these passages. Then with the remaining text, ask "can I say this in fewer words?"

B. Suggested Memoranda Formats

There are two basic formats for the traditional office memorandum. Both follow the overarching structure of most legal writing: (1) introduction, (2) facts, (3) law and analysis (application of law to fact), and (4) conclusion. The first format begins with question(s) presented and short answer(s). The second format begins with a summary, sometimes called "Executive Summary." Both formats put the drafter's prediction or conclusion for each issue at the beginning. The prediction or conclusion is what the reader is most interested in, and putting it first provides context for the rest of the memo—which will show how and why the prediction or conclusion is sound and well supported.

The first of these two memorandum formats is the more formal and traditional, featuring a question presented and short answer section in the introductory portion. This format is particularly useful when delivering the results of a traditional law firm research assignment that asks you to research the law applicable to a set of facts and present your legal analysis. This first format follows (see next page):

MEMORANDUM

TO:
FROM:
DATE:
RE.:

QUESTION(S) PRESENTED
SHORT ANSWER(S)
FACTS
DISCUSSION
Summary
Concise heading describing the first issue
Concise heading describing the second issue
Concise heading describing the third issue
And so on
CONCLUSION

The second format for a traditional memorandum is a bit more flexible and is more suited to a broader range of projects in which a memorandum might be required, including reports of discovery and due diligence review and the like. The difference is the elimination of the question presented and short answer sections, substituting in their place a single, unified summary, making this memorandum format more closely resemble that used in business and other non-legal fields.

MEMORANDUM

TO:
FROM:
DATE:
RE.:

SUMMARY
FACTS
DISCUSSION
Concise heading describing the first issue
Concise heading describing the second issue
Concise heading describing the third issue
And so on
CONCLUSION

C. Memoranda Components

1. Questions Presented

Questions presented set out the issues addressed in the memo. If you are using the traditional memo format, write a question presented for each main issue the memo addresses. Each question should identify the issue and the key facts that raise the issue and that are essential in your analysis. In the beginning, the easiest way to ensure that you do this is to use the Whether/When format: Whether *[a legal consequence results]* when *[key facts]?*

The question must strike the right balance—it must be specific enough to the case you are discussing, but general enough so it identifies the subject of the memo for "memo bank" purposes. (Your memo bank is your collection of prior memos, work product, and other authorities saved and accessible for future reference.) Thus, include the names of the parties *and* their status or relationship. "Our client Moe Smith, owner of Moe's Tavern" or "Smith's employee, bartender Jim Jones."

Also in the when portion of the question presented, make sure you describe actual specific facts rather than legal conclusions. For example, if the memo addresses validity of a will and whether the deceased was mentally incompetent at the time of its execution under the wills statute, this question is conclusory:

> Is a will valid where signed by a mentally incompetent person? (Bad —this is a conclusion—in other words the answer to this question is "of course not.")
>
> Rewrite: Whether Peter Smith's will is valid when Smith had an IQ of 70 and a blood alcohol content of .142 when he signed it.

The legal issue is whether Peter Smith's will is valid. The key facts that raise this issue are his IQ and blood alcohol content.

Your analysis of an issue may involve a large amount of specific facts. You cannot list all of them in the question presented because the question will become too long and unwieldy. You must decide which specific facts are key—essential to your analysis—and what facts should be described more generally or by category. In these cases it is often best to write the final question presented and short answer after you have written the discussion section of the memo; a rough draft should help focus you at the beginning. When describing facts generally or by category, be sure not to describe legal conclusions, however.

Say, for example, the issue is whether your client is likely to prevail in an action for trademark infringement against a rival clothing company, and there are many different facts regarding whether the defendant's use of its trademark is likely to cause confusion (an essential requirement of infringement) with the plaintiff's product. This question is conclusory:

> Whether our client, Allister Clothing Co. is likely to prevail in a trademark infringement action against J.J. Sport, where J.J. Sport's trademark is similar to Allister's trademark, and the two companies' products are similar and marketed and sold in similar ways.

The question is conclusory because similarity of the plaintiff's and defendant's trademarks, similarity of their products, and similarity of the products' marketing and sales are important legal factors that indicate likelihood of confusion. Thus, the drafter has described the facts in categories that are legal conclusions, *i.e.*, she has set out legal factors rather than specific facts.

Rewrite:

> Whether our client, Allister Clothing Co. is likely to prevail in a trademark infringement action against J.J. Sport where J.J. Sport's trademark is an Irish setter, while Allister's is a golden retriever, and both trademarks are embroidered in thumbnail size on casual sports clothes that are marketed to young men and women through TV commercials, billboards, and magazine advertisements, and sold in mall retail stores and by catalog.

In this question the drafter has set out specific facts that are key to her analysis (specifically describing the two trademarks and noting they are both embroidered on clothing), as well more generally describing other facts in categories regarding similarity of the products and similarity of marketing and sales methods.

2. Short Answers

Short answers contain your prediction for each main issue addressed in the memo. The question presented and short answer work together. The short answer must directly address and answer the question presented. It should begin with one or two words, *e.g.*: Yes, No, Probably, Probably Not, and, if there is no other option, Possibly.

After the one or two word answer, set out the basic reason or reasons in a conclusory fashion. In setting out your reasons be sure to identify any sub-issues the memo will address. You do not need to further explain your reasons in the short answer segment. For example, if your question presented is the rewritten question above regarding trademark infringement, your answer could be:

> Yes, because (1) J.J. Sport's trademark is similar to Allister's trademark, (2) the two companies' products are similar, and (3) their products and marketed and sold in similar ways; thus, J.J. Sport's use of its trademark is likely to cause confusion among consumers.

This answer identifies the sub-issues the memo will address, and is properly conclusory—it does not explain or attempt to support the basic reasons given. This is because the short answer should be just that—short.

Although the short answer should be conclusory, it must also be specific. The reader will want to know exactly why you reached each conclusion. Thus the reason(s) supporting your conclusion or prediction should be specific. Vague answers such as "No, under applicable law, our client will not be liable" do not give the reader enough information.

Finally, even worse than a vague answer is an equivocal one. In these, the reasons given are often preceded with words such as "if" "provided" or "as long as," *e.g.*: "Yes, if (1) J.J. Sport's trademark is sufficiently similar to Allister's, (2) their two products are similar, and (3) their products are marked and sold in similar ways." This answer will leave the reader wondering, "Well, are they?"

3. Summary

If your memo is in the question presented/short answer format, the summary comes at the beginning of the discussion section. Otherwise, the summary comes at the beginning of the memo. The summary provides context for the memo and should present a clear, concise, accurate road map for your analysis.

If the memo begins with the summary, drafters should lead with their prediction or conclusion on the main issues. This is not necessary if the memo begins with the question presented and short answer. Otherwise you will follow the same general format:

1. Draft a sentence that sets out what must happen in order for the client to prevail or otherwise obtain its desired result, or what must happen in order for the other side to prevail. Often this is put in terms of what the client must prove, show, or do. Sometimes it is easier to state what the other side must prove, show, or do, especially if it has the burden of proof. The summary then briefly evaluates whether and why that is or is not likely to happen. Note, if what must happen includes more than one requirement, set forth those requirements in the same order as they are addressed in the memo.

2. If a statute is involved, quote the pertinent portions in the summary. There is no substitute for the actual statutory language to reassure the reader that your discussion and conclusions are tied to reality and make sense.

3. Set out the issues and sub-issues in terms of the main law(s) governing them. Do this in the same order as you address these issues in the discussion section of the memorandum. Include a citation to authority for each main law governing an issue.

4. State your conclusion on each issue. Depending on how complex your issues are, your discussion section might set out each issue and conclusion separately, or you might set out several issues and then your conclusions on each in the same order:

> Issue 1/Conclusion,
>
> Issue 2/Conclusion,
>
> Issue 3/Conclusion.
>
> —or—
>
> Issue 1/Issue 2/Issue 3, and Conclusion1/Conclusion 2/Conclusion 3

5. With either format, set out your key supporting reasons for each conclusion.

6. Include citations to supporting legal authority for your conclusions and reasons.

7. If the matter involves important overarching laws that apply generally or to more than one issue, set them out in the summary, *e.g.*, rules of construction or underlying policy.

4. Statement of Facts

Your goal in drafting the statement of facts is to present an accurate, concise account of the events and circumstances that sets up your analysis in the discussion section.

The statement of facts must provide enough information and context for an unfamiliar reader to understand what the matter is about and what happened. The challenge is to give enough detail for the reader to have a good picture of the players and what happened, but not to get bogged down in details that are not legally relevant. On the flip side, you do not want the facts to be too bare-bones, flat, dull, or lacking in texture.

It is often said that in memoranda, the statement of facts should be objective. True enough, but (1) objective doesn't mean boring, and (2) you will be expected to "work the deal" as much as possible for your client, while informing your assigning attorneys of any problems spots or weaknesses. This means developing the basic facts into patterns, implications, and findings of fact to support conclusions of law.

a. Basics

You must include all legally material facts in the statement of facts, both the favorable and the unfavorable. In determining whether a fact is legally material, consider the research you have done, your knowledge, and your understanding of the applicable law both for and against your client. All facts necessary to analyze the issues presented must be included. Thus, if you refer to a fact in your discussion section, it must first be set out in the statement of facts. Some drafters prefer to write the discussion section first and then the statement of facts once they are clear on what facts are relevant. Others prefer to tell the story first.

Favorable Facts

(1) support your client's legal claim or defense, or

(2) provide shading or background that you think will make a court or jury favorably view your client or its position.

Unfavorable Facts

(1) undermine your client's legal claim or defense, or

(2) provide shading or background you think might make a court or jury view your client or its position favorably.

Clearly indicate the source of various facts. For example, "In his interview, Mr. Jones stated that ________." "The complaint alleges________." This is critical as, once it becomes time to use your analysis in a memorandum or brief to a court or other decision maker, it will be necessary to cite to the source of all facts. Since you have tracked down this information for your memo, make a record of where it came from now. It is easier to check sources than to rediscover them from scratch. In memos, however, as long as the source of particular facts is captured, you do not have to keep repeating the source. For example above, you would not have to put "In his interview" in front of every sentence pertaining to facts taken from Mr. Jones' interview.

b. Organization

Context first. The first paragraph of the statement of facts should provide the background and context for the memo. The client and its problem or situation as well as other important parties or players should be identified. For example, "Our client Medium Co. came to us because one of its former employees, Blaine Jones ("Jones"), has threatened to sue it for wrongful termination and employment discrimination. Jones maintains that...." Define terms for people and entities that will be referred to often in the memo. In doing so, avoid strings of initials that do not produce pronounceable acronyms—instead, use one or two words from the full name that can be pronounced. In this example, ("Jones") is the defined term for Blaine Jones. Do not use unnecessary words in defining terms, *e.g.*, (hereafter referred to as "Jones"). Putting the term in parentheses and quotation marks and capitalizing the initial letter of each word is enough to define it.

The opening paragraph in the statement of facts is important because it enables the reader to understand the subsequent details—why they're important, where they fit, and the like.

After the opening paragraph, set out the facts in a logical sequence that will make it easy for a vaguely familiar reader to understand what the case is about and what happened. Often the best sequence is chronological order. Other logical arrangements are by issue, by subject, by witness, or from the general to the specific. Be sure not to jump back and forth from issue to issue or subject to subject, etc. Set forth all facts that pertain to an issue or subject before moving on.

c. Show vs. Tell

The statement of facts should be free of conclusions and argument. Instead, set out the specific facts that would *lead* the reader to a conclusion. For example, rather that writing "The teacher completely humiliated the student," state specifically what the teacher said and did that you believe shows he humiliated the student. Avoid overreliance on adverbs and adjectives. Instead use concrete, precise terms that do not require adverbs or adjectives in order to lead the reader to reach a conclusion, *e.g.*, "In class, Mr. Burns put a 'Hello Kitty' sticker on Brad's forehead and called him a 'little girl.' Many students referred to Brad as 'Kitty' for the remainder of the semester."

Just the facts: avoid words or phrases in the statement of facts that amount to legal conclusions. For example, if the matter involves adverse possession —which has a continuity of use requirement — do not write a sentence such as "June Smith and her family used the neighboring parcel continuously starting in 1998." Also, many beginning drafters cannot resist explaining the law or making legal arguments in the statement of facts, *e.g.* "The fact the Smiths built a gazebo on the property is significant in demonstrating a hostile use." Save any legal conclusion, explanation, or analysis for the discussion section.

Use verbatim quotes from people where you want to direct attention to particular facts, or where the speaker or writer has used slang or terms that you do not want attributed to you. Avoid too many quotes, as your reader will start to skim over them. Finally, use quotation marks only for *another person's* words. Do not put quotes around *your own* words for emphasis or otherwise.

5. Main Discussion

The discussion section is the heart of the memo, where drafters show how and why their predictions or conclusions are sound and well supported. Remember though, this is different than defending a position or thesis in a college paper. Your memo will be used to make decisions, plan strategy, advise clients, and the like. So it must be thorough and accurate and cover all sides of the issues.

If your memo is in the question presented/short answer format, the discussion begins with an executive summary discussed above. Otherwise the organization for both memo formats is the same.

a. Large Scale Organization

The discussion section of a memo is based on the IRAC format (Issue, Rule/Law, Application/Analysis, Conclusion) and is composed of IRACs with each issue and sub-issue getting its own IRAC. The first step in drafting the discussion is deciding on a logical and cohesive order for addressing the issues and sub issues. This order may change during the drafting process, but it is important to think about and begin with a framework.

Start by identifying the main issues in the matter. These are the broad legal questions that need to be solved in order to address the client's problem or situation. For example, if you have been asked to research what causes of action or defenses a client might have in a situation, the main issues would be the separate causes of action or defenses you have discovered in your research. Also, if the assigning attorney has identified an issue, you should address it in the memo—even if it turns out to be inapplicable or irrelevant. If that is the case, you need to explain how and why it does not figure into the matter. The same goes for any issues that seemed obviously present in the beginning, but which your research revealed were inapplicable. You should make a record and explain why you eliminated the issues. What you do not want is for this conversation to occur:

Assigning attorney:	"This seems like a clear case of attractive nuisance. Why isn't that in the memo?"
You:	"Um, I thought so too, at first, but it turns out no."

Assigning attorney:	"Why?"
You:	"Well, I need to check back with my notes, it was last week ..."
Assigning attorney:	Tossing the memo back at you. "Yeah, do that, and fix this by the end of the day."

After you have identified the main issues, decide upon the order in which to address them. Usually it is best to begin with any threshold issues, *e.g.*, standing, jurisdiction, statutes of limitation, legality of a proposed transaction, and things of a similar nature. The remaining order depends on the issues themselves and how they relate to each other. A default order is to rank the issues from those most favorable to the client to the least favorable. Related issues that involve similar types of facts, law, and tests should be put next to each other. For example, potential tort causes of action would be addressed together before addressing potential contract causes of action or vice versa. Sometimes, it is best to start with an issue that is easily addressed and dispensed with.

The main issues will often have sub-issues. At the drafting stage you should have a good understanding of cases and applicable law. Identifying sub-issues begins with identifying the elements or factors of the applicable law and the client facts relating to them. Generally case law or a statute will set out series of elements and/or factors or a multipronged test. For example, if one of your main issues is whether your client has a cause of action for negligence, the sub-issues would be (1) duty, (2) breach of the standard of care, (3) cause in fact, (4) proximate cause, and (5) actual injury. Of these five, there may be no dispute that the client was actually injured, in which case your discussion of the negligence issue has four sub-issues: duty, standard of care, cause and proximate cause. One IRAC for each may be sufficient. However, depending on the applicable law and the facts of your case, one or more of these sub-issues may have sub-issues themselves. In other words, there may be more than one legal question that must be answered. For example, breach of the standard of care may involve (1) predicting what the standard of care is, and (2) predicting whether or not the applicable standard was met. If so, you would need an IRAC for each.

All issues and sub-issues should be identified by a point heading that concisely describes them. Also, if a memo has several main issues that consist of sub-issues, a one paragraph mini-summary for each main issue may be appropriate. The mini summary would consist of your overall conclusion on the main issue supported by your conclusions on the sub-issues with citations to authority.

Discussing the identification and organization of issues and sub-issues in the abstract is of limited value, however. This is a process that begins with your basic understanding of the law and continues with your research and legal analysis of a matter. Before you begin drafting, you should have an idea of the various IRACs that you think will comprise the discussion section of the memo—even if you have not written or even outlined them yet. Think of IRACs as building blocks and, before you start drafting, have a concrete idea of where you think they should go. In other words, begin with an explicit structure in mind. Know also, however, that this structure may change or you may need additional IRACs.

b. Small Scale Organization—The IRAC

You will draft an IRAC for each issue and sub-issue in the discussion section. Identify the issue using a point heading, which can be quite short, even one or two words, *e.g.*, "Duty" or "Proximate Cause"—as long as the heading clearly flags the issue. The heart of the IRAC will be the explanation and illustration of the rules or laws, followed by an application of them. This is where you show your work supporting your prediction or conclusion. Depending on the length or complexity of the analysis you may also have a separate conclusion at the end—the "C" of the IRAC. Often this is not required because the application should begin with your conclusion on the issue or sub-issue in its topic sentence. The IRAC form is discussed in detail in Chapter 2.

c. Rules/Laws: Identify, Explain, and Illustrate

The applicable laws should be set out and explained in order of broad to narrow, general to specific. Thus, begin with a topic sentence setting forth the basic law pertaining to the issue or sub-issue followed by a citation to supporting authority. Then you would set out and explain various requirements, factors or tests that are applicable. Laws are often explained with other laws. A requirement might be further explained with a test or series of factors used to determine if that requirement is met, or with the purpose underlying the requirement. Or you may have synthesized an explanation by identifying a common thread among cases. Explaining a law in an IRAC is *not* repeating it again in different words or engaging in academic discourse or any other college-paper-type reflection or narration. Eliminate any sentences that do not directly contribute to solving the legal issue or issues at hand.

Every law you set out and explain must be accompanied by a pin citation to the authority from which it came, *e.g.*, a case or statute. A pin cite includes not just the first page of a case, but the specific page on which the law or explanation is set forth or from which it is derived. Similarly, a pin cite to a statute includes the specific section or subsection in which it is set forth or from which it is derived. Including a pin cite with every law or explanation will help you avoid superfluous narration. Your explanations of the law must be based on specific authority to which you can directly refer the reader through citations.

Illustrating the law means including specific factual examples from cases that show how a particular requirement was met or not met, or to show when a factor or series of factors was or was not present. Specific facts and holdings are necessary to show how a law works in practice, in reality. Without them the rule/law section will read like an abstract list. Placement of illustrations depends on the laws being explained. Sometimes the laws will relate and nest so easily that you can explain them together in one paragraph and follow that with a paragraph of case examples. However, if you have a separate paragraph of illustrations but have to refer back to match which law a case is illustrating, you will need to illustrate as you go — meaning certain laws will need to be illustrated before moving to explaining others. Remember, for illustrations to be useful, they must contain the specific facts of the cases.

You need to set forth, explain, and illustrate all the laws applicable to an issue, favorable and unfavorable. If you think the other side will use a law, explanation, or case to support their position, you should include it in the rule/law section. To leave it out is to deprive readers of the information they need to make a decision, plan strategy, advise a client, and the like.

Finally:

(1) any law, explanation, or cases that you refer to in the application/analysis section must first be set forth in the rule/law section. If something is important enough that you use it in your analysis, the reader should already be familiar with it.

(2) Do not discuss client facts in the rule/law section. Set forth, explain, and illustrate all the applicable laws first, then apply them in the application/analysis section.

d. Application/Analysis

In the application/analysis portion of the IRAC you analyze whether the client facts meet or fail to meet the laws you have set forth, explained, and illustrated. Begin with a topic sentence stating your conclusion on the issue or subissue, accompanied by a pin cite to supporting authority. Be specific, direct, and concise, *e.g.*: "Here, June Smith's use of the property next door was open and notorious," not "In the present case, our client June Smith's use of the property was sufficient under applicable law." Then tell why and show how this conclusion is sound and well supported. "Tell" by making assertions, *e.g.*, that particular requirements were met, or not, or certain factors are present, or not. Every assertion must be accompanied by a pin cite to supporting authority.

"Show" by comparing and/or contrasting the client facts with those in the cases you have to illustrate the laws. (If you find that you used a case in the application/analysis section that was not in the rule/law section—go back and add it.) Be specific in your comparisons and contrasts. Sometimes you will elaborate on the facts of case; other times you will briefly remind the reader of what happened in a case. Do not expect the reader to remember a case, even if it feels like you have just written about it. Often times case names run together. Thus, although you will know exactly what happened in the *Jones, Smith*, and *Brown* cases, the readers likely will not be able to match up the facts with the case name. That means they will have to stop reading your analysis and refer back to the rule/law section—something you never want to happen because it wastes their time.

Your application/analysis section should be cohesive. This means you need to show how the facts of your client's situation relate to each other, which of those facts are most significant, and which are contributing facts and why. You do not want your analysis to appear like "and another thing..., and another..., oh yeah, here's another,..., and this one ... too."

Analyze all sides of an issue or sub-issue, both favorable and not. If your analysis is fairly strong or better, in favor of the client's position, you may do this by assessing counter arguments after your main analysis. Counter arguments are arguments you think the other side is likely to raise but have particular flaws or weaknesses that you can point out, without the need for lengthy analysis. You must be specific and incisive in responding to counter arguments. It is not sufficient to repeat points you have made in your main analysis. If you find you have done this, you may need to move the counter arguments into the main analysis.

If the issue is a close one, or the law favors the other side, you should analyze both sides in the main analysis. If the issue is close, the main analysis will be incomplete if you save addressing weakness for your analysis of counter arguments. The reader will feel sandbagged. They will finish the main analysis with the impression that the issue is favorable to the client, only to find out that this is not, in fact, the case. If the issue favors the other side, this effect is magnified. Therefore it is best to elevate these counter arguments to the main analysis. You must analyze both sides, but you need to show you are aware of the client's interests and that they are important to you.

Finally, (1) all client-specific facts you refer to in the application/analysis potion of an IRAC in the discussion section must first be set forth in the statement of facts section of the memo, and (2) any law, explanation, or case used or referred to in the application/analysis portion must first be set out in the rule/law portion.

e. Conclusion

In many IRACs a separate conclusion is not necessary because you have set forth the conclusion in the topic sentence of the application/analysis portion. However if the analysis section is particularly complex, close, or if you have assessed several counter arguments, you may need to wrap up the issue with a separate and concise statement restating your conclusion before moving on.

6. Conclusion

After the main discussion section, *briefly* set out your overall conclusion regarding the main issues in the memo and supporting reasoning. There must be nothing new — no new facts, rules, reasons, or analysis — in the conclusion. Note: sometimes, by the time you get to your conclusion, you really see things clearly and understand what's going on. So you write a longish, strong conclusion that should have been part of the main discussion. If this is the case, it is time to go back and edit or redraft the discussion with this clear understanding in mind. It also may indicate that you should go back and re-write the introduction. Most legal drafters will tell you that the best introductions in any legal document result from writing that section last.

D. Testing Your Draft with a Heading and Topic Sentence Outline

A good way to test memoranda for overall substance and organization is to create a heading and topic sentence outline. After you have completed a draft of the memo, highlight the documents headings and subheadings along with the topic sentences of every paragraph, then copy them in order into a separate document and print it out.

First, check if the headings and topic sentences identify all the subjects, issues, and points necessary to analyze the problem or matter. Thus, in the statement of facts are all the significant categories of facts clearly identified? In the discussion section, are all issues that needed to be addressed identified? Are the major or overarching applicable laws identified in the topic sentences of the rule/law paragraphs? Are your overall conclusions for each issue and sub issue set forth in the topic sentences of you application paragraphs?

If the outline reveals any ambiguities or omissions in facts or analysis, review your draft. It may be that you have left out subjects or issues that you intended to address or that you realize need to be addressed or steps in analysis may have been omitted—which mean more substantive drafting is needed. Or, you may have fully addressed the necessary subjects and issues, but the headings and topic sentences do not adequately identify them—which means revising or adding headings or topic sentences.

Second, check if the headings and topic sentences are arranged in a logical order that is easy to follow. Pared down to headings and topic sentences you should be able to tell if the memo provides context before details, puts familiar information before new information, and has an explicit structure. A heading and topic sentence outline also reveals whether the issues and sub issues are logically arranged, *e.g.*, threshold issues are addressed first, and issues and sub issues that relate to each other or that follow each other are put one after another. Also, the subjects and issues may be arranged in logical order, but some topic sentences may need transition words to make their relationship explicit.

Third, check if the headings clearly and concisely identify the subject of the section or subsection and that the topic sentences clearly and concisely identify the subject or point of the paragraph. In other words, check your headings and topic sentences first in isolation to ensure they are clear and strong, and then make sure they are accurate.

E. Research Memorandum Drafting and Reviewing Guidelines

These guidelines will aid drafters as a checklist in drafting, reviewing, revising, and editing their own memos.

1. Substance/Analysis and Organization

a. Question(s) Presented

Does the question identify the main issue(s) addressed in the memo and the key facts? *E.g.*, Whether *(legal issue)*, when *(key facts)*. Detractions from questions presented include questions that leave out important facts, questions that are too general (they do not identify the issue with sufficient specificity), or that are conclusory (they contain all or part of the answer).

b. Short Answer(s)

Does the answer begin with one word, *e.g.*, "Yes" "No" or "Probably," and directly address and answer the question presented? Does it state the basic reason(s) in a conclusory fashion? Does the answer identify the major sub-issues the memo will address? (The question should set out the overall issue, and the answer should identify the sub-issues). Detractions include answers that do not set out affirmative conclusions (watch for the words "if" and "provided that"), that do not include reason(s) in support, or that contain too much explanation.

c. Statement of Facts

Does the first paragraph provide context for the memo? Are the parties, players, and general situations identified? Are terms defined for the parties and players as necessary (if not already done in the question presented (Short Answer or executive summary)? Does the statement of facts include all legally material facts—all the facts that are referred to in the discussion section? Based on your knowledge of the law, does the statement contain all facts necessary to analyze the issues presented? Does the statement include helpful background and context facts? Does it appear that the facts are presented neutrally? Is the statement free of conclusions or argument? The statement of facts should show versus tell the reader what went on that is relevant to the question presented.

Are the facts set forth so that it is easy for a busy, unfamiliar, or vaguely familiar reader to understand what the case is about and what happened? Are the facts arranged in a logical sequence, *e.g.*, chronologically, by issue or subject, by witness, or from general to specific. Detractions include omitting facts, failing to put contextual facts in the beginning of the statement, and jumping back and forth from issue to issue or subject to subject. Set forth all facts that pertain to an issue or subject before moving on.

Does the statement of facts clearly indicate the sources of the various facts so that these sources can later be efficiently located?

d. Discussion

(i) Summary[1]

Does the summary set out the basic claim or defense—what a party will have to do, show, or prove to prevail? Does this sentence identify these re-

1. In the second memo format the summary comes at the very beginning.

quirements in the same order they are addressed in the main discussion? If a statute is involved, does the summary quote the pertinent portions of it? Are the essential governing rules for each issue set out with supporting citations? Then do you set out your conclusion for each issue, along with your essential, specific supporting reasons with supporting citations? Does the summary include any overarching rules that apply to all the sub issues?

If you are using the memo format that begins with an executive summary rather than questions presented and short answers, do you begin the summary with a brief conclusion regarding the main issue(s) addressed in the memo?

(ii) Main Discussion
Identifying, Explaining and Illustrating the Law

Do you begin with the overarching law applicable to the issue or sub issue? Do you set out the rules, elements, tests, standards, factors, and cases necessary for an unfamiliar reader to understand how and why the issue is likely to be decided? Are the laws, elements, tests, standards, factors, and cases sufficiently explained? Are they sufficiently illustrated with examples from the cases? Are they set out in a logical sequence, *e.g.*, broad to narrow, general to specific? Is every law, element, test, factor, law explanation, or case accompanied by a pin citation to a supporting authority? Is every law, element, test, standard, factor, or case that you refer to in your application first set out in the rule/law section? This includes those relevant to counter arguments. When you compare or contrast the client's facts with a case in the application section, be sure to illustrate the case first in the rule law section. Do not discuss client facts in the rule/law section.

Are the rules synthesized from the cases so that a busy, unfamiliar reader can easily understand how they work, what's important, what a court or jury will look to in deciding the issue?

Detractions from the main discussion include:

(1) omission of important laws, elements, standards, tests, factors, or cases;
(2) omission of any laws, elements, standards, tests, factors, or cases you refer to in your application section;
(3) failure to adequately explain these items and illustrate how they work;
(4) mere lists of statements from cases or descriptions of cases (a.k.a. sequential case analysis) instead of synthesis of the cases and then critical facts;
(5) discussing client facts; and
(6) failing to cite to supporting authority.

Application (Analysis)

Does each application/analysis section begin with a topic sentence with your overall conclusion on the issue or sub-issue with a citation? Is this sentence direct and specific? Are all of the material client-specific facts addressed? Are they addressed in a logical sequence, *e.g.* strongest to weakest?" Do you make clear how these facts relate and which are more significant and why? Do you both tell (make assertions with supporting citations) *and* show (compare/contrast the client's facts with the facts of the cases)? Do you use the cases effectively (by comparison or contrast) to show how and why the client facts meet or fail to meet the applicable laws, tests, standards, etc.? Have you cited to the cases while telling and showing? When discussing your client's facts, have you linked those facts to cases and cite those cases to show the reader the facts you are discussing are legally significant? Have you assessed potential weaknesses either through counter arguments or the main analysis?

Detractions from the application section of the discussion include:

(1) Omission of material client specific facts (good or bad);

(2) Failure to show how the facts relate or which facts are particularly significant and why;

(3) Discussion or reference to any laws, elements, tests, standards, factors, or cases that are not first set out in the rule/law section (if you compare or contrast the client facts to the facts of a case, be sure you have first illustrated that case in the rule/law section);

(4) Insufficient use of the cases to show whether, how, and why the client facts meet or fail to meet the applicable rules, elements, tests, standards;

(5) Insufficient citation;

(6) Failure to address weaknesses or counter arguments.

e. Conclusion

The conclusion of the memo should succinctly set out your resolution to the main issue(s) addressed by the memo, your key reasons in support, and supporting citations.

2. Paragraphs

Do your paragraphs begin with a topic or transitional sentence that identifies the subject or main point of the paragraph? Then does each sentence in the paragraph (1) relate to the topic or transitional sentence, and (2) relate to the sentences around it? The second requirement is accomplished by arranging the sentences in logical order, and by using transition words as signals, *e.g.*, however, conversely, also, moreover.

Detractions include:

(1) paragraphs without clear topic or transition sentences;

(2) sentences that do not relate to the topic identified; and

(3) paragraphs that are choppy or disconnected because the sentences are not arranged logically or smoothly, or transition words are needed.

3. Sentences and Word Choice

Are your sentences as clear, direct, and concise as possible? Always look for ways to use fewer words and to eliminate unnecessary words. Use specific, concrete words. Have concrete subjects and active predicates. Where possible have your subjects be people or entities that can act rather than concepts.

Put yourself in the position of the distracted unfamiliar reader. Are any of your sentences too long or hard to follow? Three lines of text is stretching the limit—give a hard look at sentences over 2 ½ lines, and sentences under 2/3 of a line (for choppiness). If you must have a long sentence, break it up with enumeration, *e.g.*, (1), (2), (3) or (a), (b), (c). If the reader might have to read a sentence more than once to understand what you mean, the sentence needs revision.

Eliminate any words or sentences that simply narrate the process of your analysis, *e.g.*, "This issue was addressed by the Illinois Supreme Court." Instead, state the rule, requirement, test, or standard and cite the case(s).

Avoid intrusive phrases or clauses (don't interrupt yourself).

Use parallel structure, *e.g.*, don't have present tense and past tense in the same sentence.

Avoid legalese and words or phrases you would normally not use, but do not use slang or overly casual terms.

Make sure you use the right word: *e.g.* courts "rule," and "hold" but they don't "feel" or "argue."

4. Technical

Make time to proofread. This requires time away from the document to rest and refresh your eyes and mind. Make sure there are no proofing, grammar, *Bluebook*, quotation, formatting, or style errors. If you use another source's words, you must put quotation marks around those words and pin cite to the exact page of the source from which you are quoting. To do otherwise is plagiarism.

F. Communicating the Substance of the Memorandum to the Client

You or someone in the firm will communicate to the client of the results of your research and analysis to keep the client informed and enable them to make decisions regarding their case. Some drafters rewrite the memo removing much of the citation and some of the legal analysis to make it shorter and quicker for the client to read. The problem with this option is often unnecessary time spent (and billed) converting one perfectly good document into another.

The better practice is often to send the client a copy of the memo with a transmittal or enclosure letter that (1) contains an expanded executive summary of the memo that adds an assessment of any counter arguments or potential weaknesses, (2) asks the client to carefully review the facts set out in the memo—because any conclusions and predictions are based on those facts—and to inform the drafter of any errors, omissions or additions to the facts, and (3) asks the client to contact the drafter with any questions or comments. For further discussion regarding transmittal letters see Chapter 4, section E.

Checkpoints

- Research memoranda are used to make a record of your legal reasoning and predictions and to show that they are well supported by research and analysis.
- The goals in drafting a research memo are to:
  - o solve a problem,
  - o be thorough, and
  - o be concise.
- It is important to analyze both sides of a problem in a research memo and present the good news and the bad news, the pros and the cons, the strengths and weaknesses of a client's matter.
- Memorandum formats are formal structures within which to organize the materials and parts of a memorandum; they should be learned, internalized, and followed as they represent a traditional, familiar format that the reader expects.
- The basic formats for traditional office memoranda include (1) an introduction—either questions presented and short answers, or an executive summary, (2) a statement of facts, (3) discussion section containing law and analysis (application of the law to the facts), and (4) a conclusion.
- Questions presented set out the issues addressed in the memo.

Checkpoints *continued*

- Questions presented should describe actual specific facts rather than legal conclusions.
- Short answers contain your prediction and essential supporting reason(s) on each issue.
- A short answers must directly address the question presented and should begin with one word or two words, *e.g.* Yes, No, Probably, Probably not.
- After the one or two word answer, set out the basic reason(s) in support in conclusory fashion.
- The summary or executive summary either comes at the very beginning of the memo (replacing the question presented and short answer) or at the beginning of the discussion section if using the question presented/short answer format.
- If the memo begins with an executive summary, the drafter should begin the summary with his or her prediction of the outcome of each main issue addressed in the memo.
- In drafting the summary, follow this basic format and these requirements:
    - o Draft a sentence setting out what must happen in order for the client or opposing party to prevail.
    - o If a statute is involved, quote the pertinent portions.
    - o Set out the issues in terms of the main law(s) that govern them, in the same order as those issues are addressed in the memo.
    - o Set out your conclusion on each issue.
    - o Include the key reason(s) supporting each conclusion.
    - o Include citations to supporting legal authority for your conclusions and reasons.
    - o If the matter involves important, overarching laws that apply generally, or to more than one issue, set them out in the summary.
- The statement of facts should provide an accurate concise description of the facts that sets up your analysis in the discussion section. It needs to provide enough context and information for an unfamiliar reader to understand what the matter is about and what happened.
- The statement of facts must contain all legal material facts, both favorable and unfavorable to the client, and any fact referred to in the discussion section must be included in the statement of facts.
- Begin the statement of facts with a paragraph that provides the context and background for the memo. Identify the client and their problem or situation as well as any other important parties or players.

Checkpoints *continued*

- Then set forth the facts in a logical sequence that makes it easy for the reader to follow and understand the facts, *e.g.*, chronological order, by issue, by subject, by witness, general to specific.
- The statement of facts should be free of conclusions and argument, instead describe the specific facts that would lead the reader to a conclusion.
- The discussion section is where drafters show that their predictions on the issues are sound and well supported.
- Each issue and sub issue in the memo is addressed using the IRAC format.

  I: Identify the issue or sub issue in a point heading

  R: Set out, explain and illustrate the applicable laws/rules (favorable and not), going from broad to narrow, general to specific. Provide pin citations to supporting legal authority for each law, each explanation, and each illustration.

  A: Begin each application section with a topic sentence containing your overall conclusion on the issue or sub issue, with a pin cite to legal authority supporting it.

  Then tell why and show how your conclusion is sounds and well supported:

  Tell by making assertions, supported by legal authority, that the client's facts meet or fail to meet the various rules, tests, standards, requirements set forth in the rule/law section, or by making assertions supported by legal authority that relevant factors are or are not present in your client's facts.

  Show by comparing and/or contrasting the facts of your clients case with the facts of cases used in the rule/law section.

  o Assess both the strengths and weaknesses of the client's case, either in the main application/analysis or through assessing counter arguments.

  C: A separate conclusion after the application may be necessary if the analysis is complex, close, or contains several counter arguments. Otherwise, you may omit it because the topic sentence of the application section contains your conclusion on the issue of sub issue.

- Test your memorandum for overall substance and organization by creating and reviewing a heading and topic sentence outline.
- Once you have a complete, quality draft, thoroughly assess the memo using the memorandum guidelines.
- Make time to print and proofread the memo separately before turning it in.
- Often the results of your research will be communicated to the client by sending the memo to the clients along with a transmittal letter. Keep in mind when drafting the memo that it will be read by others than the assigning attorney —including the client.

Chapter 6

Memoranda of Points and Authorities or Briefs in Support of or Opposition to Motions in the Trial Court

Roadmap

- The purpose of a memorandum of points and authorities ("MPA") or brief in support of or opposition to a motion in the trial court is to persuade the court to take or not take the action requested in the motion.
- To draft an effective MPA or brief in support of a motion, you must first know exactly what relief you are seeking or opposing; drafting a proposed order is one way to accomplish this end.
- Effective MPAs and briefs feature a message that is delivered well and a simple solution for the trial court to implement.
- MPAs and briefs are comprised of a caption, a preliminary statement, a statement of facts, a discussion or argument section, and a conclusion. Each portion has its distinct purpose.
- Drafting statements of fact involves accurate, compelling storytelling. Statements of fact should contain all relevant facts, even those that are unfavorable, which should be deemphasized. For each fact an accurate citation to the record or to an exhibits is critical.
- Drafting the discussion or argument section involves showing the court how to rule in your favor and why it should do so. The discussion section should be drafted in the form of a series of CRACs, one for each issue and sub-issue.
- The conclusion section of an MPA or brief in the trial court is a simple, short restatement of what you are asking the court to do. Typically one does not restate the reasons for doing so in any degree of detail.

A. Purpose, Audience, and Goals—Developing and Delivering Your Message

—The purpose of a motion and supporting MPA or brief is to request and persuade a court to do something. On the flip side, the purpose of a MPA or brief in opposition to a motion is to persuade the court to deny the request. Many different types of motions are filed in the trial court—ranging from the complex, *e.g.*, motions for summary judgment in civil cases and motions to exclude evidence on constitutional grounds in criminal cases, to the relatively simple, *e.g.*, a motion to compel responses to interrogatories. In all instances, though, a motion is a request that the court do something specific—from dismissing a complaint with prejudice to extending a discovery deadline.

The primary audience for trial court memoranda is the trial court judge, a law clerk, or court attorney. These persons and their roles vary from jurisdiction to jurisdiction. In some jurisdictions certain judges are assigned to hear motions in all cases prior to trial, while different judges are assigned to preside at trial. Thus, the judge that hears motions in a case may not be the same judge that tries the case. In other jurisdictions cases are assigned to specific judges who both hear motions and preside over trials in the cases they have been assigned. Or, particular types of motions will be assigned to certain judges or other decision makers. For example, a case may be assigned to judge for trial, while discovery motions in the case are heard by a commissioner or magistrate.

Law clerks and court attorneys also fill different roles and have varied experience. Sometimes they are straight out of law school with a one- or two-year clerkship. Other times they are veteran attorneys with permanent positions. If the latter, the permanent law clerk or court attorney is likely to be the primary audience for memoranda in support of or opposition to a motion.

Thus, your readers will have a variety of different perspectives and experience. Assume, however, that all these persons in their various roles have one thing in common: they have a heavy workload and deal with a large number of cases and matters—only one of which is yours. They will have little time to read your supporting or opposing memoranda. Thus, you will need to be clear and concise regarding what you want the court to do and why it should do it. All too often attorneys lose sight of this goal and allow their motions and oppositions to become their "masterpieces," or receptacles for lengthy argument and blather.

Other people will also read trial court memoranda in support of or opposition to motions: co-counsel and opposing counsel, possibly the client, appellate court judges and their law clerks, or court attorneys. Good drafters focus on the primary audience—the very busy trial court judge, law clerk, or court attorney.

The goals in drafting memoranda in support of or opposition to a motion are to (1) make the court want to rule in your favor and (2) make it easy for the court to do so. Remember, the purpose of memoranda to the trial court is to *persuade* the court to act in a certain way. Persuading is different than wining an argument or proving that you are right. Think: sales and marketing versus arguing and rhetoric.

The first step in making the court want to rule in your favor and making it easy to do so is to have a clear understanding of exactly what relief you are seeking. If you represent the movant, an excellent way of doing this is to draft the proposed order you are seeking first, before the memorandum of points and authorities or brief. This focuses your thinking on exactly where you are going and ensures that your supporting memorandum addresses all topics that you wish included in the court's order. The proposed order can even be used as an exhibit to the motion itself in order to make it clear to the court exactly what you are asking for.

Developing a Message: To effectively package and market your points and arguments, you need to develop a theory, theme, or pitch for your case. This is the message you send to the court that justifies your position and motivates the court to rule your way. Your message provides the framework for the discussion and focuses your drafting. A compelling message can be described in just one or two lines—similar to a slogan or tag line in advertising. Only instead of "Coke: it's the real thing" it could be "The plaintiff not only assumed the risks, he embraced them," or "The police did not honor the defendant's right to silence, they undermined it."

Messages are not pulled out of thin air. They evolve through research, review, and synthesis of cases and other authorities. Thus, as you research and analyze the law and facts, look for common threads and strengths that emerge, and be thinking of how your case should be packaged. When you start your first draft, have an idea of your theory, theme, or pitch and test it in the drafting process. This will help focus your writing and keep you alert to alternative, possibly more compelling, messages.

Delivering your Message: Delivering your message and making the court want to rule in your favor involve a combination of telling a compelling story in your statement of facts followed by a discussion of the law that sells and supports the message. The discussion section shows the court how and why the law and facts compel a ruling in your favor. You will focus on the strengths of your position, but also address, dispel, or minimize difficulties or weaknesses, *e.g.*, cases, facts, or arguments your opponent will use attempting to persuade the court in his favor. Ignoring weaknesses or difficulties will undermine your position. If you do not address them, the court will hear about them only from your adversary.

Making it easy for the court to rule in your favor will help make the court want to do so. Busy trial courts are drawn to clear, simple solutions. In other words, a persuasive memorandum solves problems rather than creates them. Present your message and make your points as clearly and concisely as possible. This means spending extra time to make complex arguments appear as simple as possible and editing out unnecessary sentences and words. In other words, you need to work harder to make it easier for your reader.

Also make sure your memoranda are easy to read visually—that the font size is large enough, that the headings are clear and concise, and that there is enough white space between paragraphs. Tabulated format, numbered subparagraphs, and bullet point lists are often effective means of presenting individual points concisely. Proofing errors are also a distraction and make a document difficult to read.

B. MPA or Brief Formats

Most courts have specific local rules regarding the format for memoranda of points and authorities or briefs in support or opposition to motions. Thus, always consult and follow local rules when drafting and filing any document in the trial court. In general, however, motion memoranda follow this format:

(1) a caption that includes the title of the document,

(2) a preliminary statement,

(3) a statement of facts (sometimes called "factual and procedural background" if both underlying and procedural facts are relevant to the motion or opposition),

(4) a discussion or argument section, and

(5) a conclusion.

C. Motion Components

1. Preliminary Statement (if allowed)

Unless forbidden by local rules, an MPA or brief to the trial court should begin with a brief preliminary statement that sets the context and provides a road map for the document. Preliminary statements are similar to executive summaries in office memoranda, except that preliminary statements advocate a position rather than predict a result. The preliminary statement should clearly communicate what the drafter would like the court to do, and why the court should do it. Optimally, the preliminary statement is one to one-and-a-half pages long. It is usually the first thing a judge law clerk or court attorney will read, and is the drafter's first opportunity to deliver the message. Like the introduction to a research memorandum, it is often most effective if drafted last, after the rest of the memorandum to the trial court.

In a memorandum in *support* of a motion, begin the preliminary statement with a specific request to the court, *e.g.*, to enter summary judgment dismissing the complaint, to exclude particular evidence, and the like. In a memorandum in *opposition*, begin the preliminary statement with an assertion (a polite one) that the court should deny the other side's request. Then in both cases state the grounds for the motion or the opposition, *i.e.*, very briefly explain the reasons the court should rule in your favor, along with citations to supporting authority. Set forth your supporting reasons in the same order as they are addressed in the discussion or argument section. Difficulties or weaknesses are usually not addressed in the preliminary statement unless they are central to your discussion. Finally, define terms for people and entities that will be referred to often in the memo. In doing so, avoid strings of initials that do not produce pronounceable words—instead, use one or two words from the full name that can be pronounced.

The following is a preliminary statement to a complex 20-page memorandum in support of motion for relief from stay in a bankruptcy court dealing with discharge and notice issues under case law based upon *Mullane v. Central Hanover Bank & Trust Co.*, 339 U.S. 306 (1950):

> PRELIMINARY STATEMENT
>
> The Norton Towers Homeowners Association, Inc., ("Norton") and the individual plaintiffs request this Court to grant their Motion for Relief From Stay allowing them to pursue their state law claims and facilitate recovery against any applicable insurance policies. This motion should be granted for the following reasons:
>
> First, neither Norton nor the individual plaintiffs had a claim under 11 U.S.C. § 101(5)(a) because they had no exposure to, or relationship or contact with the debtor and its products prior to confirmation of the plan. *In re Rosenfeld*, 23 F.3d 833, 838 (4th Cir. 1994). Therefore, their state law claims were not discharged, barred, or otherwise compromised through the bankruptcy proceedings. *In re Rosenfeld*, 23 F.3d at 838. Moreover, even if their post-confirmation state law causes

> of action qualified as a claim under § 101(5)(a), they were not discharged or barred through the bankruptcy proceedings because notice by publication is not constitutionally adequate notice to a potential future claimant. *See Bosiger v. U.S. Airways*, 510 F.3d 442, 451 (4th Cir. 2007). Finally, the discharge injunction does not apply for the purpose of collection against an insurer who is a non-debtor and is also liable for the debt. *See In re Mann*, 58 B.R. 953 (Bankr. W.D. Va. 1986). Norton and the individual plaintiff may still proceed nominally against the debtor in order to seek derivative recovery against the insurer. *In re Jason Pharm., Inc.*, 224 B.R. 315 (Bankr. D. Md. 1998). There being no prejudice to the estate, relief from stay should be granted.

This preliminary statement (1) identifies the three grounds supporting the request for relief; and (2) includes citations to relevant Fourth Circuit authorities as the matter was pending in a district within the Fourth Circuit where it was a matter of first impression.

2. Statement of Facts or Factual and Procedural Background

Next comes the statement of facts. If the motion touches on procedural issues or prior court rulings, you will include a description of procedural facts as well as underlying or client specific facts with a heading such as "Factual and Procedural Background." For example, a motion to compel responses to interrogatories would detail when they were served and any extensions of time that were given. Prior court rulings that relate to the issues in the motion should also be included. Thus, a memorandum in support of or opposition to a motion for summary judgment would note if the court had denied a motion to dismiss for failure to state a claim and the reasons given. It is important to be accurate when describing prior rulings and their basis. Attorneys lose credibility with decision makers when they appear to misconstrue prior rulings or put words in the court's mouth that were not originally there.

If the procedural facts and underlying facts are lengthy, each would go under separate headings, *e.g.*, "Procedural Background" and "Factual Background." If there are no prior rulings and the motion is based solely on the underlying facts of the case, they are set forth under the heading "Statement of Facts."

a. Purpose and Goals of the Statement of Facts

Think of drafting the statement of facts as accurate storytelling. Your purpose and goals are to tell a compelling, concise, and accurate story that will make the court want to rule your way, and give it enough information to do so. Many, if not most, of the legal rules you will be seeking to invoke in the discussion or argument section involve flexible standards that will be applied to the facts to reach a desired outcome. The statement of facts develops and reinforces your message and sets up your analysis in the discussion section. The statement should provide enough information and context for an unfamiliar or vaguely familiar reader—a judge, law clerk, or court attorney—to easily see what the case is about and what happened. You want the reader to be interested and ideally, sympathetic—or at least understanding.

We use the term "compelling" in context. Your underlying facts may not be riveting; they may be technical, tedious, or, even, in the abstract, dull. Or your client may not be seen as sympathetic, for example, if you represent BigCo. in a serious personal injury case in which you are moving for summary judgment based on the expiration of the statute of limitations. Your goal still is to tell the story so that the facts (1) are as easy to follow and as accessible as possible and (2) promote your message.

The scope of the statement of facts will depend on the issues addressed in the motion. For example, in a motion to dismiss based on lack of personal jurisdiction over your client, the statement of facts would focus on your client's contacts with the forum state, while briefly describing what the underlying case is about.

Some drafters prefer to write the statement of facts first—to tell the story and prepare for the analysis in the discussion of argument section. Others prefer to write the discussion section first and then the statement of facts after they are clear on what facts are relevant. Preferences also vary from case to case. Our recommendation is to begin with the section that seems easiest to you.

b. Dealing with Favorable and Unfavorable Facts

The statement of facts must include all legally material facts, both favorable and unfavorable. In determining whether a fact is legally material, consider the research you have done, your knowledge and understanding of the applicable law both for and against your position, and your message or theory of the case. Any fact you refer to in the discussion or argument section must be included in your statement of facts. Similarly, any facts you know your opponent will use should be included. You may include or omit any subjective (not legally material) facts—favorable and unfavorable. Your decision whether to include subjective facts, either good or bad, will often depend on your message—how you are packaging the case. Finally, as a guide, remember that your statement of facts cannot be misleading through omission, inaccurate description, or otherwise.

In general, favorable facts support your client's legal claim or defense (legally material facts), or provide shading or background that you think will make a court or jury favorably view your client or its position (subjective facts). Unfavorable facts are those that undermine your client's legal claim or defense (legally material facts), or provide shading or background you think might make a court or jury unfavorably view your client or its position (subjective facts).

Although the statement of facts must include all legally material facts, favorable and unfavorable, you do not have to handle them equally. Rather, you will emphasize favorable facts and de-emphasize unfavorable ones. This is done through placement, tone, and treatment.

i. Placement

The first step in deciding placement of facts is to assess your case and decide which facts are favorable and which are not, and why. Keep a list either in your mind, on screen, or on paper of (1) facts that support your legal positions or provide shading or background you think will make the court want to rule in your favor, and (2) facts that undermine your legal position and/or support the other side's, or provide shading or background you think might make the court want to rule against you. Knowing the strengths and weaknesses in the facts is essential to good legal story telling.

Once you have assessed which facts are favorable and which are unfavorable, you are ready to start drafting. Place favorable facts in positions of emphasis, *e.g.*, at the beginning of a section, paragraph, or sentence, or at the end of these with a solid build up. Conversely, bury damaging facts in the middle of the narrative or the middle of paragraphs or sentences. Sometimes, unfavorable facts can be de-emphasized by being joined or juxtaposed with favorable facts. However, make sure you do not taint your favorable facts in doing so.

Always, at a minimum, set forth all the facts the court will need to rule in your favor. This requires a thorough understanding of your theory of the case and the applicable law, including any tests, elements, requirements, or factors. Make sure you have corresponding facts for each.

ii. Tone and Treatment

Emphasizing favorable facts and minimizing unfavorable facts is not just a matter of where you place them, but of what you say about them and how you say it. For favorable facts, use the active voice, concrete subjects, and active predicates, *i.e.*, employ all the sentence writing techniques described in Chapter 2 regarding clarity and getting and keeping the reader's attention. On the other hand, distance and minimize unfavorable facts with the passive voice, *e.g.*, "An accident occurred." Sentences containing unfavorable facts can and should be dull—accurate but not commanding attention. Avoid, however, couching unfavorable facts in confusing sentences that a reader may have to read more than once to understand. This will unbury those facts.

Word choice is critical. Favorable facts should be set forth in vivid, specific terms that convey as much meaning as possible, without going overboard, e.g. "attack" versus "incident." Specific concrete words are more effective than adjectives and adverbs. They also take up less space. You may use your own words to characterize facts as long as those words are accurate. Your goal is to tell a compelling story without going too far and appearing overwrought or overly dramatic. We suggest using a "might readers roll their eyes?" test for assessing this.

In treating unfavorable facts, use words that are bland and general, without being inaccurate. This is the time to use terms like "incident," "event," "occurrence," "matter," and the like. Be sure though, not to be so general as to be absurd. For example if a person demanded money in an armed robbery, do not describe the event as a "conversation."

In treating favorable or unfavorable facts maintain a professional tone. You do not want to appear to be belittling or arguing with the other side. This undermines your position and signals to the court that it needs to solve your problem rather than your solving a problem for the court.

c. Organization

Although favorable and unfavorable facts are treated differently in terms of placement, the overall organization of the statement of facts in a memorandum to the court is similar to that in an office memorandum. The first paragraph should provide the background and context so the judge, law clerk, or court attorney can better understand the subsequent details; why they're important, where they fit, and the like. It should include the parties and any other significant players and the general situation giving rise to the motion or opposition. Then, mindful of placement of favorable and unfavorable facts, tell the story in a sequence that will (1) make it easy for an unfamiliar or vaguely familiar reader to understand what the case is about and (2) best deliver your message. A common sequence is chronological order. Other logical arrangements are by issue or subject, by witness, or from the general to the specific. As always, be sure not to jump back and forth between issue to issue or subject to subject. Include all facts that pertain to an issue or subject before moving on. If the statement of facts is long or complex, break it up with short descriptive headings that identify the topic, issue, or subject of the facts discussed.

d. Citing to the Record and Providing Support for the Statement of Facts

In an office memorandum it is enough to simply note the sources on which the facts are based. In a memorandum to the trial court, however, any fact you describe should be accompanied by a cite to the court file that indicates where the document can be located, usually a docket number, *e.g.*, "Complaint, Docket No. 3." For facts that are based on documents that are not in the trial court file, you will need to provide them as an exhibit to the memorandum or an authenticating declaration and cite to them, *e.g.*, "(Exhibit 4, 10/20/2010 Letter from Donna Looper to Nancy Rapoport.)" Also, if not voluminous, consider attaching supporting documents as exhibits even if they are in the court file. This will make it easier for the judge, law clerk, or court attorney to locate and review them.

The documents you use and cite to will be made part of the record and, absent a sealing order, open to the public. Thus, the sources for the facts in the statement of facts should not be private or privileged, *e.g.*, client interviews, inter-office memos, letters between other attorneys in the firm and the client, and the like. Public documents and sources include pleadings in the file, sworn declarations, deposition transcripts, and letters to or from the opposing party or counsel.

e. Show vs. Tell

In telling a compelling story in your statement of facts, avoid conclusions and argument. Rather, set out the specific facts that would *lead* readers to a conclusion, ideally so that they think they came to the conclusion on their own. This is much more compelling than your telling them what to conclude, which often triggers resistance. So rather than writing, "The defendant committed a heinous crime," state specifically what the defendant did. Use adjectives and adverbs sparingly. Instead use concrete, precise terms that do not require further description to lead the readers to the conclusion you want them to reach.

Also be sure not to describe facts such that they become legal conclusions, *e.g.*, "When the plaintiff put on her skis, she assumed the risk that she might be injured by fellow skiers," or "The defendant voluntarily waived his right to silence, and then spoke to the police." Save these types of statements for the discussion or argument section. Concentrate on telling an accurate, compelling story or painting a picture for the court.

f. Conclusion

In the statement of facts you are telling a story, a true one. It must be accurate and contain all legally material facts, but how you tell the story depends on whose it is and the message you want to send the court. Your statement of facts should both set up your analysis and make the court want to rule your way. We discussed the "roll the eyes test" for going overboard and appearing too dramatic. On the flip side is the "eyes glazed over test." Passing this test means doing all that you can to simplify technical or complicated facts so they become accessible and easy to grasp. Also, do not pack your statement of facts with quotations, especially block quotations, as readers tend to skip over them. Use just your best quotes for special emphasis and/or to support a compelling statement or characterization you have made.

Always remember that you are telling a story to and painting a picture for *the court* versus arguing with the other side. Keep your tone professional, never smug or snotty.

D. Discussion or Argument

1. Purpose and Goals of the Discussion or Argument Section

In the statement of facts you have set forth the facts the court will need to rule in your favor in such a way that it will want, or at least be inclined, to do so. The purpose and goals of the discussion or argument section are to show the court *how* to rule in your favor and *why* it should. Here is where you explain the law and apply it to your facts to compel a favorable result. We recommend titling this section "Discussion" because that term implies that you are explaining the state of law as it actually is, versus arguing your version of it. Also, "Discussion" is often the term courts use for their explanation and application of the law, and it is wise to align yourself with the court.

Showing the court how to rule in your favor involves making your points as clearly and concisely as possible. This often means organizing complex information so that the busy reader can quickly and easily understand it. Chapters 1 and 2 discuss tools to help you accomplish this as a drafter. These include (1) putting context before details, (2) going from broad to narrow and general to specific, (3) linking new information with familiar information, and (4) having an explicit structure. The structure of the discussion section of a trial court brief is based on the CRAC format (Conclusion, Rule/Law, Application/Analysis, and Conclusion). Similar to the IRAC format used in office memoranda, the CRAC format is designed to deliver information in the most straightforward manner and is the format most readers expect. Also important in organizing complex information is deciding on a message—the theory, theme, or pitch for the case—which will enable you to package the details and focus your drafting. You are selling the court a solution you want it to implement. Before a court will implement your solution, it needs to understand how it works; thus you must lead the court from point A to point B in a straightforward manner, not take it through a maze.

Clear simple solutions (particularly to complex issues) tend to be persuasive in their own right, which is a good start. You add to this in the discussion section by telling and showing the court *why* it should implement your solution and rule in your favor. This requires thorough and sophisticated knowledge of the law and authorities and how they affect your facts. There is no substitute for sound research, analysis, and preparation. With that foundation you will be able to:

(1) Recognize strong points and arguments and make the most of them;

(2) Understand and overcome or minimize weaknesses in your positions;

(3) Understand the hierarchy of your authorities and use them to your best advantage, and

(4) Organize your arguments persuasively and coherently.

All these accomplishments combine to further persuade a court to rule your way.

2. Organizing Your Discussion or Argument Section

a. *Main Sections*

In a memorandum in support of a motion, every independent ground on which you base your request becomes a main section in the discussion. If, for example, a motion to dismiss is based on lack of personal jurisdiction, lack of subject matter jurisdiction, and improper venue, each of these grounds would get its own section. In a memorandum in opposition to a motion, each independent reason the court should deny the request should get its own section. The main sections of supporting and opposing memoranda will usually be similar in subject matter. However, the drafter of the opposing memorandum is not obligated to follow the supporting memorandum's organization. In both supporting and opposing memoranda, each main section is preceded by a heading that identifies the issue addressed in the section.

Ordering your main arguments (sections): If you have more than one independent reason why the court should rule in your favor, you should almost always put your strongest argument first, the next strongest second, etc. The judge, law clerk, or court attorney will read your memorandum quickly, and first impressions are important and will influence the decision-maker's remaining impressions. Your strongest argument is the one that delivers your message most effectively. It contains the highest ranking and most on-point cases and makes the most of your facts.

Which argument is strongest and which arguments are stronger than others may become obvious to you in the research and analysis stage, or the hierarchy may not be clear until you have tested your argument in the drafting and revision stages.

Sometimes, however, drafters must lead with arguments other than their strongest, for example, when the strongest argument is dependent on first establishing another element or requirement. Or a court may not be able to understand the stronger argument unless it is preceded by a simpler argument that helps set the context for the stronger, but more detailed and complicated argument.

Finally, if you have two arguments that you think are of equal strength, lead with the one that is most consequential—that would give you the most relief. For example, in a motion to dismiss based on lack of personal jurisdiction and improper venue, the argument that the court does not have personal jurisdiction over your client would go first.

b. Subsections

An independent ground or reason the court should rule your way may have sub-issues that each merit discussion. For example, a ground for your motion or opposition might contain several elements or requirements that must be established; each element would get its own CRAC and subheading. Or for clarity's sake you may need to divide a complex argument with several types of legal support into subsections, each with its own CRAC and subheading. Division of an argument into subsections may become obvious during the research and analysis stages. Or, during the drafting stage you may find that you need to break up a long argument into subsections.

In general, if a matter merits a paragraph or more discussion of the law, and then a paragraph or more of application of the law to your facts, it should become a subsection and get its own heading and a separate CRAC. On the other hand, be careful not to subdivide your argument unnecessarily or excessively. Too many subsections and headings can break up the flow of an argument. Finally, if you use subsections, do not have a main argument with just one subsection under it. A single, stand-alone subsection is not a subsection at all.

Ordering your subsections requires balancing clarity with strength. Ideally, the subsection with the strongest arguments goes first. If this interrupts the flow or logic of the main argument, or if your strongest argument is dependent on one in another subsection, the strongest material may have to come later in the discussion. A discussion section that is quickly and easily understood is most important. In order to be persuaded by an argument, a court must first understand it.

If a main section/argument contains subsections, it is common to put a "mini summary argument" after the main section heading and before the first subheading that sets forth your overall conclusion on the main argument, supported by your conclusion for each of the subsections, in the order you discuss them, with citations to authority for each.

3. Make the Structure Explicit

Before you start to draft a trial memorandum, decide what your main arguments are and have a plan regarding what order to put them in. Also have an idea of which argument should be divided into subsections and in what order those subsections should go. This may change as you draft and revise, but it is important to start with a structure in mind. Then make that structure explicit with headings, subheadings, CRAC, well-organized paragraphs, sentences, and appropriate transitions.

4. Reviewing and Ranking Cases and Other Authorities

By the time you are ready to start drafting the discussion section, you will have an idea of which cases and authorities you will use in your sections and subsections. Review them carefully so that you have thorough and comfortable knowledge of their holdings and important facts, as well as any laws, tests, factors, and the like, they contain. Complete and sophisticated knowledge of how the cases and other authorities help or hurt your cause is essential in drafting good arguments.

Once you have reviewed the cases you are considering using, rank them with your message in mind. Whether you prefer to think of it as your theory of the case, theme, or pitch, the message determines how you package and sell your points and arguments to justify your position and motivate the court to rule your way.

For each section and subsection you plan to draft, determine which:

- Cases you will use to set out your basic laws or tests;
- Cases have compelling language that you will want to quote or paraphrase;
- Cases have facts that you want to use to analogize or distinguish the facts in your case;

- Cases are useful simply because the court ruled the same way you want the trial court to rule.

It is likely that the same case or cases will be useful in more than one category. These cases go to the top of the heap and will be featured in your argument. If there are cases you thought you might use that did not make any of these categories, put them aside. It is likely you will not use them in your discussion. Do not throw them away yet, because a use for them may be triggered as you draft your arguments. What is important is that you start with a plan regarding which cases you are going to use and why. This will focus your writing and prevent you from cluttering up your memorandum with extraneous discussion and case citation.

Also examine and rank the cases you think are harmful because:

- they set forth rules that are detrimental to your cause;
- they have damaging language that you can imagine the other side quoting; or
- their facts and holding could undermine your theory of the case.

Here, too, the same case or cases might satisfy more than one category. These go to the top of the "must legally assail and/or factually distinguish" heap. Resist the urge to ignore or dismiss cases that might be damaging, because the opposing side certainly will not.

Also, be sure that the authority you intend to use is still good law. This means Shepardizing™ or Keyciting™ your authorities, and having enough knowledge of the law and subject matter to recognize if, for example, a case was decided before a change or shift in the law.

Finally, all cases and authorities are not created equally. Be clear on where in the hierarchy of authority they fall. First note whether the case or other authority is controlling—does it come from an appellate court or a court of last resort in the trial court's jurisdiction? Is a statute or ordinance from the state or county in which the trial court is situated? Authority that is not controlling, *e.g.*, cases and statutes from other jurisdictions and secondary sources such as treatises, is merely optional. Optional authority is sometimes referred to as "persuasive authority"—which is a misnomer, because optional authority is only persuasive if the court decides it is. For further discussion regarding the hierarchy of authority see Chapter 3, section (A)(1).

Then for each section and subsection, rank the controlling authorities among themselves, *e.g.*, cases from courts of last resort in the jurisdiction are ranked higher than appellate court cases.

As drafters become more experienced this all will become second nature and happen automatically.

5. Drafting Your Argument

There are two cardinal rules to live by in drafting the discussion or argument section of your trial court memorandum:

1. *Keep it simple*—In general your reader, be it the trial judge, law clerk, or court attorney, is extremely busy and pressed for time. They may be reviewing and working up as many as 20 motions at a given time. You want to grab their attention and make it easy for them to rule or recommend ruling your way.
2. *Stick to your theory of the case, theme, or pitch*—This is the essence of your memorandum, your message. It should guide how you organize your arguments, what cases you use, how you use them, and how you use your facts.

The discussion or argument section is comprised of CRACs (Conclusion, Rule/Law, Application/Analysis, Conclusion), each of which help deliver your message to the court and persuade it to rule in your favor. Each main argument without subsections is addressed using a CRAC, and each subsection within a main argument gets its own CRAC.

C: Conclusion—The Heading

Each section and sub-section is preceded by a heading that concisely sets forth the conclusion you want the court to reach on the issue or sub-issue. The main function of a heading in a trial memorandum is to act as a sign post that identifies the main point of the section or subsection for the reader. Phrasing the heading in the form of a conclusion makes it persuasive. Drafters should resist the urge to cram their arguments and supporting reasons in headings because this usually makes the headings long and unwieldy. Also, readers tend to skip over lengthy headings—those more than 3 lines. If you can set forth your conclusion and fundamental reason in support in less than 3 lines, do so. Otherwise you are better off saving the fundamental reason for the topic sentence that immediately follows the heading.

If you are having difficulty drafting a heading, skip it and move on to explaining and applying of the law on the issue or sub-issue. After you have finished, the exact conclusion you want the court to reach will become much clearer.

R: Rule/Law—Identifying, Explaining, and Illustrating the Law

Begin every rule/law section with a topic sentence that sets forth the conclusion you want the court to reach and the fundamental reason why, accompanied by a cite to the strongest supporting authority. This may feel repetitive to the heading, but probably will not be if your heading is of manageable length. By including a citation to authority, you are backing up the conclusion with law.

The topic sentence elaborates on the heading, without becoming bogged down in details. The goal is to be simple and compelling. Use concrete, descriptive words, and the active voice.

Next set forth and explain the law, standards, tests and/or factors in a way that supports your argument. For every law, include a pin cite to the authority from which it came. Similarly, every explanation of the law should be followed by a pin citation to the authority from which it came or on which it is based. This shows readers you are not making it up and enables them to look up the case or other authority for themselves. Quote where you think the language is particularly compelling, but limit block quoting as readers often skip over block quotes. If you do block quote, it may be useful to include a summary of the quote either immediately before or after it to ensure that its content is communicated effectively.

Be sure to illustrate the law and explanations with examples from the cases. Illustrating the law means including specific factual examples from cases that show how a particular requirement was met or not met or to show when a factor or series of factors was or were present, or not. Specific facts and holdings are necessary to show how a law works in practice. Without them, the rule/law section will be merely abstract. Placement of illustrations depends on the laws being explained. Sometimes they will relate so easily that you can explain them together in one paragraph and follow that paragraph with a paragraph of case examples. Other times you will need to illustrate as you go, meaning certain laws will need to be illustrated before moving to explaining others.

Identifying, explaining, and illustrating the law in a way that best delivers your message requires thorough and sophisticated knowledge of the authorities and how they affect your facts. First you need to draft in a logical order that is easy to understand. This usually means going from broad to narrow and general to specific, as in an office memorandum. At the same time you want to focus on the most favorable aspects of the law (be it rules, standards, tests, factors, etc.) and highlight your strongest cases. Knowing what all these are, how they relate, and how they affect your case is critical. There is no substitution for thorough research, analysis, and preparation.

As you explain and illustrate the rules to advance your side, it is important not to ignore law, explanations, or cases on which the other side will rely. Your goal is to diminish their impact. This means distinguishing them on their facts or assailing them legally. (See below regarding dealing with adverse authority).

Every law, explanation, or case that you refer to in the application section of your CRAC must first be set forth in the rule/law section. Also, do not discuss the facts until the application section. Readers have a hard time following a piecemeal analysis in which the drafter states a law and applies it; states another law and applies it, etc. Instead, set out, explain, and illustrate all the laws applicable to an issue or sub-issue, then apply them.

A: Application/Analysis

Begin each application section with an overall assertion of whether facts in your case meet or fail to meet the basic law you have set forth in the rule/law section, with a pin cite to your strongest authority. Here, you are telling the court specifically the result you would like it to reach based on the law and facts. Thus, make your overall conclusion specific: "The court has personal jurisdiction over the defendant" rather than general: "The defendant meets the above tests and factors."

Then, in order of broad to narrow, strongest to weakest:

A. *Tell* the court why the facts in your case meet or fail to meet the laws you have set out and explained, with pin cites to supporting authorities (these are your "assertions"), *e.g.*, The defendant had numerous and systematic contacts with Texas, including monthly business trips, leasing a summer home, and renting a post office box. *See McDermott v. Cronin*, 31 S.W. 2d 617, 619 (Tx. Ct. App. 2000) (defendant established minimum contacts with the forum by using a Texas mailing address on both correspondence and contracts).

B. *Show* the court how the facts in your case meet or fail to meet the laws you have set out and explained by comparing and contrasting them to facts of the cases cited in the rule/law section of your CRAC. Here you will show the court how your facts are (1) the same or similar to cases that held in your favor, and (2) unlike the facts of cases that did not. Remember, a good contrast can be just as persuasive as a comparison. Be sure to pin cite to these cases as you discuss them and the facts of your case. This shows that the client specific facts you are highlighting are legally significant, and enables the reader to go to the exact page and find the facts of the case you are comparing or contrasting. The goal in the application section is to show the court that your conclusions and assertions are sound and well supported by the law and the facts.

Avoid a mechanical application of the various laws, tests, factors, etc. in the order they are set out in the cases. Look at your facts and decide which are the most compelling. Perhaps several combine into a central theme. Highlight these facts or theme and show they meet or violate a rule or requirement as explained in the cases. This is the time when you can use some of the descriptive words you concluded were too over the top for your statement of facts. You still want a professional tone, however—you do not want to appear overwrought. Ask yourself: "Would my reader roll her eyes at this?"

Dealing with Adverse Authority

You will need to address adverse cases in the controlling jurisdiction. This is different than addressing counter arguments in an office memo. Deal with adverse authority by distinguishing it on its facts, and/or assailing it legally, which may involve showing its reasoning was flawed, that the court misinterpreted prior caselaw, that it was decided before a change in the law, or that the case is an outlier—that few other courts have cited it or ruled the same, etc. There are many reasons a case may be "wrong." A good lawyer and drafter is able to identify these reasons and explain them coherently.

In general, first try to distinguish a case on its facts, because trial courts are more apt to distinguish a case than say it is wrong if they can do so. This means showing how its facts are different than those in your client's case and why that is significant. But do not be afraid, if you have grounds, to show how and why a case is legally incorrect.

Try to minimize the impact of an adverse case by putting it in the middle of your argument rather than at the beginning or the end. Avoid ending your argument on a low note. Finally, try to deal with an adverse case as swiftly as possible.

Note: In memoranda to the court, avoid *articulating* a possible argument on the other side. Thus, eliminate sentence structures like: "The (defense/prosecution) might argue, relying on ________, that ________", or sentences that begin with: "An argument could be made" or "It could be said," etc. It is the other side's responsibility to make its own arguments, and you do not want to articulate or highlight opposing arguments (indeed, you may state the argument better than they do).

Final Words on Discussion/Argument

1. State What You Want;
2. Tell Why;
3. Show How.

E. Conclusion

In the conclusion section of an MPA or trial brief, remind the court in simple, compelling terms what you want it to do, and why it should. Some jurisdictions limit what can be contained in a conclusion. If so, follow this guidance strictly. In any event, the conclusion should seldom, if ever, exceed a single three to five sentence paragraph.

F. Create a Heading and Topic Sentence Outline

A good way to test memoranda to the trial court for overall substance and organization is to create a heading and topic sentence outline. After you have completed a draft of the MPA or trial brief, highlight the document's headings and subheading along with the topic sentences of every paragraph, then copy them in order into a separate document and print it out.

First check if the headings and topic sentences identify all the subjects, issues and points necessary to analyze the problem or matter and persuade the court to rule in your favor. Thus, in the statement of facts are all the significant categories of facts clearly identified? In the discussion section, are all issues that needed to be addressed, and all points and arguments that needed to be made, identified? Are the major or overarching applicable laws identified in the topic sentences of the rule/law paragraphs? Are your overall conclusions for each issue and sub issue set forth in the topic sentences of your application paragraphs?

If the outline reveals any ambiguities or omissions in facts or analysis, review your draft. It may be that you have left out subjects, issues, points, or arguments that you intended to address or that you realize need to be addressed, or steps in an analysis or argument may have been omitted—which mean more substantive drafting is needed. Or, you may have fully addressed the necessary subjects and issues, but the headings and topic sentences do not adequately identify them—which means revising or adding headings or topic sentences.

Second, check if the headings and topic sentences are arranged in a logical order that is easy to follow. Pared down to headings and topic sentences you should be able to tell if the MPA provides context before details, puts familiar information before new information, and has an explicit structure. A heading and topic sentence outline also reveals whether the issues and sub issues are logically and persuasively arranged, *e.g.*, threshold issues are addressed first, and issues and sub issues that relate to each other or that follow each other are put one after another, and that, where possible, the strongest arguments are placed first, followed by the next strongest, etc. Also, the subjects and issues may be arranged logically in persuasive order, but some topic sentences may need transition words to make their relationship explicit.

Third, check if the headings clearly and concisely identify the subject of the section or subsection in the form of a conclusion, and that the topic sentences clearly and concisely identify the subject or point of the paragraph. In other words, check your headings and topic sentences first in isolation to ensure they are clear and strong, and then make sure they are accurate.

G. Trial Court Memorandum Statement of Facts Drafting and Reviewing Guidelines

Examine your statement of facts for the following:

1. Substance/Analysis
2. Organization
3. Sentence Structure, Word Choice, Tone
4. Paragraph Structure
5. Technical Aspects: Proofing, Grammar, *Bluebook*, etc.

Each of these is discussed separately below.

1. Substance/Analysis

Does the statement of facts include all legally material facts? Does it include helpful or compelling background and emotional (subjective) facts? Based on your research and knowledge of the law, does the statement contain all facts necessary to rule in your favor? Have any facts pertaining to any relevant legal issue, element, or factor been omitted?

Does the statement of facts provide enough information and context for an unfamiliar or vaguely familiar reader to understand what the case is about and what happened?

Does the statement of facts promote your theory, theme, or pitch and deliver the message you want to send to the court?

Does the statement of facts set up your analysis in the discussion or argument section? Is every fact you refer to in the discussion or argument section set forth in the statement of facts?

2. Organization

Organization is particularly important in the statement of facts. First make sure you have set forth the facts, including background facts so that the reader will understand what the case is about and what happened. Then check to see if the favorable facts are put in positions of emphasis—at the beginning of the section, paragraph, or sentence, or at the end with a solid build up. Check to see if unfavorable facts are de-emphasized—buried in the middle of the section, paragraphs, or sentences, or effectively joined or juxtaposed with favorable facts.

Overall, is the story you have told easy to follow and as compelling as the underlying facts allow?

If complex, have you broken up the statement of facts with short, descriptive subheadings to aid the reader in finding topics and to provide some relief for the eyes?

3. Sentence/Word Choice, Tone

Sentence structure and word choice are also critical in drafting the statement of facts. First, check for sentences that are confusing or hard to read and understand. This is a detraction for both favorable and unfavorable facts. (Indeed, when dealing with an unfavorable fact, you do not want the reader to have to read your sentence more than once.) Then check to see if favorable facts are described using compelling, specific, and descriptive words, in active sentences with concrete subjects and active predicates. Also see if unfavorable facts are effectively de-emphasized by use of the passive voice and flat general terms.

Is the tone compelling, yet professional? Is it subtle in its partisanship? Detractions would be an overly emotional, angry, combative, or smug tone; or, conversely, a tone that is too flat or seemingly uninvolved. Any tone that suggests the drafter is putting himself in the place of the court, or commanding the court, is detraction as well.

4. Paragraph Structure

The guidelines for critiquing paragraphs in the statement of facts are the same as with all legal writing only with an eye toward emphasizing favorable facts and de-emphasizing unfavorable facts. Paragraphs should begin with a topic or transitional sentence. Every sentence in the paragraph should (1) relate to the topic/transitional sentence, and (2) relate to the sentences around it. The second requirement is accomplished by arranging the sentences in a logical progression, and, often, by using good transition words that signal where you are going with the sentence, *e.g.*, thus, accordingly, moreover, conversely, nevertheless.

Also check for effective placement and emphasis of favorable facts, and effective burying of unfavorable facts within the paragraphs.

Detractions include paragraphs without clear topic or transition sentences; sentences that do not relate to the topic identified; paragraphs that are choppy or disconnected because the sentences are not arranged smoothly or because transition words are needed; and, of course, paragraphs that fail to effectively emphasize favorable facts or that emphasize or fail to minimize unfavorable facts.

5. Technical Aspects: Proofing, Grammar, *Bluebook*, etc.

This category involves attention to detail. Student drafters should avoid leaving points on the table because they have not had time to proofread thoroughly or ensure their cites are in perfect *Bluebook* form. The rule applies with the same force in the real world. A document that has distracting proofing and *Bluebook* errors and that suffers from inconsistent formatting will undermine the document's persuasiveness and the drafter's credibility.

Some points on the technical editing checklist:

- Check for widows and orphans—opening and ending lines of paragraphs that are stranded alone on their own page. There should always be at least two lines of a paragraph on a page. If not, change the page break.
- Keep headings with the text to which they relate. Two lines of text together with the heading is the minimum preferred.
- Check that pages are numbered consecutively.
- Examine the font size used. 12 point is standard, although 14 point is becoming increasingly the norm for federal appellate courts for ease of reading.
- Check margins (at least one-inch around); use of defined terms where appropriate.

Finally, check that you have strictly complied with all requirements of the local rules of the court. Some may surprise you. For example, a court may require that all documents filed with it begin on the second line of a 28-line double spaced page, on every page. Why? Because the documents are bundled in two-hole punched file folders and, when the folder gets thick, one cannot turn back enough of the pages above to see the first line on the page. Know the local rules and follow them to a fault. There will be hyper-technical members of the clerk's office staff that will refuse to file your documents if they are out of compliance.

H. Trial Court Memorandum Discussion/Argument Drafting and Reviewing Guidelines

Examine your Discussion or Argument section for:

(1) Substance/Analysis,

(2) Organization,

(3) Sentence Structure, Word Choice, Tone,

(4) Paragraph Structure, and

(5) Technical—Proofing, Grammar, *Bluebook*, etc.

1. Substance/Analysis

In this category, look at content and persuasiveness. Do you demonstrate a thorough and sophisticated knowledge and understanding of the subject matter and applicable laws, rules, standards, tests, factors, and cases? Are the laws, rules, standards, tests, factors, and cases necessary to enable a court to rule in your favor all present? Are the cases used effectively to highlight and focus the reader's attention on favorable facts? Are the client specific facts used effectively to persuade court? Are adverse cases effectively distinguished or legally assailed? Are the headings informative, compelling and easy to read? Does the discussion promote the theory of the case, theme, or pitch?

The ultimate question is: "Does the court have enough legal and factual information to rule in my favor and would it be persuaded to do so?"

Also assess your citation to the cases. Every law, rule, standard, test, factor, and fact you describe must be accompanied by a pin citation to the case from which it came, so readers can go to the exact page of that case or exact subsection of the statute and see for themselves. In addition, when comparing or contrasting the client specific facts with those of a particular case, you must cite to the exact pages of that case where those facts are set out or discussed.

Detractions include:

(A) Omission of important laws, rules, standards, tests, factors, or cases;

(B) Not recognizing or highlighting useful cases, laws, rules, standards, tests, factors, facts from the cases, or client facts;

(C) Not distinguishing or critically analyzing flaws in adverse cases;

(D) Spending too much time on weaker points;

(E) Dull, lengthy recitation of the facts in the cases, or dull, lengthy, mechanical application of the laws; or

(F) Sequential analysis and application of the cases—the writer should synthesize the cases and highlight significant favorable factors and facts.

2. Organization

First check if you have organized the discussion or argument in a logical manner that is easy to follow. Do the sections/arguments follow the theory of the case? If there is more than one main argument, are the arguments set forth in a compelling and logical order? If the arguments are divided into subsections, does this help your understanding, or is the flow interrupted? Do general, overarching rules come first, followed by discussion of factors and facts from the cases? Do the paragraphs logically follow each other, with informative topic or transitional sentences?

Next assess whether the arguments are arranged persuasively. Are the most helpful cases in positions of emphasis? Are the client specific facts placed or woven in strategically, so that the reader can easily see how they meet or fail to meet any applicable test or rule? Are unfavorable facts and cases put in positions of de-emphasis, *e.g.*, in the middle of the argument or paragraph?

The ultimate questions: Would unfamiliar or vaguely familiar readers understand the discussion or argument? Would they be persuaded by it?

3. Sentence/Word Choice/Tone

First, check for sentences that are confusing or hard to read and understand. Then check that favorable laws, rules, standards, tests, factors, and cases are set forth using compelling, specific, and descriptive words, in active sentences with concrete subjects and active predicates. Also see if unfavorable facts, tests, factors, or cases are effectively de-emphasized by use of the passive voice, and flat general terms.

Assess the tone: is it compelling, persuasive, yet professional? This is argument, and thus the drafter can use works that were too overboard for the statement of facts. Still, the drafter must ask "is the reader likely to roll her eyes?"

Detractions include an overly emotional, angry, combative, smug, or partisan tone; or conversely a tone that is too flat, seemingly uninvolved. Any tone that suggests the lawyer is putting herself in the place of the court or commanding the court is detraction as well.

4. Paragraph Structure

The well-written, persuasive paragraph is the key component of the discussion or argument. Make sure the paragraphs begin with an informative and compelling topic or transition sentence that clearly identifies the point the writer is advancing. Then every sentence in the paragraph should (1) relate and support the topic/transitional sentence, and (2) relate to the sentences around it. The second element is accomplished by arranging the sentences in a logical progression and, often, by using good transition words that signal where you are going with the sentence, *e.g.*, Thus, Accordingly, Moreover, Conversely, Nevertheless.

Check for emphasis of favorable facts and law and de-emphasis of unfavorable facts and law.

Detractions include paragraphs without clear, compelling topic or transition sentences, sentences that do not relate to the topic identified; paragraphs that are choppy or disconnected because the sentences are not arranged smoothly or because transition words are needed, paragraphs that fail to effectively emphasize favorable facts or law, or that emphasize or fail to minimize unfavorable facts or law.

5. Technical: Proofing/Grammar/*Bluebook*, etc.

This category assesses attention to detail. Drafters should proofread thoroughly to ensure their cites are in perfect *Bluebook* form and there are no grammatical, punctuating, or other proofing errors. Also double check to make sure that all local rules regarding form and formatting have been complied with. See section (G)(5) of this chapter for a proofreading checklist.

The Basic Structure: CRAC

Under this format, for each issue and sub-issue:

C—**Conclusion:** Identify the issue by setting forth the conclusion you want the court to make. Do this in your headings and the topic sentences that come immediately after your headings.

R—**Rules/Laws:** Set forth and explain the applicable rules or law in order of broad to specific/general to narrow (describing factors is part of explaining). Illustrate the law and your explanations with factual examples from the cases. Set forth, explain and illustrate the law so as to advance your position. Do not ignore—but rather diminish—the importance or impact of rules, factors or cases that you know the other side will rely on. Remember, often detailed or narrow laws are used to explain broader ones.

Think of the Rule/Law section as Law/Law-Explanation/Law-Illustration section.

A—**Application/Analysis:** Begin with your conclusion—that the facts of your case meet or fail to meet the basic law you have set forth in the rule/law section, with a cite to your strongest supporting authority. Then in order of broad to narrow, strongest to weakest:

1. *Tell* the court why the facts meet or fail to meet the laws you have set out and explained and illustrated, with citations to supporting authorities (these are your "assertions"), and

2. *Show* the court how the facts meet or fail to meet the laws you have set out and explained and illustrated by comparing and contrasting them to the facts of the cases cited in the rule/law section—be sure to pin cite to these authorities as you discuss them and the facts of your case.

Also distinguish and diminish any factors or cases you know the other side will rely on. The goal is to show the court that your conclusions and assertions are sound and well supported. Think of the application as the "tell and show" section.

Remember: Do not introduce or refer to any new rules, explanations, factors, cases, or facts in the Application/Analysis section. They must first be introduced in the Rule/Law section or the Statement of Facts.

C—**Conclusion:** If necessary because the analysis is lengthy and/or complex, tell the court again the conclusion you want it to make and why, with a cite to your essential authorities.

Checkpoints

- The purpose of a MPA or brief in support of or opposition to a motion in the trial court is to persuade the court to take or not take the action requested in the motion.
- The audience for an MPA or trial brief is a judge, law clerk, or court attorney. Their experience and expertise will vary. One thing they all have in common: a heavy work load—a large number of cases, only one of which is yours.
- The goals in drafting MPAs or briefs in support of or opposition to a motion are to make the court want to rule in your favor and make it easy for the court to do so.
- To draft an effective MPA or brief in support of a motion, you must first know exactly what relief you are seeking or opposing; drafting a proposed order is one way to accomplish this end.
- Effective MPAs or briefs feature a message that is delivered well and a simple solution for the trial court to implement.
- Developing a Message: to effectively package and market your points and arguments, you need to develop a theory, theme, or a pitch for your case.
- MPAs and briefs are comprised of a caption, a preliminary statement, a statement of facts, a discussion or argument section, and a conclusion. Each portion has its distinct purpose.
- The preliminary statement sets the context and provides a road map for the MPA or brief. It is similar to an executive summary in an office memo, except that it advocates a position rather predicts a result.
- Drafting the statement of facts is a matter of accurate storytelling. Your goal is to tell a compelling, concise, and accurate story that will make the court want to rule your way and give it enough information to do so.
- The statement of facts develops and reinforces you message and sets up the analysis in the discussion section.
- The statement of facts must include all legally material facts, both favorable and unfavorable.
- Emphasize favorable facts by:

  o placing them at the beginning of a section, paragraph or sentence, or at the end of these with a solid build up, and

  o describing them using the active voice, concrete subjects, and active predicates.
- Minimize unfavorable facts by

  o placing them at the in the middle of the narrative or the middle of paragraphs and sentences, and

Checkpoints *continued*

  - o describing them in words that are bland and general—as long as they are accurate.
- Maintain a professional tone in describing the facts, favorable and unfavorable.
- Although favorable and unfavorable facts are treated differently in terms of placement, the overall organization of the statement of facts in MPAs and trial briefs is similar to that of an office memo. The first paragraph should provide the background and context so that the reader con better understand the details. The statement of facts should be arranged logically so that the readers can easily understand what the case is about and the message you are delivering.
- The statement of facts should be free of conclusions and argument, and must contain any fact referred to in the discussion section.
- Any fact set out in the statement of facts must be accompanied by a citation to the trial court record or to an attached exhibit.
- The purpose of the discussion or argument section in a MPA or trial brief is to *persuade* the court to rule your way. This is different than trying to win an argument or show that you are right.
- We recommend using the term "discussion" rather than "argument" in your heading. Discussion implies that you are explaining the state of the law as it is, versus arguing your version of it.
- Persuading the trial court involves showing it how to rule in your favor and why it should so.
- Where possible, provide the court with simple solutions that are easy to understand and implement.
- Showing the court why it should rule your way requires thorough and sophisticated knowledge of the law and authorities and how they affect your facts.
- In an MPA or brief in support of a motion, every independent ground on which you base your request becomes a main section in the discussion.
- In an MPA or brief in opposition to a motion, every independent reason the court should deny the request becomes a main section in the discussion.
- Ideally the section with the strongest most persuasive points and arguments goes first, the next strongest second, and so on.
- Sometimes you may need to lead with arguments other than your strongest, *e.g.*, when the strongest argument is dependent on first establishing another requirement, or where a court might not be able to understand the stronger argument unless it is preceded by a simpler argument.
- Before you begin drafting review and rank your authorities, and make sure they are still good law.

Checkpoints *continued*

- In drafting the discussion section of an MPA or trial brief, remember to:
  - o Keep it simple, and
  - o Stick to your theory, theme or pitch — the essential message you want to deliver.
- The discussion section is composed of CRACs (Conclusion, Rule/Law, Application/Analysis, Conclusion). Each main argument without subsections is addressed using a CRAC, and each subsection within a main argument gets its own CRAC.
- The conclusion section of an MPA or brief in the trial court is a simple, short restatement of what you are asking the court to do. Typically one does not restate the reasons for doing so in any degree of detail.
- Test your MPA or trial brief for overall substance and organization by creating and reviewing a heading and topic sentence outline.
- Once you have a complete quality draft, thoroughly assess the MPA or trial brief using the statement of facts and discussion/argument guidelines set out in this chapter.
- Make time to print and proofread the MPA or trial brief separately before filing it or turning it in.

Chapter 7

Appellate Briefs

Roadmap

- The purpose of an appellate brief is to persuade a court to reverse or affirm a judgment or order below. An appellate brief should not attempt to retry the case.
- An appellate brief should show:
  - that there was or was not error below — that the decision below was incorrect or correct under the applicable standard of review; and
  - that the error requires reversal because the error was not harmless, or does not require reversal because the error was harmless.
- An appellate brief is made up of separate components, usually prescribed by local rules of procedure. Typical components include a statement of issues on appeal, tables of contents and authorities, statement of the case, statement of facts, summary of the argument, discussion or argument with headings and subheadings, and a conclusion.
- The issues on appeal should specifically identify the alleged error or lack of error below. Often whether an error was harmless or reversible is not identified as a separate issue on appeal since it is generally always an issue.
- The statement of the case should set out the relevant procedural history of the case and should also contain the essential reasons why the decision below should be reversed or affirmed. Accurate citations to the record for each fact or document are essential.
- The statement of facts should tell an accurate story that will make readers want to adopt your legal positions and that gives them enough information to be able to do. Accurate pinpoint citations to the record for each fact are essential.
- The purpose of the discussion or argument is to show readers how to rule in your client's favor and why they should do so. This involves making your points as clearly as possible, which usually means organizing complex information so that readers can understand it as easily as possible. It also involves showing why your positions are the better alternative.
- The conclusion section of an appellate brief is usually short reiteration of the request for the relief that you seek.

A. The Purpose, Audience, and Goals of an Appellate Brief

The purpose of an appellate brief is to persuade the court to reverse or affirm a judgment or order below. A judgment terminates the lawsuit and sets forth the parties' rights and obligations. For example, a judgment may be entered in favor of the defendant dismissing the lawsuit with prejudice, or entered in favor of the plaintiff and awarding damages. An order is a command by the court that allows, requires, or forbids something from occurring. Most appeals are required to be from judgments or final orders to avoid piecemeal appeals.

The party appealing from the judgment or order is usually called the "appellant" especially if the appeal is by right, *e.g.*, an appeal of a final judgment to an intermediate appellate court. However, if a party must petition for review or certiorari in order to proceed, that party is often called the "petitioner." The party opposing the appeal is usually called the "appellee" or the "respondent." It is important to check local rules to make sure you refer to your client with the correct term. In this book, we use the term appellant for the party seeking reversal of a judgment or order, and appellee for the party opposing the appeal and seeking affirmance of the judgment or order.

1. Audience

The audience for appellate briefs will be an intermediate appellate court or a court of last resort. The focus and role of each are somewhat different. The focus of an intermediate appellate court is chiefly on error correction. Courts of last resort also correct errors, but in addition, make policy, make new law, and extend or clarify existing law much more than intermediate courts.

Unlike the trial court, in both intermediate appellate courts and courts of last resort the audience includes more than one decision maker (usually at least three), and you will need to persuade a majority of them to reverse or affirm. Thus, keep in mind that some of your audience may lean favorably toward your position from the outset, some may be hostile, and some may be neutral —and it is often the neutral decision makers who will cast the deciding vote.

a. Intermediate Appellate Courts

The vast majority of appeals are to intermediate appellate courts. At the intermediate level, cases are usually heard and decided by a three-judge panel. One judge is usually assigned as the "writing judge," and this person and a law clerk or court attorney will be the primary audience for the brief. In most cases, you will not know who the writing judge is until the opinion is issued, however. The other two judges on the panel (and perhaps their law clerk or court attorney) will also review your brief. The writing judge will change if the other two judges do not agree with his or her analyses or conclusions regarding the appeal. In that case, one of the other two judges on the panel will issue the opinion.

The writing judge on the intermediate appellate level will likely spend more time reading the brief than a trial judge spends reviewing a memorandum in support of or opposition to a motion. The person who will probably spend the most time with your brief, however, is the judge's law clerk or the court attorney who is charged with working up the appeal. Working up an appeal involves reading the briefs, reviewing the record on appeal, researching and analyzing the law, and then preparing a bench memorandum or drafting an opinion for review by the judges on the panel. The law clerk or court attorney will probably have and take more time to review your brief than the person assisting a trial judge, but your matter will be one of many they are working on. Thus, you will still want to be as concise and direct as possible. This means working hard on your drafting to ensure your organization is easy to follow and that your points and arguments are easy to grasp—even, or especially, if they are complex.

Since the focus and function of intermediate appellate courts is primarily on error correction, the appellate briefs should concentrate on whether the correct law was applied and whether it was applied correctly. Hence, arguments would focus on what the correct law *is* rather than what the correct law *should be*. Policy argument may help support arguments regarding which law is correct or how a law is correctly applied, but they should not be your primary support.

Sometimes an intermediate appellate court will be in the position of making new law or clarifying existing law, *e.g.*, where a statutory scheme is new or recently amended. Also, some intermediate appellate courts are more inclined and in a better position to make policy, *e.g.*, United States Courts of Appeals. In general, though, the primary focus of the appellate brief in an intermediate appellate court will be whether, under existing law, there was error below.

Also keep in mind that intermediate courts of appeal are much more likely to affirm the judgment or order of the trial court than reverse it. Indeed, one study indicates that in the past decade, the affirmance rate in the United States Court of Appeals was approximately 90%. Chris Guthrie & Tracey E. George, *The Futility of Appeal: Disciplinary Insights into the "Affirmance Effect" on the United States Courts of Appeals*, 32 Fla. St. U. L. Rev. 357, 358 (2005).

b. Courts of Last Resort

If the appeal is heard by a court of last resort, *e.g.*, the United States Supreme Court or a state supreme court, your brief will be read by as many as nine decision makers (usually referred to as "justices") as well as their law clerks or court attorneys. The number of justices sitting on courts of last resort varies, *e.g.*, the United States Supreme Court has nine, the California Supreme Court has seven, and the Tennessee Supreme Court has five. In some courts a writing judge may be tentatively assigned before the case is heard; in others the writing judge is decided after the matter is heard and the judges have conferred. One thing is certain: your brief will have a significantly larger primary audience than in an appeal to an intermediate appellate court. Also, if review is discretionary, it is guaranteed that a certain amount of the primary audience thinks that the issues presented are significant. (Not all appeals to courts of last resort are discretionary. For example, review by the California Supreme Court is automatic in cases in which the death penalty has been imposed.)

Since courts of last resort have a more expanded role than intermediate appellate courts, they will entertain and, indeed, expect policy arguments to aid them in determining the law, making new law, and clarifying existing law. Justices and their law clerks or court attorneys will also have and take more time reviewing your brief. However, it is important to make your points and arguments as clearly as possible. You will still need to show whether or not there was error and why. Policy arguments involve demonstrating why your position is the better one among choices. In order for policy arguments to be effective, drafters must first convince the court that their basic legal positions are sound and well supported.

Generally, courts of last resort are not as likely to affirm as intermediate appellate courts. In fact, during the same period that the United States Court of Appeals affirmed 90% of their cases, the United States Supreme Court *reversed* 64% of its cases. Chris Guthrie & Tracey E. George, *The Futility of Appeal: Disciplinary Insights into the "Affirmance Effect" on the United States Courts of Appeals*, 32 Fla. St. U. L. Rev. 357, 358 (2005).

Briefs in moot court competitions are often styled for the United States Supreme Court, but are read and scored initially by lawyers or law students. In these competitions it is essential that the briefs be easy to read and understand. Readers may have long, multiple factor scoring sheets, but the reality is that most will rank the briefs based on their overall impression, ease of reading experience, and technical errors like typographical and citation form errors, and assign scores accordingly. As the rounds advance, it is more likely that actual judges will be scoring the briefs, and briefs with the more sophisticated and artful arguments should prevail. However, to make it to the advanced rounds your brief must be easy to read and free from error.

2. Goals

If you are representing the appellant, your goals in drafting the brief are to convince a majority of the judges or justices deciding the case that:

(1) there was error below—that the decision below was incorrect under the applicable standard of review, that is, *it was incorrect to the appropriate degree*, and

(2) that the error requires reversal—that the error *matters* because it sufficiently affected the result below. In other words, it must be reversible or prejudicial and not harmless error.

When representing the appellee or respondent, your goals in drafting the brief are to convince a majority of the judges or justices deciding the case that:

(1) there was no error below—that, at minimum, the decision at issue *was not incorrect to the appropriate degree*, and

(2) even if there was error, that error was harmless—that it does not warrant reversal because it did not sufficiently affect the result below.

Accomplishing These Goals: Developing a Message

As with trial briefs, drafters of appellate briefs to both intermediate appellate courts and courts of last resort should develop a message through which to package and market their arguments. To develop an effective message, focus on the judgment or order being appealed. If you represent the appellant, ask: How is it vulnerable? What are the essential weaknesses and flaws that you think warrant reversal? How do they relate to each other? How might you link them? If you conclude there is only one ground for reversal, how do you best describe it so it will quickly and easily resound with readers? If you represent the appellee, what shields the judgment or order from attack or makes it irreversible? Since you will already know the appellant's grounds for appeal, ask: What are the flaws or weaknesses in those grounds? Is there a fundamental flaw that permeates them?

Going through this process will help you to package and organize your arguments, and will focus your drafting. Your mission is to file a cohesive brief that, *as a whole*, persuades the court to reverse or affirm the decision below, rather than a brief that constitutes an assortment of arguments.

Finally, an overarching goal for both appellant's and appellee's counsel is to draft a brief that the appellate court adopts in whole, or in large part, as its own opinion in the case. This demonstrates that the drafter has persuaded the court and made it very easy for the court to rule in her client's favor by adopting their positions.

For further discussion on developing a message in persuasive drafting, see Chapter 6, section A.

B. Standards of Review and Reversible versus Harmless Error

The standard of review on appeal is the filter through which the decision below is evaluated. Sometimes it is enough merely to show the decision below was wrong; other times you must show it was "clearly wrong," or an "abuse of discretion," and so on. Deciding whether there was error is only the first step in the appellate court's decision making process, however. If the court finds error, it must next decide whether the error requires the judgment or order to be reversed, *i.e.*, whether the error is reversible or harmless. This inquiry requires evaluating whether and how the error affected the overall result.

1. Standards of Review

Despite the many articulations of the standards of review that are discussed below, the human mind generally only applies two: deferential and non-deferential review. Deferential review is generally applicable to factual determinations and matters within the trial court's discretion. This makes sense as the jury, court, or agency below is the body that received the evidence and made its factual findings accordingly. A reviewing court is not in a position to have enough information to reliably review every nuance of the proceedings below. Similarly, the deferential standard of abuse of discretion is reserved for decisions particularly within the trial judge's province such as courtroom management matters.

Non-deferential review is a different story. Non-deferential review is usually applicable to questions of law. In these situations, the reviewing court is in just as good a position as the court below to pass on these issues.

However, even when the standard of review is non-deferential, at the intermediate appellate court level there is an unwritten presumption of correctness in favor of the trial court. This presumption is generally not present or not as strong in the case of discretionary review of cases in courts of last resort.

Keeping in mind the observation that there are probably really only two basic standards of review in practice—deferential and non-deferential—spread along a spectrum, here are four basic standards of review as well as the one used by the Tennessee Appellate Courts:

(1) *De Novo* (Wrong);

(2) Presumption of Correctness (Tennessee) (Pretty Wrong);

(3) Clearly Erroneous (Very Wrong);

(4) Substantial Evidence (Very Wrong);

(5) Abuse of Discretion (Very, Very Wrong).

If the applicable standard of review is not satisfied, the decision or action below will be upheld.

De Novo: *Wrong*

Under the *de novo* standard, the appellate court reviews the question anew, on its own, with no deference given to the lower court's decision on the matter. The court need only find that the decision below was incorrect. The appellate court is under no constraints. It does not have to give any nod, respect, or deference to the court below.

De novo review typically applies to questions of law, for example, the proper interpretation of a statute or the determination of whether a statute is constitutional. Typical statements of this standard of review are: "This is a question of law which we review *de novo*" or "We independently review whether *x* applies to juveniles."

Presumption of Correctness (Tennessee): Pretty Wrong

Apart from the four standard standards of review discussed above and below that permeate the Federal and many state court systems, some jurisdictions have their own enunciations of their standard of review. When faced with a differently enunciated standard of review, it is important to understand its nuances, both as the standard is stated and as it is applied — remember to watch what courts *do* as well as what they *say*. Tennessee appellate courts, for example, afford a trial court's findings of fact "a presumption of correctness, which is overcome only when the preponderance of the evidence is contrary to the finding of fact."

This standard of review applies to a Tennessee state trial court's findings of fact. There appears to be a lot of wiggle room in the wording of this standard, which affords the appellate court more flexibility should it choose to use it and deniability should it choose not to do so. On one hand, there is a presumption of correctness. On the other hand, the appellate court may conclude that the evidence preponderates the other way.

We have included the Tennessee standard of review as an example of the many permutations of standards among the various jurisdictions. It is important in each appeal to correctly articulate the standard used in the jurisdiction. Not only might it make a substantive difference (as in the case of Tennessee), even if it is only a matter of "semantics," articulating a different standard than the one used by the court will reflect poorly on the drafter and his or her brief.

Clearly Erroneous: Very Wrong

A finding is clearly erroneous where the appellate court is said to be "left with the definite and firm conviction that a mistake has been made." As long as the findings are plausible, they will not be set aside, even if the appellate court would have reached a different result.

The clearly erroneous standard generally applies to trial court findings of fact in the federal system and elsewhere. A typical enunciation of this standard of review is "Although we might have found differently, we cannot say that the trial court's findings are clearly erroneous."

Substantial Evidence: Very Wrong

When the substantial evidence standard is used, the appellant must show that the decision or finding is not supported by "substantial evidence"—often referred to as evidence that is reasonable, credible, and of solid value. The appellate court reviews the issue in the light most favorable to the finding and makes all reasonable inferences in the finding's favor. This standard may sound rather favorable to the appellant, but as a practical matter, it is not. The appellant must show there is *no* substantial evidence to support the decision or findings. Often the court, aided by the respondent, can find *some* substantial (reasonable and credible) evidence in the record. The substantial evidence standard often applies to findings of fact made by a jury and, in California and many other jurisdictions, also to findings of fact made by the trial court.

Abuse of Discretion: Very, Very Wrong

Under the abuse of discretion standard, the appellate court must conclude that the court below abused its discretion in making the decision. The court must find that the decision below was very, very wrong. This usually means the trial court acted arbitrarily, capriciously, or "outside the bounds of reason."

This standard often applies to sanctions, courtroom management issues, protective or sealing orders, or decisions regarding whether or not to admit certain evidence. Although difficult, the standard is not impossible to meet, and often comes down to the court not doing its job. For example, "a district court may abuse its discretion by ignoring a material factor that deserves significant weight, relying on an improper factor, or even if it mulls over the proper mix of factors, by making a serious mistake in judgment." *Siedle v. Putnam Inves., Inc.*, 147 F.3d 7, 10 (1st Cir. 1998). In the *Siedle* case, the trial court rescinded an order sealing the record "after a brief colloquy with counsel" without writing a decision or otherwise stating its reasons. The appellate court reversed, stating "In this instance, we discern no evidence that the district court identified and balanced the interests at stake, or that the court endeavored to determine whether any information contained in Siedle's filings actually fell within the ambit of the attorney-client privilege. In the circumstances at hand, these omissions amounted to an abuse of discretion." In other words, the court below had not done its job.

2. Reversible versus Harmless Error

If the appellant successfully convinces the appellate court that there was error under the applicable standard of review, the court then determines if the error requires reversal of the judgment or order below.

In appeals where the court has concluded that the jury's or trial court's finding of facts are clearly erroneous or not supported by substantial evidence, this process is compressed. Findings of fact that are not plausible (under the clearly erroneous standard) or unsupported by any reasonable or credible evidence (under the substantial evidence standard) cannot stand, and judgments or orders based on them will be reversed. In other words, if an appellant shows error under the clearly erroneous or substantial evidence standards, reversal is automatic.

Also, certain errors, called "structural errors," require automatic reversal because they render a trial fundamentally unfair or the verdict fundamentally unreliable. For examples of errors involving fundamental unfairness, *see Johnson v. United States*, 520 U.S. 461, 468, 117 S.Ct. 1544, 137 L.Ed.2d 718 (1997) (complete denial of counsel); *McKaskle v. Wiggins*, 465 U.S. 168, 104 S.Ct. 944, 79 L.Ed.2d 122 (1984) (denial of self-representation at trial); *Waller v. Georgia*, 467 U.S. 39, 104 S.Ct. 2210, 81 L.Ed.2d 31 (1984) (denial of public trial), *Tumey v. Ohio*, 273 U.S. 510, 47 S.Ct. 437, 71 L.Ed. 749 (1927) (biased trial judge). Regarding unreliability, an erroneous jury instruction that misdescribed the prosecution's burden of proving guilt beyond a reasonable doubt was held to require automatic reversal because "it vitiate[d] all the jury's findings" leaving a reviewing court "to engage in pure speculation—its view of what a reasonable jury would have done." *Sullivan v. Louisiana*, 508 U.S. 275, 281, 113 S.Ct. 2078, 124 L.Ed.2d 182, 190 (1993).

If the court determines the error is structural, it will automatically reverse the judgment below. The term automatic is a bit misleading to the extent it implies that this is a quick and easy process. On the contrary, structural error analyses and arguments are often complex.

If the error did not involve insufficient evidence or was not structural, the court will engage in a harmless error analysis to determine whether and how much the error affected the result at the hearing or trial. The tests used to determine if an error requires reversal or is merely harmless depend on the type of error involved. For example, if the error relates to a right protected by the United States Constitution in a criminal matter, the government must prove beyond a reasonable doubt that the error did not contribute to the defendant's conviction; otherwise, the judgment must be reversed. *Chapman v. California*, 386 U.S. 18, 26 (1967). However, if the error involves only a state rule, a more lenient harmless error standard may be applied. For example, in California cases involving errors of state law, the appellant must show it is reasonably probable that he or she would have received a more favorable result or verdict if the error had not been committed; otherwise the judgment will be affirmed. *People v. Doolin*, 87 Cal. Rptr. 3d 209 (Cal. 2009). In both instances, however, appellate courts weigh the significance of the error against all the other evidence. Whether the error is reversible/prejudicial or harmless is a matter of degree.

It is important to keep in mind this two-step process when drafting an appellate brief: First the court determines whether there was error under the applicable standard of review. If yes, it then considers whether the error requires reversal, which depends on what type of error was committed. With decisions based on insufficient evidence under the clearly erroneous or substantial evidence standards, or structural errors, reversal is largely automatic. In other cases, the court conducts a harmless error analysis under varying standards—depending on the type of error committed. Thus it is possible to win the battle (convince the court there was error below), but lose the war (fail to convince the court that the error requires reversal) and vice versa.

C. Appellate Brief Formats

Always check the most recent rules of the court in which the appeal is pending before drafting your brief. Most appellate court rules state exactly the format required for appellant opening briefs, appellee responding briefs, and appellant reply briefs. These rules will include the sections required in each brief, as well as length and type face requirements. It is particularly important to know the page limitation before starting to draft the brief so that you are sure to come within it.

D. Summary of Typical Appellate Brief Components

Statement of Issues on Appeal. This section identifies the legal questions presented in the appeal. First and foremost, make sure the issues are clear. We recommend using the "whether (legal question), when (essential facts)" format taken from the office memorandum, discussed in Chapter 5 (C)(1).
Tables. These contain the table of contents and authorities cited in the brief. Fill in the page numbers last or code all headings and citations for your word processor's automatic table creation utility. Refer to your appellate rules of court for the order in which to list the authorities.

Statement of the Case. This is where you set out the pertinent procedural history of the case, telling the appellate court what is being appealed, the nature of the action, what happened below, the parties involved, and why the matter has come before the court. It is also your first opportunity to state your reasons why the judgment should be reversed or affirmed—in setting forth or responding to the grounds for appeal.

Statement of Facts. This is where you set out the relevant facts that were heard or considered by the court or jury in rendering a decision. You are limited to evidence in the record and must provide cites to the appellate record for every fact you describe. Some jurisdictions require the statement of the case (procedural facts) and the statement of facts to be set forth in one section usually called "The Statement of the Case." If this is the case, the procedural facts should come first to establish context and background.

Summary of the Argument. The summary of the argument provides the road map for the brief and is where drafters deliver their message—their theory, theme, or pitch—for reversal or affirmance of the judgment or order. First tell the court what you want it to do—affirm or reverse—and then the grounds for that action. Clearly and concisely state the legal and factual basis for your appeal or response citing the most important legal authorities.

Discussion/Argument with Headings and Subheadings. The discussion section forms the heart of the appellate brief. Like the trial brief discussion section, this is where you show the court in detail how to rule in your favor and why it should. Showing the court how to rule in your favor involves presenting your points clearly and showing that your positions are sound and well supported. Showing the court why it should rule in your favor involves convincing the court that your points and positions are not only sound, but also that they are the best way to resolve the issues (or at least that they are better than the opposite side's). Headings flag the issues in a way that summarizes and advances the main point made in each section.

Conclusion. In this section drafters briefly remind the court of what they want it to do (affirm or reverse) and, if court rules allow, the main reasons in support.

E. Drafting the Components of the Appellate Brief: Order and Timing

The table of contents and the table of authorities should always be drafted or generated last, after the rest of the brief is complete, to ensure the entries and the corresponding page numbers are accurate. *Any* change made in the brief, no matter how small or minor may cause the pagination to change.

The sequence in which the other components are drafted varies from lawyer to lawyer. Some proceed in loose order from beginning to end, starting with the statement of issues, followed by the statement of the case, statement of facts, and the discussion/argument, and then go back and draft the summary of the argument and the headings once the analysis and arguments have gelled. Others begin with the headings as a way of outlining the argument, and then draft the statement of the case and the statement of the facts to set up the argument they have outlined, and then draft the summary of the argument and the discussion/argument section. Some draft the discussion/argument section first. There are risks in drafting the discussion/argument before the statement of facts because the drafter may mistakenly rely on and include facts in her analysis that are not actually in the record. For example, she may be quite certain that a witness made a particular statement, but later be unable to find it in the trial transcript.

No matter what order you choose to draft the appellate brief, approach the process as a series of discrete smaller tasks rather than one giant, looming job. It is best to start drafting as soon as possible and calendar enough time to complete each task well before the filing deadline. Do not wait until you think you have found all the cases and all the answers—because you will not know what additional cases you need and what all the questions may be until you start drafting. Also leave plenty of time to proofread the appellate brief. Once you are sure it is error-free, the tables of contents and authorities can be generated. Generating tables often takes longer than expected and often reveals proofing errors such as alternative spellings of the same case that will need to be corrected.

If you are not sure where to begin, start with one that seems easiest, *e.g.*, a particular subsection of the discussion. For more discussion on the drafting process, see Chapter 2 and Chapter 6, section D.

F. Individual Components

1. Issues on Appeal

The Statement of Issues on Appeal describes the issues the court is being asked to address and decide.

If you represent the appellant, the issues on appeal should identify the individual grounds on which you believe the judgment or order below should be reversed. If the same attorneys that handled the case at the trial level are handling the appeal (and this is often a mistake as new counsel can bring an unbiased eye to the record), their initial reaction may be that there are many, many errors or that the court or jury "got it wrong." It is important, however, to isolate the issues and errors that are likely to result in reversal because the case cannot be retried on appeal. This requires examining the record objectively with the various applicable standards of review and harmless error standards in mind.

In other words drafters must first identify a specific *error*. Then they need to examine the likelihood that that error will mandate a reversal. This involves assessing the type of error involved and applicable harmless error standard. For example, it may be clear that a court erred in admitting certain evidence, but whether this error would require reversal depends on the strength or impact of this evidence compared to all the other properly admitted evidence. Did the court erroneously admit your client's confession, or did it allow equivocal hearsay testimony from one of many witnesses?

Counsel for the appellant should then phrase the grounds on which they are appealing the judgment or order as issues on appeal. For each ground set out the legal question the court must decide to find error along with the factual context. Appellants generally control the issues to be decided on appeal since the issues reflect the grounds for appeal. Counsel for appellees, however, are not bound by appellants' choice of wording. Rather they will state the issues on appeal so as to advance their reasons for affirming the judgment or order. What is essential for both appellants' and appellees' statements of the issues is that the issues be set out clearly, specifically, and not in a conclusory fashion.

Whether any error is reversible or harmless does not have to be set forth in the issues on appeal. However, if counsel for the appellant or appellee wants to emphasize this as an issue or advocate a particular standard they should add it to the statement of issues.

Statements of issues on appeal are much like questions presented in an office memorandum. They set out the legal question for the court to decide along with the essential facts that raise the question. We recommend using the "Whether/When" format: Whether (a legal result occurs), when (essential facts)? The question should appear neutral, but think: what ruling do you want the court to make and what *concise* facts support the ruling.

An example of a Statement of Issue on Appeal from Appellant's counsel:

> "Whether a confession is inadmissible on the ground that the defendant's Sixth Amendment right to counsel was violated when police continued questioning him after he stated "I'm thinking I should speak to my attorney."

The first, "Whether," part of the statement of issue contains the ruling the appellant wants the court to make along with the legal ground therefore, and the second, "when," part of the statement contains the essential facts that raise the issue.

Appellee's counsel may phrase the issue this way:

> Whether a confession is admissible under the Sixth Amendment where police ceased questioning the defendant after he stated, "I want to talk to my attorney."

Both statements of the issue identify for the court that the legal issue is whether the defendant's confession was properly admitted under the Sixth Amendment pertaining to the right to counsel. However, the counsel for the appellant and counsel for the appellee have focused on different facts that they considered essential to resolving the issue: appellant's counsel on what happened when the suspect *initially mentioned* an attorney, and appellee's counsel on what happened when the suspect later stated he *wanted to speak* with his attorney.

Also, neither statement of the issue is conclusory. Conclusory statements occur when the facts are described in such a way that a particular answer is mandated. In other words, do not overstate by answering your own question; do not assume the very point that you are trying to make.

Examples of conclusory statement of issues on appeal:

> Appellant: Whether a confession is inadmissible when the police violated the defendant Sixth Amendment's right to counsel by continuing to interrogate him after he invoked his right to counsel. (If the statement is posed this way, the answer has to be yes in favor of the appellant).

> Appellee: Whether a defendant's confession is admissible under the Sixth Amendment where the police honored his right to counsel once he invoked that right. (If the statement is posed this way, the answer has to be yes in favor of the appellee).

Both questions are conclusory because the central issue is *whether* and *when* the defendant invoked his right to counsel.

Also, resist the urge to cram in so many supporting facts that your statement of issue becomes long and muddled. If this happens, your readers will stop reading and skip over it.

If you are having trouble formulating your statement of issues on appeal, put that task aside and revisit it after you have drafted other portions of the brief such as the statement of the case or discussion/argument section.

2. The Statement of the Case

The statement of the case in an appellate brief sets forth the relevant procedural history of the case. Its purpose is to tell the appellate court what is being appealed and to describe the nature of the action, the parties, and how and why the matter has come before the court. The statement of the case is also the first opportunity for drafters to deliver their message—to set forth their essential reasons why the decision below should be reversed or affirmed. Thus, although the statement of *facts* should be free of legal conclusions or argument, in the statement of the *case,* you may and should advance your legal positions in describing the grounds for appeal or stating the reasons the decision should be affirmed.

Statements of the case in both appellants' and appellees' briefs should begin with a description of the decision being appealed from, *e.g.*, a conviction of first degree murder after a jury trial, a summary judgment dismissing appellant's personal injury suit, an order denying certification of a class action, and the like. If representing the appellant, include the date of judgment or order was entered, state when the notice of appeal was filed and set forth the grounds on which you are appealing the decision. Appellants need to set forth the relevant dates to show the appeal was timely filed.

If you are representing the appellee, you may follow your description of the decision being appealed with the reasons it should be affirmed or, if the statement of the case is relatively short, you may set out the reasons to affirm at the end of the statement—try it both ways and choose. The appellee does not have to repeat the appellants' grounds for appeal, nor is it necessary to include the dates the judgment was entered or the notice of appeal filed unless you are challenging the appellate court's jurisdiction based on failure to file a timely notice of appeal.

Next, this is the typical order for setting forth the additional information in the statement of the case:

1. Briefly describe the nature of the action if it is not already clear from the description of the decision being appealed;
2. In chronological order, set out the pertinent acts and pleadings that led up to the decision, *e.g.* the filing of a motion to exclude the appellant's

statement to police, the opposition to the motion, and the hearing on the motion;

3. Set out the court's ruling or decision and its basis (if given) or the jury's verdict. (Often it is unnecessary to repeat the jury's verdict if it is set forth in the beginning of the statement in describing the judgment being appealed); and
4. If representing the appellant, briefly elaborate on the reasons the decision should be reversed. If representing the appellee, set forth the reasons the decisions should be affirmed, or elaborate, as necessary, on the reasons you gave in the beginning of the statement of the case.

For every procedural act described and document filed, provide a cite to the appellate record so that the judge, law clerk, or court attorney working up the case can easily locate the pleading or other document detailing the action. Also, in the statement of the case, define terms for the parties and other persons or entities you refer to frequently in the brief.

Statements of the case vary in length and complexity depending on what happened procedurally in the court or courts below. In some cases the proceedings are simple and straightforward. In others they may be complex and contain the source of the reversible error.

The following are examples of simple preliminary statements in an appeal of a judgment of conviction of first degree murder after a jury verdict. The issue is the admission of statements the appellant made to police.

Appellant's version:

> On March 15, 2009, Appellant Steven Turner ("Mr. Turner") was convicted of murder in the first degree after a jury verdict. (Record on Appeal "R" 978) Mr. Turner filed a notice of appeal on April 12, 2009 (R 981). He appeals his conviction on the ground the court erroneously admitted his statements to police that were obtained in violation of his right to silence under the Fifth amendment and *Miranda v. Arizona*, 384 U.S. 436 (1966). Prior to trial, Mr. Turner moved to exclude statements he made to police on the grounds they were improperly obtained while he was in custody and after he invoked his right to silence. (R 677) The government opposed the motion. (R 679). After a hearing on the matter (R 688), the trial court denied Mr. Turner's motion to exclude concluding that the statements were voluntary and thus admissible. (RT 690). The statements were admitted into evidence at trial and considered by the jury. (RT 967).
>
> Mr. Turner maintains on appeal that the trial court erred in admitting his statement to police because "voluntariness" is not the stan-

dard for admissibility of statements obtained from persons who are in police custody and have invoked their right to silence. Rather, after a person has invoked his right to silence under *Miranda*, police must "scrupulously honor" his right to cut off questioning. *Michigan v. Mosley* 423 U.S. 96 104 (1975). Police failed to scrupulously honor Mr. Turner's right to cut off questioning, rather, they undermined it. This error requires reversal of Mr. Turner's conviction because Appellee cannot prove that admission of these damaging statements did not contribute to the jury's verdict. *Chapman v. California*, 386 U.S. 18, 26 (1967).

Appellee's version:

Appellant has appealed his conviction by jury of first degree murder in the stabbing death of Shawn Martin ("Mr. Martin"). (Record on Appeal "R" 976–78). Appellant was indicted for first degree murder after stabbing Mr. Martin in the back and through the heart. (R 3). Prior to trial, Appellant moved to exclude statements he made to police from evidence at trial. (R 677). The People opposed this motion. (R 679). The trial court, after holding an evidentiary hearing (R 688) and considering the moving and opposition papers as well as the oral argument from counsel, denied the motion, (RT 690) After a six-day jury trial, the jury found Appellant had committed first degree murder. (R 900-910).

Appellant's conviction should be affirmed because his statements were given freely and voluntarily in compliance with the Fifth Amendment. *Michigan v. Mosley*, 423 U.S. 96 104 (1975); *Miranda v. Arizona*, 384 U.S. 436 (1966). Moreover, any error in admitting the statements was harmless: The evidence at trial against appellant was overwhelming and the statements were merely cumulative and did not contribute to the verdict. *Chapman v. California*, 386 U.S. 18, 26 (1967).

Both appellant's and appellee's statements of the case are accurate and supported by citations to the record, but their messages are different. Appellant's statement focuses on the police officers' conduct and the admission of appellant's statements at trial. Appellee's focus is more diffused—on the nature of the crime, all that the court considered before ruling on the motion, and the length of the trial. The treatment of appellant's ground for appeal is almost matter of fact—implying "all is fine."

In sum, use the statement of the case both to explain the pertinent procedural history to the appellate court, and to deliver your message. The statement of the case is often the first opportunity to package and market your positions, be sure to make the most of it.

Statement of the Case Drafting and Editing Checklist

1. Does the statement of the case begin with the specific decision or action being appealed, *e.g.*, a particular judgment or final order? Does the appellant's statement include the date the judgment or order was entered?
2. In the appellant's brief, is the description of the action or decision being appealed followed by the grounds for appeal? The appellee may choose to state the reasons the decision should be affirmed here or at the end of the statement of the case.
3. Does the statement of the case briefly describe the nature of the case?
4. Does the statement of the case set forth the pertinent parties, persons, and entities and define a term for each?
5. Does the statement of the case set out the pertinent pleadings, hearings, and other acts that led up to the decision with citations to the record for each?
6. Does the statement of the case state the rulings or decisions below and their basis, if given?
7. In the appellant's brief does the statement of the case then briefly elaborate on the grounds/reasons the judgment or order should be reversed? In the appellee's brief does the statement of the case then set forth the reasons the order or judgment should be affirmed, or elaborate, as necessary, on the reasons given in the beginning?
8. Is the statement of the case easy to follow: does it clearly explain what is being appealed, the nature of the case, the pertinent parties and other players, and how and why the matter has come before the appellate court?
9. Does the statement of the case effectively deliver the drafter's message—the essential reasons the judgment or order should be reversed of affirmed?
10. Is the statement of the case free from any grammatical, punctuation, formatting, or proofing errors?

3. The Statement of Facts

a. Goals

In the statement of the case, you described the procedural posture of the matter and stated your essential reasons why the decision below should be reversed or affirmed. Thus, when readers turn to the statement of facts, they will probably know the nature of the case, the parties, and your basic legal positions. Your goal in drafting the statement of facts is to tell an accurate story that will make readers want to adopt your legal positions and that gives them enough information to be able to do so.

While readers at the trial court level may have been vaguely familiar with the case, readers on the appellate level will usually know nothing about the case except for what you and your opponent tell them and what they find in the record. Appellate court readers must be able to easily understand from the statement of facts what the case is about and what facts form the basis of the appeal. They can only be persuaded by a story they can follow.

Keep your message in mind as you draft and package the statement of facts. This will focus your drafting and help you tell an accurate story that is both easy to understand and persuasive.

Show versus tell: The statement of facts should lay out the specific details that will lead readers to the conclusion you want them to reach. It is much more powerful if they feel they have reached the conclusion themselves than if you tell them what to conclude. Save legal conclusions and argument for the discussion/argument section. Describe the underlying story in the statement of facts.

Finally, keep in mind the overarching goal of having the court adopt your brief in large part as their opinion—this should help keep you on track in drafting a statement of facts that is easy to follow, accurate, and tells the story in a compelling, professional way.

b. Material Facts in the Record

The record consists of the documents from the proceedings below that the parties have designated to be in the record. Procedures for designating the record vary by jurisdiction, but the basic process is the same: The appellant makes an opening designation of the record, the appellee then gets to counter designate, and the clerk of the lower court transmits the record, as designated, to the appellate court. The degree to which the clerk independently assembles the record or to which the parties are involved in selecting, copying, and binding the documents varies by jurisdiction. The process usually takes place shortly after the notice of appeal is filed to initiate the appeal.

You must include all legally material facts in the record, both favorable and unfavorable. Only facts in the record may be included in the statement of facts in an appellate brief. This means only the facts that were presented to, heard, or considered by the court or jury below can be described in the statement of facts. Thus, for example, a witness must have testified to a fact at trial, or a document containing a fact must have been presented to the court as an exhibit, in order for those facts to be used in the statement of facts. This is why we recommend drafting the statement of facts earlier on in the drafting process—to ensure that all the facts you intend to use in the discussion/argument section are included in the statement of facts and in the record that you designate on appeal.

In addition, every fact set forth in the statement of facts must be accompanied by a citation to the record that enables the person working up the appeal to look up testimony of a witness or review the document containing the facts described. Portions of the record on appeal are described and cited slightly differently depending on the jurisdiction. Often court rules tell attorneys what terms to use. For example, in some jurisdictions, documents filed with the trial court are contained in the "Clerk's Transcript" on appeal, and witness testimony is contained in the "Reporter's Transcript." In other jurisdictions the documents filed with the trial court are contained in what is referred to as "the Record", and witness testimony is contained in what is referred to as "the Transcript." Be sure to use the terms the particular appellate court expects and to clearly indicate which portions of the appellate records you are referring to in your citations.

On appeal you should have a good idea of the material facts—those that pertain to the issues on appeal. These are facts that support or undermine the appellant's grounds for appeal or that support or undermine the appellee's reasons for affirming the decision below. Any fact referred to in the discussion/argument section must be included in the statement of facts. Also, each side will want to include any background or shading facts that help convey the drafter's message.

As with briefs to the trial court, your goal is to emphasize favorable facts and to minimize or diffuse unfavorable facts. You should not omit unfavorable facts from the statement of facts. Not only is this misleading, but you can be sure that any facts unfavorable to your side will be included and emphasized in your opponent's brief. Drafters emphasize favorable facts and deemphasize unfavorable facts through (i) the overall organization of the statement of facts, (ii) placement of individual facts, and (iii) tone and treatment of individual facts.

i. Overall Organization

Tell the story in the order you want to tell it—the order that best conveys your message and places your positions in the most favorable light. This means a logical and persuasive order. Often in appellate briefs, different sets of facts go to different issues, and thus it makes sense to organize the statement of facts by issue. Which issue you begin with depends on your message and the impression you want the readers to have.

For example, in the appeal of the murder conviction addressed in the discussion of statements of the case above, there are two sets of underlying facts: (1) facts (evidence presented to the court) pertaining to police obtaining the suspect's statements, which are relevant to whether the trial court erred in admitting those statement, and (2) facts (evidence presented to the jury) pertaining to the underlying crime, which are relevant to whether any error in admitting the statements was reversible or harmless.

Counsel representing the appellant would probably begin with the facts regarding the police obtaining their client's statements and emphasize any police misconduct. Their goal would be to focus the attention of the readers on the actions of the police.

Counsel representing the appellee would probably begin with a description of the underlying crime using and citing evidence other than the appellant's statements and follow with the appellant's arrest and questioning by the police. Not only is this order chronological, it emphasizes the appellant's crime—which was stabbing the victim to death—and all the evidence against the appellant other than his statements.

Where facts are organized by issue or subject, it is usually best to break them up with short subheadings that describe the issue or subject the facts pertain to. Headings serve as useful sign posts and help make a longer or complex statement of facts easier to follow and easier on the eyes.

Note: The statement of the case should have already set out the nature of the case as well as the parties. However, the first paragraph in the statement of facts should still establish the context for the story that best delivers the drafter's message. In the above example, the appellant would make the context the police interrogation, while the appellee would make the context the underlying crime.

ii. Placement of Individual Facts

Drafters also promote their message in smaller scale organization by placing favorable facts in positions of emphasis, *e.g.*, at the beginning of a section, paragraph or sentence, or at the end with a solid build up. They de-emphasize damaging facts by placing them in the middle of the narrative or the middle of paragraphs or sentences. Sometimes, unfavorable facts can be de-emphasized by being joined or juxtaposed with favorable facts. However, be sure to test these sentences for overall impression to make sure favorable facts are not undermined in doing so.

iii. Treatment and Tone

Just as in briefs to the trial court, emphasize favorable facts by using the active voice, concrete subjects, and active predicates when describing them. In other words, employ all the sentence writing techniques you have learned so far regarding clarity and getting and keeping the reader's attention.

On the other hand, distance and minimize unfavorable facts with the passive voice. Although you do not want to couch unfavorable facts in confusing, hard-to-read sentences that will call attention to them , your sentences involving unfavorable facts can and should be dull—accurate, but not commanding attention.

Favorable facts should be set forth in vivid, specific terms that convey as much meaning as possible, without going overboard, *e.g.*, "the stabbing" versus "the incident." You may use your own words to characterize facts, including paraphrases of direct quotes, as long as your words are accurate. In treating unfavorable facts, use words that are as bland and general as possible, without being inaccurate. This is the time to use terms like "incident," "matter," etc. Also avoid terms that are used in cases that are unfavorable to your side.

Note, however, it is possible to be too artful in the placement and treatment of unfavorable facts. For example, burying an unfavorable fact so deeply that the drafter appears to be hiding something, like a fatal flaw in their position. Or describing a fact with so bland or vague a term that it becomes absurd, *e.g.*, referring to a fatal stabbing as a "contact." Also, when emphasizing favorable facts, be sure as a drafter to maintain a professional tone and not to stray into the realm of pulp fiction. To test your drafting for effective deemphasizing of unfavorable facts and emphasizing favorable facts, employ the "Will readers roll their eyes?" test. A court will not adopt your statement of facts in its opinion if the statement goes overboard.

iv. Final Words

In the statement of facts you are telling a story, a true one. It must be accurate and contain all legally material facts, but how you tell it depends on whose story it is. As in trial briefs, avoid simply summarizing the transcript or using a repetitious question and answer format. Also, do not pack your statement of facts with quotations. Use just your best quotes for special emphasis or to support a compelling statement or characterization you have made. Expect that the appellate court or its staff will read the transcript. Your goal is for the court to read it with your narrative in mind. This is the case even if the appeal presents primarily questions of law in a court of last resort. The statement of facts will give the appeal context, and how you tell the story will still leave an impression with your readers. For further discussion regarding statements of fact see Chapter 6, section (c).

c. Appellate Brief Statement of Facts Drafting and Editing Guidelines

Examine the statement of facts for the following:

- Substance/Analysis
- Organization
- Sentence Structure, Word Choice, Tone
- Paragraph Structure
- Technical—Proofing, Grammar, *Bluebook*, etc.

i. Substance/Analysis

Does the statement of facts include all legally material facts as well as helpful or compelling factual background or shading of the facts? Does it contain all facts necessary to rule in your client's favor? Have any facts pertaining to any relevant legal issue, element, or factor been omitted?

Does the statement of facts provide enough information and context for an unfamiliar reader to understand what the case is about and what happened?

Does the statement of facts promote your message—your theory, theme, or pitch for reversing or affirming the judgment or order?

Does the statement of facts set up your analysis in the discussion or argument section? Is every fact you refer to in the discussion or arguments section set forth in the statement of facts?

Does the statement of facts provide clear citations to the appellate record for every fact set forth, described, or alluded to?

ii. Organization

Overall, is the story you have told as easy to follow and as compelling as the underlying facts allow?

First, make sure you have set forth the facts, including background facts so that the reader will understand what the case is about and what happened. Then confirm that you have told the story in the order that best promotes your message. Do you begin with facts that create the initial impression you want your readers to have? Are favorable facts put in positions of emphasis—at the beginning of the section, paragraph or sentence, or at the end with a solid build up? Check to see if unfavorable facts are de-emphasized or diffused—placed in the middle of the section, paragraphs, or sentences, or effectively joined or juxtaposed with favorable facts.

If complex, have you broken the statement of facts up with short, descriptive subheadings to aid the reader in finding topics and to provide some relief for the eyes?

iii. Sentence Structure, Word Choice, Tone

First check for sentences that are confusing or hard to read and understand. This is a detraction for both favorable and unfavorable facts. (Indeed, when dealing with an unfavorable fact, you do not want the reader to have to read your sentence more than once.) Then check to see if favorable facts are described using compelling, specific, and descriptive words in sentences with concrete subjects and active predicates. This also goes for favorable/unfavorable rulings and reasons. Are unfavorable facts deemphasized by use of the passive voice, and flat, general terms?

As with statements of facts in trial briefs, check that the tone is compelling, yet professional? Is it subtle in its partisanship? Detractions would be an overly emotional, angry, combative, smug, or partisan tone; or conversely a tone that is too flat, and seemingly uninvolved. Any tone that suggests the lawyer is putting herself in the place of the court or commanding the court is a detraction as well. Apply the "Will my readers roll their eyes?" test for treatment of both favorable and unfavorable facts.

iv. Paragraph Structure

The guidelines for critiquing paragraphs in the statement of facts are the same as with all legal writing only with an eye toward emphasizing favorable facts and deemphasizing unfavorable ones. Paragraphs should begin with a topic or transitional sentence. Every sentence in the paragraph should (1) relate to the topic/transitional sentence, and (2) relate to the sentences around it. The second requirement is accomplished by arranging the sentences in a logical progression, and, often, by using good transition words that signal where you are going with the sentence, *e.g.*, thus, accordingly, moreover, conversely, nevertheless.

Also check for effective placement of emphasis of favorable facts, and effective de-emphasis of unfavorable facts within the paragraphs.

As always, distractions include paragraphs without clear topic or transition sentences; sentences that do not relate to the topic identified; paragraphs that are choppy or disconnected because the sentences are not arranged smoothly and/or because transition words are needed.

v. Technical Aspects: Proofing, Grammar, etc.

This category involves attention to detail. Student drafters should avoid leaving points on the table because they have not had time to proofread thoroughly. The rule applies with the same force in the real world. A document that has proofing and citation errors is distracting to readers and reflects poorly on the drafter and his or her positions and arguments.

Some points on the technical editing checklist:

- Check for "widows and orphans"—opening and ending lines of paragraphs that are stranded, alone, on their own page. There should always be at least two sentences of a paragraph on a page. If not, change the page break.
- Check that pages are numbered consecutively.
- Examine the font size used. 12 point is standard, although 14 point is becoming increasingly the norm for federal appellate courts for ease of reading.
- Check margins (at least one-inch around); use defined terms where appropriate.

Finally, check that you have strictly complied with all requirements of local appellate court rules.

4. Discussion or Argument

a. Purpose and Goals

The purpose of the discussion or argument section in the appellate brief is to persuade a majority of the members of the court to reverse or affirm the judgment or order below. You are challenging or defending a decision or action that has already occurred—not starting with a clean slate. Thus, the discussion section should focus on identifying or refuting reversible error. This often means addressing what feels like just the tip of the iceberg and leaving out a variety of things you believe the court or the other side did wrong below. This is one of the reasons appellate courts require a statement of issues on appeal—to focus the attorneys on the issues that matter.

As with trial briefs, the goals of the discussion section in appellate briefs are to show the court *how* to rule in your favor and *why* it should. Showing the court how to rule in your favor involves making your points as clearly as possible, which usually means organizing complex information so that the readers can understand it as easily as possible. Although readers on the appellate level will generally have more time to spend with the briefs than readers at the trial court, you are still competing for your readers' time and attention. See Chapters 1 and 2 for methods of accomplishing this, including (1) putting context before details, (2) going from broad to narrow and general to specific, (3) linking new information with familiar information, and (4) having an explicit structure.

When drafting the discussion section, envision the opinion you would like the court to issue and *draft it like that.* The best thing that can happen to the drafter of an appellate brief is to find that their brief has been turned into the opinion issued by the court—make it easy for the court to do this by drafting an easy-to-follow, legally sound, persuasive brief.

The structure of the discussion section of an appellate brief, like that of a trial brief, is based on the CRAC format (Conclusion, Rule/Law, Application/Analysis, and Conclusion), which is designed to deliver information in the most straightforward manner. In some appeals, particularly those to courts of last resort, the emphasis is on the rule/law portion. For example, a decision regarding (1) which law applies, (2) the interpretation of existing law, (3) the articulation of a new law, or (4) the extension or reining in of the law, may dictate or heavily influence the resolution of the issue. In these situations, the application section will be short and straightforward. Do not leave out it out, however—be sure to concisely connect the dots for the readers so they do not have to do so themselves. Issues on appeal may be factually intensive, as well. For example, whether an error in admitting certain evidence at trial is reversible depends on the harmless error standard applied and all the other evidence admitted at trial as compared to the evidence admitted in error. This will often entail a thorough, detailed application section.

For further discussion regarding the CRAC structure and drafting arguments using this structure, see Chapter 1, section F and Chapter 6, section D (5).

b. Persuading the Appellate Court

Persuading the appellate court involves showing that your positions and arguments are (1) sound and well supported by authority, and (2) the better choice.

First and foremost, persuading the court involves drafting arguments that are clear and easy to follow. Even when the argument is complex, your job is to make it as easy as possible for the readers to grasp. Courts are reluctant to implement solutions they do not readily understand. As on the trial court level, showing the appellate court that your positions are sound and well supported requires thorough and sophisticated knowledge of the law and authorities and how they affect your case so that you (1) recognize strong points and arguments and make the most of them, (2) understand and overcome or minimize potential weaknesses in your positions, and (3) understand the hierarchy of your authorities and use them to your best advantage.

Showing the court that your positions and arguments are the better choice often starts with exposing and exploiting the weaknesses in the other side's arguments and showing they are incorrect, unsound, or not well supported. In other words you demonstrate that your position is better because it is correct and sound, while your opponent's is not.

Using policy to persuade:

Your audience will include at least several decision makers and you should assume that some will consider both positions tenable. Thus, showing that your positions are the better choice will involve making what are often referred to as "policy arguments." Unfortunately this term often leads law students and new lawyers to approach these arguments too abstractly, using lofty terms and phrases. This should not be the case. Policy arguments are concrete but larger reasons why the court should adopt a tenable legal position. They show the court that your position advances a particular goal and/or that the other side's position will undermine this goal or cause harm.

The policy goals could be furthering the underlying purpose of the statute or legislation at issue; promoting the efficient administration of the courts; encouraging safety; promoting freedom of alienation and property rights, and the like. Potential harms could be unknown, unintended consequences; foreclosing access to the courts; creating a "slippery slope;" creating a disincentive to free market behavior, and the like. Our point is that potential policy arguments are numerous and varied. Your mission as the drafter is to explore the various goals your positions may promote, and the potential harms the other side's positions may cause, and find the ones that best package your message, that best advance your purpose in persuading the court to affirm or reverse. This involves having solid knowledge and understanding of both positions and the authorities supporting them. Look for potential policy arguments in case law—in majority opinions, concurrences, and dissents (earlier dissents can become later majority opinions), and legislative history— particularly legislative comments to statutes. Once you have decided on the policy arguments you think you will use, research them further, finding law review articles or cases in other jurisdictions that further explain or promote them.

Often, beginning drafters will find an oft-stated policy their position would promote and simply chant it in their argument, *e.g.*, "This question is better left to Legislature." This is not enough. Rather, drafters should acquire thorough and sophisticated knowledge regarding the policies they use in their arguments so that they can clearly identify them and explain them, show why and how they are valuable, and exactly how their position furthers those policies, or the other side harms them. It is often best to approach this process using the CRAC format. As the C—Conclusion—identify the policy and state that your position promotes it. In the R—Rule/Law section—explain how and why the policy you have identified is valuable using case law, legislative history, law review articles, etc. In the A—Application/Analysis section—tell why and show how your position promotes that policy. In the final C—Conclusion section—again identify the policy and how the drafter's position supports it.

Keep in mind in drafting the discussion section that your goal is to persuade a majority of the members of the court that affirming or reversing the decision below is the correct and best thing to do.

c. Organizing the Discussion and Using Point Headings

i. Main Sections

Each separate issue on appeal becomes a main section in the discussion section of the brief. Often reversible versus harmless error gets its own main section at the end of the brief.

The discussion in appellate briefs should begin with any threshold issues. These are issues that must be decided before the court can reach the merits of the appeal. Examples include whether one of the parties had standing to bring suit, whether there was personal jurisdiction over the parties at trial, or whether a matter is appealable. After any threshold issues, the discussion usually begins with the issue/section that contains the drafter's strongest and most persuasive argument for reversing or affirming the decision below, then the issue/section with the next strongest arguments, and so on.

An exception might be if the strongest arguments will have the smallest consequence, for example an argument that would result in the appellant's lengthy criminal sentence being reduced by one month, or that would result in a small change in the award of damages. These types of arguments usually go at the end of the brief.

Which section contains the most persuasive arguments may be obvious as you review the decision or action below, the record, and the authority cited to and relied on by the court. Sometimes this hierarchy may not be clear until you have tested your arguments in the drafting and revision stages.

If you have more than one section that you think contain arguments of equal strength, lead with the one that is most consequential—that would give you the most relief. Thus, on appeal a section regarding an error that would require automatic reversal of the entire judgment would come before an alleged error subject to a harmless error analysis and that would lead to reversal of only a portion of the judgment, *e.g.*, an adjustment in the award of damages.

ii. Subsections

Each separate issue on appeal may have sub-issues that each merit discussion, *i.e.*, that each gets its own CRAC and a subheading. If, for example, several elements of a test must be established to show that a court did or did not err, each element deserves its own subsection where it can be separately addressed. Or for clarity's sake you may need to divide a complex argument with several types of legal support into subsections, each with its own CRAC and subheading. Division of an argument into subsections may be obvious from the beginning. Or, while you are drafting the discussion, you may find that you need to break up a long argument into subsections.

In general, if a matter merits a paragraph or more of discussion of the law, followed by a paragraph or more application of the law to your facts, it should become a subsection and get its own heading and a separate CRAC. On the other hand, be careful not to subdivide your argument unnecessarily or excessively. Too many subsections and headings can break up the flow of an argument. Also, a short subsection may look skimpy or flimsy on its own, which could undermine the overall point you are making. If you use subsections, do not have a main argument with just one subsection under it. A single, standalone subsection is not a subsection at all.

As with trial briefs, ordering your subsections requires balancing clarity with strength. Ideally, the subsection with the strongest arguments goes first. If this interrupts the flow or logic of the main argument, or if your strongest argument is dependent on one in another subsection, the strongest material may have to come later in the discussion. A discussion that is quickly and easily understood is most important. In order to be persuaded by an argument, a court must first understand it. Also remember the basic rules regarding organization in ordering your subsections: general to specific, broad to narrow.

If a main section contains subsections, it is usual to put a mini summary argument after the main section heading and before the first subheading that sets forth your overall conclusion on the main argument, supported by your conclusion for each of the subsections, in the order you discuss them, with citations to authority for each.

iii. Explicit Structure

Before you start to draft the discussion, decide what your main arguments are and have a plan regarding in what order to place them. Also have an idea of which arguments should be divided into subsections and in what order those subsections should appear. This all may change as you draft and revise, but it is important to start with a structure in mind. Then, make that structure explicit with headings, subheadings, CRAC, well organized paragraphs, sentences, and appropriate transitions.

iv. Drafting Headings and Subheadings

Headings flag the issues discussed in the sections and subsections in a way that summarizes and advances the main point made in each. Each heading and subheading serves as the "C" in the CRAC format. The heading should tell the court what you want it to do or the conclusion you want it to reach, and the essential reason why. Headings should be a maximum of three lines of text, and ideally shorter. Readers tend to skip over lengthy headings. Thus do not try to pack in too much information in your headings or you will frustrate their purpose.

Headings are a good way to test the logic and flow of the discussion section. Indeed, they form the table of contents and serve as an outline for the discussion. After you have drafted them, arrange your headings in order in a separate document—headings with subheadings, etc. Do the headings make sense when read together? Would an unfamiliar reader be able to easily grasp your basic arguments from reading the headings? Does it appear that your strongest section and your strongest arguments come first and go in descending order? Do the headings easily and effectively deliver your message?

Also, your headings should be formatted so that they are easy to read. Traditionally main point headings have been set single spaced using all caps, which can be difficult to read. Also single spaced, underlined text appears cramped and is often difficult to read. Using italics is usually better. In other words, beware of cluttering up your headings with too many word processing tools—*e.g.*, the bold, all-caps, underlined heading. For further discussion regarding persuasive headings see Chapter 6, section D(5).

d. Statements of the Standard of Review

Each main section of the discussion should contain a statement of the standard of review that applies to the type of error addressed. If the standard of review is undisputed, this portion can and should be short: State the standard and include a citation to authority, then briefly describe what it is. If representing the appellant, describe the standard using terms found in case law in which the standard was met and cite those cases. If representing the appellant, describe cases in which the standard was not met and cite those cases. Often, the same standard of review will be described slightly differently depending on whether the court concluded it was met or not.

Sometimes the standard of review on an issue will be contested, in which case, this portion will require its own CRAC. C—Conclusion: set forth the standard you want the court to adopt. R—Rule/Law: Set forth and explain the two different standards including the type of issues and situations to which they apply and why, and A—Application/Analysis: tell why and show how the error at issue is the type that requires or merits the standard of review you advocate.

5. Summary of the Argument

Most appellate courts allow, and many require, that the discussion or argument portion of the brief begin with a summary of the argument. Drafters should always include one if allowed. The summary will help readers to better follow the discussion section, and it will deliver your essential messages to the readers before they tackle the details. They are similar in purpose to the preliminary statements in trial briefs discussed in Chapter 6, section C (1).

Begin the summary with a request of the relief you want and state why you're entitled to it, *e.g.*, The judgment should be reversed/affirmed because (1) and (2). This is your essential pitch—what the court should do and why. Also be sure to include citation to the strongest authorities supporting each point. Then, in the same order as your discussion or arguments section, set forth your supporting reasons with citations to authority for each reason. It is often best to draft the summary of the argument toward the end—after you have drafted and revised the main discussion/argument and tested it with a heading and topic sentence outline.

G. Heading and Topic Sentence Outline

As with trial briefs, after you have completed a first or second draft of your appellate brief test its overall substance and organization by creating and reviewing a heading and topic sentence outline as described in Chapter 6, section F.

H. Appellate Brief Discussion/Argument Drafting and Reviewing Guidelines

Examine your Discussion or Argument section for:

(1) Substance/Analysis

(2) Organization

(3) Paragraph Structure

(4) Sentence Structure, Word Choice, Tone

(5) Technical—Proofing, Grammar, *Bluebook*, etc.

1. Substance/Analysis

In this category, look at content and persuasiveness. Do you demonstrate that your positions are sound and well supported? Have you addressed the rules, tests, factors, and cases necessary to enable a court to rule your favor? Are the cases used effectively to highlight and focus the reader's attention on favorable facts? Are the facts used effectively to persuade the court? Is adverse authority effectively distinguished or used to legally assail adverse cases? Are policy arguments used effectively to show that your positions are the better choices? Are the headings informative, compelling, and easy to read? Does the argument promote the theory of the case, theme, or pitch? Have you made it easy for a court to adopt your discussion in its opinion? Do headings clearly identify the issue and main point made in each section and subsection?

The ultimate question is: would a reader conclude that my positions are (1) sound and well supported, and (2) the better choice?

Also assess your citations to the cases. Every rule, test, factor, and fact you describe must be accompanied by a pinpoint citation to the case from which it came, so that readers can go to the exact page of that case or exact subsection of the statute and see for themselves. In addition, when analogizing or distinguishing the facts of your case with those of a particular judicial opinion, you must cite to the exact pages of the opinion where those facts are stated or discussed.

Detractions include:

(A) Omission of important rules, factors, or cases;

(B) Not recognizing or highlighting useful cases, rules, tests, factors, facts from the cases, or client specific facts;

(C) Not distinguishing or critically analyzing flaws in adverse cases;

(D) Spending too much time on weaker points;

(E) Dull, lengthy recitation of the facts in the cases, or dull lengthy mechanical application of the law;

(F) Sequential analysis and application of the cases—you should synthesize the cases and highlight significant favorable factors and facts;

(G) Policy arguments that are undeveloped, abstract, or hard to quickly grasp.

(H) Headings that are too long or difficult to follow.

2. Organization

First, check if you have organized the discussion or argument in a logical manner that is easy to follow. Do the sections/arguments follow the theory of the case? If there is more than one main argument, are the arguments set forth in a compelling and logical order? If an argument is divided into subsections, does this help your understanding, or is the flow interrupted? Do general, overarching rules come first, followed by discussion of factors and facts from the cases? Do the paragraphs logically follow each other, with informative topic or transitional sentences? Are the headings effective signposts that make the discussion section easy to follow?

Next assess whether the arguments are arranged persuasively? Are the most helpful cases in positions of emphasis? Are the client facts placed or woven in strategically, so that the reader can easily see how they meet or fail to meet any applicable test or rule? Are unfavorable facts and cases put in positions of de-emphasis, *e.g.*, in the middle of the argument or paragraph?

The ultimate questions: Will unfamiliar readers understand the discussion or argument? Will they be persuaded by it?

3. Paragraph Structure

The well-written, persuasive paragraph is the key component of the discussion or argument. Make sure the paragraphs begin with an informative and compelling topic or transition sentence that clearly identifies the point the writer is advancing. Then every sentence in the paragraph should (1) relate and support the topic/transition sentence and (2) relate to the sentences around it. The second element is accomplished by arranging the sentences in a logical progression, and often, by using good transition words that signal where you are going with the sentence, *e.g.*, thus, accordingly, moreover, conversely, nevertheless.

Detractions include paragraphs without clear, compelling topic or transition sentences; sentences that do not relate to the topic identified; and paragraphs that are choppy or disconnected because the sentences are not arranged smoothly and/or because transition words are needed. And, of course, paragraphs that fail to effectively emphasize favorable facts or law, or that emphasize or fail to minimize unfavorable facts or law are also detractions.

4. Sentence, Word Choice, and Tone

As with any legal document, first check for sentences that are confusing or hard to read and understand. Then check to see that favorable rules, tests, factors, and cases are set forth using compelling, specific and descriptive words, in active sentences with concrete subjects and active predicates. Also see if unfavorable facts, tests, factors, or cases are effectively de-emphasized by use of the passive voice and flat general terms.

Assess the tone: is it compelling, persuasive, yet professional? Keep in mind that an overarching goal is for the court to adopt your language in its opinion. Apply the "would readers be likely to roll their eyes?" test. Detractions include an overly emotional, angry, combative, smug, or partisan tone or, conversely, a tone that is too flat, and seemingly uninvolved. Any tone that suggests the lawyer is putting herself in the place of the court or commanding the court is detraction as well.

5. Technical: Proofing, Grammar, *Bluebook*, etc.

This category assesses attention to detail. Student drafters should avoid leaving points on the table because they have not had time to proofread thoroughly or ensure their cites are in perfect *Bluebook* form. Drafters in the real world should also not let these distractions undermine the substance of their appellate brief and their credibility as an attorney. See section (c) (v) of this chapter for a proofing checklist.

Appellate Brief Final Editing Checklist

Overall Tone: Check throughout. Look for an engaged and professional tone. Every articulation of a rule, rule explanation, or case illustration should be put in a way that advances the author's side. Avoid words and sentences that appear bossy, caustic, or over the top, *e.g.*, "obviously."

Overall Sentence/Word Choice: Check throughout. Mark any sentences that are hard to follow. Then note long sentences for unnecessary words—chaff. Watch for jumps between past and present tense. Past tense is usually best, and is required for events, like testimony that has already occurred.

Style: Check for use of full names/titles with a defined term at first reference; record cites, proper citation of authorities.

Identify or Refute Error:

1. Appellant: Have you shown (a) that the decision below was incorrect under the applicable standard of review and (b) that the error was not harmless?
2. Respondent: Have you shown (a) that the decision below was correct or at least not incorrect, under the applicable standard of review and (b) even if there was error, that error was harmless.

Remember: With rare exceptions, an appeal is not about re-trying the case below. It is, at best, about error correction. In some courts like the United States Supreme Court, it is usually not even that, it is almost solely about policy.

Checkpoints

- The purpose of an appellate brief is to persuade a court to reverse or affirm a judgment or order below. An appellate brief should not attempt to retry the case below.
- The audience for the appellate brief will be an intermediate appellate court or a court of last resort. Both these courts include more than one decision maker (judges or justices) and you will need to persuade a majority of them to reverse or affirm.
- The vast majority of appeals are to intermediate appellate courts, whose focus in mainly on error correction. Intermediate appellate courts are much more likely to reverse and judgment or order from the trial court than reverse it. Appeals to intermediate appellate courts are usually heard by three judge panels.
- Courts of last resort also correct errors, but in addition make policy, make new law, and extend or clarify existing law much more than intermediate appellate courts. Courts of last resort are less likely to affirm than intermediate appellate courts.
- An appellate brief should show:
    - o that there was or was not error below—that the decision below was incorrect or correct under the applicable standard of review; and
    - o that the error requires reversal because the error was not harmless or does not require reversal because the error was or was not harmless error.
- An overarching goal in drafting an appellate brief is for the court to adopt it in large part as its opinion.
- The standard of review is the filter through which the decision below is evaluated.
- Although there are many different articulations of standards of review, the human mind generally applies one of two: either deferential or non-deferential to the decision or action below.
- The four basic standard of review are
    - o *De Novo* (the decision below must merely be wrong).
    - o Clearly Erroneous *(*the decision below must very wrong).
    - o Substantial Evidence *(*the decision below must very wrong).
    - o Abuse of Discretion (the decision below must very, very wrong).
- There are many other permutations and articulations of standards of review among the jurisdictions, and it is important to articulate the correct standard.
- If the appellant successfully convinces the court there was error below, the court then determines if the error requires reversal of the judgment or error below.

Checkpoints *continued*

- Certain errors, such as factual findings that are clearly erroneous or not supported by substantial evidence or structural errors, require automatic reversal. Otherwise the court will engage in a harmless error analysis to determine whether and how much the error affected the result at the hearing or trial.
- Thus, it is possible to win the battle (convince the court there was error) and lose the war (fail to convince the court that the error requires reversal) and vice versa.
- An appellate brief is comprised of separate components, usually prescribed by local rules of procedure. Typical components include a statement of issues on appeal, tables of contents and authorities, statement of the case, statement of facts, summary of the argument, summary of the argument, discussion or argument with headings and subheadings, and a conclusion.
- The tables of contents and authorities should be drafted or generated last. Lawyers vary in the order in which they draft the other components. What is important is to approach the drafting process as a series of discrete tasks rather than one giant job.
- The statement of issues on appeal should specifically identify the alleged error or lack of error below. We recommend using the whether/when format.
- The statement of the case should set out the nature of the case, the relevant procedural history of the case, and should also contain the essential reasons why the decisions below should be reversed or affirmed. The statement of the case is the drafter's first opportunity to deliver their message. Accurate citations to the record for each fact or document are essential.
- The statement of facts should tell an accurate story that will make the reader want to adopt your legal positions and that gives them enough information to be able to do so.
- The purpose of the discussion or argument section is to show the reader how to rule in your client's favor and why it should do so. This involves making your points as clearly as possible, which usually means organizing complex information so that the reader can understand it as easily as possible.
- When drafting the discussion section, envision the opinion you would like the court to issue and *draft it like that.*
- Persuading the appellate court involves showing that your positions are (1) sound and well supported by authority, and (2) the better choice.
- Showing the court that your arguments are sound and well supported requires thorough and sophisticated knowledge of the law and authorities and how they affect the facts in the record.
- Showing that your positions and arguments are the better choice involves:
    - o exposing and exploiting the weaknesses of the other side's arguments, and
    - o using policy arguments.

Checkpoints *continued*

- Policy arguments are concrete but larger reasons why the court should adopt a tenable legal position. They show the court that your position advances a particular goal and/or the other side's positions will undermine this goal or cause harm.
- Each separate issue on appeal becomes a main section is the discussion section of both the appellant's and the appellee's brief. Often reversible versus harmless error gets its own section at the end of the brief.
- The structure of the discussion section is based on the CRAC (Conclusion, Rule/Law, Application/Analysis, Conclusion) format and is comprised of a series of CRACs. With some issues on appeal the focus will be on the rule/law portion, *e.g.*, if the issue is which law applies, or whether a particular law is valid. On the other hand, other issues on appeal may be factually intensive, such as whether a factual finding is clearly erroneous.
- Before you begin to draft have an idea of what your main arguments are and where they should go. Also have an idea of which arguments should be divided into subsections with their own point headings and CRAC format. This may change as you draft and revise, but it is best to begin with a structure in mind.
- Test your appellate brief for overall substance and organization by creating and reviewing a heading and topic sentence outline, described in Chapter 6, section F.
- Once you have a complete quality draft, thoroughly assess the appellate brief using the statement of facts and discussion/argument guidelines set out in this chapter.
- Make time to print and proofread your appellate brief separately before filing it or turning it in.

Chapter 8

Transactional Documents

Roadmap

- Transactional documents create a record of the parties' deal while simultaneously creating mechanisms to foster agreement, encourage performance, and provide for enforcement and dispute resolution.
- Transactional documents represent the documentation of the terms and stages of the parties' relationship and range from early agreements on fundamental terms, to interim documents such as term sheets and letters of intent, and the final, binding transactional documents.
- Transactional documents have a distinct structure like other forms of legal drafting, and that structure should be followed and employed to produce practical, precise contracts and instruments.
- Contractual precision requires accuracy, completeness, and exactitude—which refers to an absence of ambiguity and unintentional vagueness. Much can be accomplished in this regard by focusing on using the active voice and uniformly using the word "shall" for duties and "may" for rights and privileges.
- Transactional documents generally contain these components: title; introductory paragraph; recitals; definitions; core provisions—consideration, covenants, conditions; risk allocations—representations and warranties; closing provisions; events of default and remedies; boilerplate; signature blocks; and exhibits and attachments.
- Preparing transactional documents requires constructive collaboration of attorneys and clients from all sides of the deal in commenting on and revising drafts.

A. Purpose, Audience, and Goals of Transactional Documents

Drafting transactional documents like contracts and other instruments such as deeds, bills of sale, security agreements, and deeds of trust, is a process of creating a record of the parties' deal and simultaneously creating mechanisms to foster agreement, encourage performance, and provide for enforcement and dispute resolution. This means that there are at least three audiences that you must bear in mind while drafting: the parties' lawyers, the parties themselves, and an unidentified future decision maker, like a judge or a jury.

These goals and the different audiences are in a state of conflict and must be balanced. In the first instance, contract drafting and negotiation is a process in which the legal drafter seeks to memorialize the terms of the parties' deal and gain mutual agreement to all of its terms. At each stage in the contract drafting process, the deal is being subtly adjusted and renegotiated. It is a process of fostering agreement and making a record of that agreement.

Once that is accomplished, however, the transactional document must encourage performance. In other words, there have to be enough conditions and other provisions ordering performance in the document to act as carrots and sticks to encourage the parties to voluntarily perform their side of the deal. These carrots and sticks are not just events of default and remedies provisions. Rather, the contract should feature conditions to each party's performance based upon the other party's performance, time lines, walk-away rights, and price adjustments if compliance is not forthcoming in a timely manner, escrows to hold funds beyond the sole control of one party, and the like. Generally, the drafter should seek to provide for enforcement and dispute resolution on terms agreed to by the parties and *not* under the default rules that are provided by statutes or the common law. The contract drafting process is one in which you can define most if not all of the terms of the parties' relationship from beginning to end if you choose to do so. It is an opportunity not to be wasted.

There is, however, an unhappy truth: after the contract is negotiated and signed, the next thorough review of its provisions will likely be by someone trying to break the contract or sue over the transaction. This is especially the case today, when contracts are chopped, sliced, diced, packaged, bundled with others and sold or assigned to a trustee or agent whose job it is to seek enforcement at a later date, when none of the original parties are involved. They have all moved on or, if still involved, their memories will have grown hazy. You will be left having to seek enforcement of what is on the page, the terms that are included in the document—and somebody is going to be trying to break or avoid those terms. Given this situation, it is imperative that you have drafted the document so that it can stand up *on its own* to hostile critical review. An essential means of ensuring that the document survives this sort of scrutiny intact is to ensure that a person of reasonable intelligence who knows nothing about the transaction can understand the deal after one reading of the contract. That is likely to be all the time a judge, law clerk, court attorney, or jury has to devote to it.

This can be achieved by drafting practical, precise documents in plain English that reflect all the terms of the deal and are devoid of ambiguity and the unintentional use of vagueness. The specific methods for achieving this are discussed later in this chapter.

B. Structure and Context of Transactional Documents

The structure of the contract is essentially the same as that of other work product of legal drafting: introduction, statement of facts, statement of rules and application of the rules to the facts, followed by a conclusion. For this reason, just as most letters, motions, briefs, and opinions have the same structure, so do most contracts.

1. The Form of Transactional Documents

The standard sections of a contract are listed below and are not subject to that much variation, although they may be reordered. The definitions section, for instance, often is moved to the end when it is very lengthy.

A. Title
B. Introductory Paragraph
C. Recitals or Background Facts
D. Definitions
E. Core provisions—Consideration, Covenants, Conditions
F. Risk Allocations—Representations, Warranties, Indemnities, Guaranties
G. Closing Provisions
H. Events of Default & Remedies
I. Boilerplate
J. Signature Blocks
K. Exhibits & Attachments

2. The Context of Transactional Documents

Each of these components of a contract is discussed below in more detail, but first consider the context of transactional documents.

Transactional documents represent the documentation of the terms of a relationship between parties. Like all relationships, the parties' relationship has a beginning, middle, and an end. Transactional documents are drafted to reflect the stage of the relationship to which they relate. Therefore, the legal drafter must keep in mind the present stage of the relationship as well as those stages that are to come in the future.

For example, in the purchase and sale of a substantial asset such as a business or a home, there are typically seven stages of the parties' relationship. First, the parties meet and, second, reach a preliminary agreement on fundamental matters like the identity of the assets to be sold and the purchase price and method of payment (cash, stock, deferred payments over time, etc.). It is usually at the third stage that legal drafters become involved, although many benefits can accrue to parties that involve legal counsel earlier in the process, or at least consult with them for coaching on what their strategies and tactics may be in steps one and two.

The third stage is the preparation of interim transactional documents, such as term sheets or letters of intent. The key issue at this stage of the relationship is to determine whether or not the interim transactional documents are meant to be binding or if they are simply tentative reflections of the terms and deal structure that the parties have been discussing and are intended to promote clarity and understanding in those discussions, but not bind the parties. Often even the most tentative term sheets contain some provisions that are intended to be binding, such as confidentiality provisions and covenants to return documents and other things if the transaction is terminated. Whatever the degree of bindingness that is intended, the preliminary documents should make that explicit in their provisions. Due diligence—the process of factual and legal verification of things like the parties' due formation, their capacity to contract, the legal state of title to assets, the number, amount, and status of claims against a party or its assets, and the like—usually begins at this stage of the relationship.

The fourth stage of the typical transaction is the preparation of final, binding transactional documents, such as a purchase and sale agreement. These final documents contain all the operative provisions and will either be structured as a *sign and close* deal where the parties sign the agreement and almost immediately exchange consideration (think of buying a used car for cash under a sale contract) or a *delayed closing* deal where, after the signing, the parties have pre-closing duties to perform that are conditions to the closing. These duties and conditions typically include access agreements and due diligence rights as well as conditions based upon third party reports or approvals. Due diligence typically continues after these final documents have been signed by the parties.

The fifth stage of the typical transaction is closing, which will have happened simultaneously with the fourth stage in a sign and close deal. But closing is not the end of the story. Most sophisticated purchase agreements include post-closing covenants and conditions that provide for post-closing adjustments to the purchase price, post-closing indemnities for breaches in representations and warranties, and the like. So, the sixth stage of the typical transaction is the post-closing adjustment period.

The seventh stage of the transaction is, hopefully, not typical at all: litigation over the deal. At this point, the litigators will review the record that the transactional attorney has created in the first six stages of the parties relationship, which will form the basis for this seventh stage.

It is helpful to keep these observations about the typical form and context of transactional documents in mind when drafting them. This will allow you to prepare the proper sort of document, in the proper form, at the proper time. All of this is very useful in bringing the transaction safely through the first six typical stages and also to allowing your client's rights to be vindicated should the transaction enter the seventh stage.

3. Macro-Organizational Tips

The same organizational and drafting rules applicable to other forms of legal drafting and discussed in prior chapters apply with equal force to contracts and other transactional documents. Include general provisions before specific ones, e.g., state the "what" before the "how." Place important provisions before lesser ones. State rules before exceptions. Use separate sections/subsections for each concept, and include meaningful headings for each section. For further discussion regarding drafting organizational strategies see Chapter 2, section A.

4. Practical and Precise Documents

Contractual precision requires accuracy, completeness, and exactitude. Exactitude refers to an absence of ambiguity and unintentional vagueness. The terms "ambiguity" and "vagueness" should not be confused.

Ambiguity occurs when a word or phrase is capable of meaning two or more things. For example, if a contract provides that one party "shall pay x and y $100,000." It is unclear whether x and y are *each* to receive $100,000 or if x and y are to receive a *total* of $100,000 to share. Another common source of ambiguity is the unclear pronoun reference. When the transactional drafter sees a pronoun, it is best to ask whether a defined term for a party cannot be inserted in its place. Defined terms are, after all, a sort of very specific, private pronoun created by the drafter.

Vagueness, on the other hand, is a lack of clarity. It is often intentionally used in legal drafting when the parties are unable to agree on a provision governing what is thought to be a rare or unexpected event without incurring costs that are not justified due to the low probability of the event happening. Consider, for example, the standard prevailing party attorney fee shifting clause, which provides for an award of "reasonable fees and costs." While a party may want to quantify or cap the amount of a fee award by specifying a not-to-exceed figure, this is likely to be unacceptable to the other party. Rather than running up their current fees negotiating a provision that everyone hopes will never be used—everyone is optimistic at the inception of most deals—the attorneys comprise on the "reasonable attorneys fee" language. But vagueness should not be used inadvertently or unintentionally. Transactional drafters should closely examine their documents and question the impact and wisdom of including every "reasonable" or "material" or similar word that is used. In fact, a good general rule is to examine and question the impact of and need for all adverbs or adjectives in a transactional document.

Much can be accomplished in the way of producing practical, precise documents simply by focusing on using the active voice and uniformly using the word "shall" for duties and "may" for rights and privileges. The standard conventions are:

- "Shall"—Specifies duties (mandatory, imperative).
- "Shall not"—Specifies prohibitions.
- "May"—Specifies rights, options (permissive).
- "Will"—Reserved for the predictive (future).
- "Is"—for statements involving no actor (*e.g.*, choice of law).

A prominent enemy of contractual precision is the overburdened provision, the provision that attempts to do too much. Just as in other drafting tasks where you use separate IRACs, CRACs, and paragraphs to explore or explain each sub-issue, transactional documents should contain separate sections for each task they are to accomplish. The rule should be to subdivide as much as possible rather than the opposite. Defined terms, information schedules, and supplemental documents and worksheets can be used to unpack overburdened provisions.

5. Consistency

Consistency, consistency, consistency is the rule in all legal drafting, and especially so when it comes to transactional documents. If you are going to say something one way in one part of the contract, say that something the same way every time you say it in the contract.

Further in this vein, question the need for strings of synonymous or nearly synonymous words like "sell, transfer, and convey." Would the word "transfer" or "transfer ownership" cover the topic? But not all doublets and triplets can be discarded easily. An example is the requirement the seller of real estate "execute and deliver" a deed to the property to the other party. A deed that is executed but not delivered (or delivered but not executed) is ineffective to transfer title. But examine doublets and triplets and other lawyerisms to make sure that they are necessary and that you understand what they mean and accomplish.

C. Contract Components

1. Title

The title of any contract is generally found on the first page, top, center of the contract in all caps. Generally accepted format is to use a generic title such as "Employment Contract" or "Agreement and Plan of Merger" augmented by the parties names or, in the case of real estate, the address of the building or other project. Often the date is included. For example, "Lease," or "Lease of 1111 B Street," or "Lease of 1111 B Street by and between Tricor Real Estate Holdings LLC and Hubble Eyewear dated as of November 1, 2011" would all be generally accepted forms. Use of the "as of" form for dates avoids the need to make sure dates are updated or changed when negotiations take longer or shorter than expected.

2. Introductory Paragraph

The introductory paragraph is not numbered and usually includes the full names of the parties, the date of the agreement, and the nature of the agreement. Many times the introductory paragraph is used to define the agreement, the parties, and other matters. The generally accepted form is:

> This [name of agreement] (the "[defined term]") dated as of [date] is between [name of party 1, including form (LLC, Inc., etc.)] ("[defined term]") and [name of party 2, including form] ("[defined term]"). So, this Real Property lease of 101 Magnolia Boulevard (the "Lease") dated as of June 1, 2010, is between Alden Realty, LLC ("Landlord") and Deloit Chicken, Inc. ("Tenant").

3. Recitals

Recitals are generally included after the title and before the substance of the agreement, usually in lettered paragraphs. This section sets the context for the transaction. Recitals are a place where the background facts of the transaction and the relationship of the parties can be stated, where additional terms can be defined, and where additional agreements and instruments can be referenced if they are important to the overall context of the transaction of which the particular agreement is a part. Keep in mind that recitals may be treated as stipulated facts or admissions of a party in later litigation.

It is common for the recitals to close with a statement in an un-numbered and un-lettered paragraph to the effect that "[Wherefore] the parties agree as follows:". The "wherefore," although common, can be eliminated as an anachronistic transition.

The agreement then continues with numbered paragraphs, often after the centered title, in all caps "AGREEMENT." One school of thought is that the first of these numbered paragraphs should be a statement that the parties agree that the recitals, above, are true and correct, because they appear above the title "AGREEMENT." Although this is also probably anachronistic, formalist legalisms die hard.

4. Definitions

Defined terms are tools that can increase the clarity of contract provisions by removing extraneous matter that is not essential but is necessary to the provision. They also can decrease the length of the document if, but for their use, long, detailed descriptions would need to be repeated often.

If the agreement is to feature many defined terms, it is useful to collect them and locate them in a single section, generally at the beginning or end of the agreement, where they are listed in alphabetical order. When defining terms, use common sense. Do not include substantive terms—those that create rights, duties, privileges, or immunities—in the definitions. That is not what defined terms are for, and doing so will make the agreement confusing and possibly deceptive. Do not define terms that are used in their normal English sense, and do not define terms to mean something completely different than they mean in their normal sense. The first is unnecessary; the second is confusing.

Define terms to narrow their meaning from their normal sense to the specialized sense in the agreement at hand, e.g., defining "affiliate" with its securities regulation meaning of "controlled by," "controlling," or "under common control with" sense. Define terms to broaden their technical meaning to match their normal sense, *e.g.*, defining "trademarks" to include trade dress, service marks, and goodwill. Also, if a term has been defined, use it only in its defined sense in the balance of the document. To do otherwise creates ambiguity.

Defined terms can also be used—although they should not be—to cloud meaning and create misimpressions. They do this by preying upon the natural tendency of most people to read a document and give the words meaning at face value rather than stopping and checking meanings by referring to a long list of complicated definitions in another part of the document. Examples could include terms like "Paid in full," which is defined as payment in stock of a non-public company, valued by an arbitrator, or "Immediately," defined as within 90 days of receipt of a written request.

5. Core provisions — Consideration, Covenants, Conditions

Covenants are the parties' promises and duties under the agreement. They should be contained in provisions that are clearly labeled and structured as covenants and should include a specified consequence for failure to perform.

Covenants should be drafted in the active voice — subject, verb, then object — and should be based on the convention of using "shall" to designate duties — "may" is used to designate rights or privileges. For example, "Seller shall deliver the deed to Blackacre to Escrow Agent no later than December 1, 2011; failure of Seller to do so shall be cause for Buyer to terminate this agreement under section 10.08."

Covenants should clearly state what party is to do what, for whom, when and the like.

i. Major Covenants: Consideration

Consideration

The next section is the meat of the contract, at least from the client's point of view. This is the section that contains the main promises of the contract, the covenants that constitute the bargained-for consideration. Examples include payment of rent in exchange for the right to use a space, payment of the purchase price in exchange for the right to receive goods, and the like. These major covenants are usually straightforward and the simplest provisions to draft.

ii. Other Covenants

Apart from the major covenants that form the heart of the deal, especially in the minds of the clients, most agreements contain additional covenants, especially if there is a delay between the time the agreement is signed and when it closes, such as with the typical sale of a home or business. This structure is called a "delayed closing" deal to distinguish it from a "sign and close" deal such as the purchase of a used car for cash where one signs the contract of sale, hands over the cash, and the dealer hands over the car keys and causes the buyer's name to be placed on the car's title. For example, in the typical sale of a home, the buyer and the seller sign a contract of sale, but the closing usually takes some time later. This allows the parties to take care of document preparation and to clear the various conditions to closing that prudent home buyers and sellers include in the contract. These conditions to closing are either satisfaction of covenants (promises) by one or both of the parties or the occurrence of an event, such as receipt of a third party approval, like a bank's approval of a loan application.

These other covenants are typically the province of the lawyers, not the clients. They are part of the lawyer's job in structuring the transaction so that the parties are obligated, at the right time, to undertake all their duties, make applications, permit and conclude inspections, give approvals, and the like.

iii. Conditions

Conditions are events, including performances by the parties, that must occur before a duty becomes ripe or is discharged or modified. They are contractual switches that, when flickered, turn duties on and off. In contrast, covenants are the duties themselves. Continuing with the sale of a home example from the last subsection, typical conditions to closing include the buyer obtaining financing for a portion of the purchase price, the seller providing evidence of marketable title, the buyer obtaining a title policy, the seller obtaining and the buyer approving a termite report, and the like. For each of these conditions, there should be a corresponding covenant by one or both parties to take steps to ensure that the condition will be met. So, if the buyer obtaining financing is a condition, the seller should also insist on a covenant that the buyer will promptly and in good faith submit an application for that financing and use its best efforts, or commercially reasonable efforts, to gain approval. It is also wise to include an "out" or a termination provision if one party does not perform its pre-closing covenants within a certain time or it becomes clear that a condition to closing will not be met. Remember, in most jurisdictions, if it is unclear if a provision is both a covenant and a condition or simply a covenant, it will be construed as merely a covenant. This means that performance of the duty can be excused and non performance merely compensated with damages, if provable. The lesson: make conditions explicit. If the satisfaction of a duty of a party is a condition to the other party's duty to itself perform, say so.

Conditions—and, remember, satisfaction or performance of a covenant can be a condition—are transactional mechanisms that control the performance of the parties under the contract. They should be crafted to give rise to additional duties at the appropriate time, which, in turn, are conditions to further covenants and duties. To continue the example, a contract for the sale of a home may be contingent (conditioned) upon several steps of performance. The buyer's obligation to close may be conditioned upon several items, such as:

A. The seller providing a termite report on the home from a licensed termite inspector showing no "Part B" or serious, ongoing infestation;

B. The buyer approving a home inspection report from a qualified, licensed home inspector, with that approval not to be unreasonably withheld;

C. The seller being able to furnish good and marketable title as demonstrated by providing a title insurance policy with no exceptions from a nationally recognized title company with the buyer and its source of financing as beneficiaries.

In that case, the contract should also impose a duty upon:

A. The seller to engage a suitable termite inspector within 10 days of the parties' signing the contract and to arrange for the inspection within 30 days and delivery of the report within 45 days.

B. The buyer to engage a suitable home inspector within 10 days of the parties' signing the contract and to arrange for the inspection within 30 days and delivery of the report within 45 days;

C. The seller to cooperate reasonably with the buyer and the home inspector to allow the buyer to satisfy its obligations in item "B" above.

D. The seller to obtain the requisite title insurance policy within 30 days of the parties' signing the contract.

Each of these additional duties should be a condition to the other party's duty to perform its pre-closing duties. Should either of the parties fail to complete these additional duties within the prescribed time periods, the other side should be excused from performing its covenants and have the option of backing out of the contract, perhaps receiving some form of liquidated damages as a result of the party's breach. Of course, the party in whose favor a condition runs may always grant a waiver or an extension of time within which to satisfy the condition.

Generally, one party wants to impose many conditions and the other only a few. Also, typically, the party with the least leverage or bargaining strength will want those conditions to be objective and the other, with more leverage, will favor more subjective conditions that make performance or closing subject to its (good faith) satisfaction of the subjective standard. In an agreement for the sale of a company, for example, the seller generally desires to have very few objective conditions—it views the transaction as its time to harvest its rewards and wants the deal to close and to obtain the purchase price—while the buyer will favor an approach that gives it as many subjective conditions that it can deem satisfied in its discretion as possible—by doing this, the buyer obtains more control over the transaction and can determine that it wants to abandon the transaction or renegotiate the purchase price as pre-closing due diligence progresses.

When drafting conditions, especially subjective ones, take care to define the standards to be used and the identity of the person that will make the determination as to whether the condition has been met. Often terms like "material adverse change," "material adverse event," "best efforts," "commercially reasonable efforts," and the like are left vague and undefined. If this is done intentionally because the cost of reaching agreement on their definitions is too high relative to the benefit to be gained by doing so, that is fine. But they should not be left inadvertently undefined, which is an invitation to unforeseen litigation with its attendant expense and delay.

Finally, remember that conditions must be workable. Consider the notion of a "no material adverse change in financial position as of the closing date" condition to closing in the acquisition of a business. In any business other than the most tiny, there is no way to know the financial condition of the business on a particular day. There are reporting delays and the time needed to process the information reported into financial statements. As a result, the material adverse change condition in this example can never work; it will be waived at closing. Better would be a no material adverse change as of a pre-closing date coupled with a bring-down certificate restating the representatives and warranties as of the closing date and a post-closing adjustment to the purchase price of any pre-closing material adverse changes that come to light in the next accounting period, perhaps to be funded out of an escrow into which a portion of the purchase price is placed.

6. Risk Allocations—Representations and Warranties

Although covenants and conditions can and are used to allocate risk, such as by placing the duty to obtain third party consents or financing on a particular party, the primary contractual mechanism for allocating risk is through the use of representations and warranties. Although the distinction between the two is blurring, it is good to know the classic, common law definition of a representation and a warranty and to focus on the purpose that each was developed to serve. One can then master the modern draft-around techniques that alter the traditional rules.

A "representation" is a statement of presently existing facts that is intended to induce reliance and action by a party, such as entering into a contract. Think of a representation as an advertising claim. An incorrect representation will give rise to a cause of action for rescission or damages in most jurisdictions. Unless otherwise specified, classically, representations terminate at closing.

A "warranty" is a statement made about certain facts whereby the warrantor promises to ensure that those facts are as stated. A breached or incorrect warranty will give rise to an action for damages. Unless otherwise specified, classically, warranties survive closing.

That said, transactional lawyers have been drafting around these distinctions for a long time. First, often the representations and warranties in a contract are combined so that, for example, a seller "represents and warrants that [statement of fact]." The combined provision is the first step in blurring the distinction between representations and warranties drawn by the common law. The second step is for the drafter to provide that "all representations and warranties will survive closing." The blurring is then complete.

Keep in mind that it is certainly possible to qualify representations and warranties and to provide that specific representations and warranties terminate at or survive until particular times. For example, the seller of land may be willing to represent and warrant that there is no contamination on the property as long as that representation and warranty does not survive closing—the buyer will have time by then to have had tests done to confirm the condition of the land and can rescind pre-closing if he desires, based upon the representation. Further, the parties may contract to specify or narrow the remedies that will be available for breach of a representation or a warranty. In most jurisdictions—and with certain exceptions, notably under certain sections of the Uniform Commercial Code and some consumer protection laws—the representations and warranties in a contract are subject to almost boundless possibilities for modification and customization.

The normal development of representations and warranties in the transactional drafting process is for the party with the most leverage in the deal to have its attorneys draft the initial proposed documents, including blanket, clean representations and warranties, *i.e.*, broad ones with no qualifications or outs such as "there are no claims outstanding or threatened against the company." The other side typically responds by proposing limits on those representations and warranties by inserting materiality thresholds ("there are no claims for more than $5,000 outstanding or threatened against the company") or referencing schedules with exceptions on them ("other than as listed on schedule 2.3.4, there are no claims for more than $5,000 outstanding or threatened against the company").

Knowledge qualifiers, especially those that define a company's knowledge to mean that of an individual or set of individuals, are also common ("To the best of the seller's knowledge,....."). When using a knowledge qualifier in a deal between non-individuals (companies), it is important to specify what the knowledge of the company consists of and whether or not the company has any duty to perform a review or investigation to inform itself prior to making the representation. Undefined references to a company's "knowledge" are a recipe for discovery fishing trips and litigation should disputes later arise.

7. Closing Provisions

Closing provisions are a simple but important matter. These are the provisions that provide who is to deliver what documents to the closing or escrow, in what condition, signed or approved by whom, when, and the like. They are generally a series of covenants and conditions, performance of which trigger other covenants and conditions, until all the consideration has been assembled and is ready to be exchanged or distributed from escrow.

8. Events of Default and Remedies

Contracts often feature specific sections that specify events of default, procedures for declaring a default, and remedies available to the non-defaulting party upon declaration of default. In contracts courses, law students study common law rules regarding remedies, calculations based on expectation measures, limits on damages such as the need to prove that the damages were reasonably foreseeable at the time of contracting, and can be proved with certainty, and the availability of specific performance. This is all well and good, but the events of default and remedies section of the contract is a chance to draft around the common law rules or harness them to your client's advantage.

Default is a broader concept than breach. Begin the default section by listing what events are "events of default." Events of default usually include things that would be a breach of the contract—like non-payment of an amount due, but they can include many things that would give your client insecurity but not be considered a breach. Examples include failure to insure collateral, declining financial performance ratios, defaults under contracts or obligations, termination of licenses or permits and the like. When you read in the business press that a company had to negotiate a waiver of a "financial covenant default," the reporter is saying that the company's financial condition had changed so that it was no longer in compliance with a financial covenant—maintaining a current asset to current liability ratio of 1.75:1, for example—and had to negotiate a waiver of the lender's right to declare a default for that failure. Cross-default clauses, where a default under another contract can be an event of default under your contract, even if the other agreement is one entirely separate from the one that you are working on, are also common. For example, a working capital loan from a bank might feature the termination of a franchised business's franchise agreement as an event of default. Breach of a representation or warranty can also be an event of default. These examples do not exhaust the possibilities.

Although it is possible to draft the contract such that the occurrence of an event of default automatically puts the other side in default, this is not the norm and it is generally not prudent. Better to retain flexibility by requiring the default-declaring party to issue a notice of default concerning the event of default in order to place the other party in the legal state of "being in default." As a practical matter, most if not all jurisdictions require some form of notice of the default prior to exercise of remedy. The content, manner, and method of providing this notice can be specified in the document. It is also possible to include a period in which the defaulting party may cure or correct the event of default, in which, case the defaulting party can reset things and no longer be considered in default. These provisions should be followed by ones that specify the available remedies, how remedies are to be selected, and whether they are cumulative or mutually exclusive. Remedies include termination, foreclosure or surrender of collateral or other property, and the like.

9. Boilerplate

"Boilerplate" refers to the seemingly standard provisions at the end of a transactional document, before the signature blocks. Calling them "boilerplate" is misleading in that they can be very important, especially when a dispute later arises under the contract. These terms commonly include choice of law, choice of forum (note that choice of venue provisions are unenforceable in some jurisdictions), severability, integration or merger, execution in counterparts, notice, and the like.

Do not simply incorporate standard provisions into your boilerplate without thought and analysis. When reviewing contracts drafted by others, do not just skim the boilerplate. Pay attention to these provisions, think them through, and draft them to aid in the interpretation of the contract and its enforcement in favor of your client.

10. Signature Blocks

Signature blocks are the place in the document where the parties indicate their assent to the deal. There are only a few issues that must be addressed with regard to them. First of all, the right parties must be named—simple as this sounds, in this day of separate entities in conglomerates, joint ventures, and hastily formed acquisition subsidiaries, it is easy not to know the exact name of the entity until shortly before signing. It is even a good idea to confirm that each non-individual entity listed as a party has been properly formed prior to its signing the agreement.

Signature blocks for an individual person, look like this:

	Example:
[defined term for the party]	Seller
______________________________	______________________________
[party name, typed], [capacity if other than self] [if the party's address does not appear elsewhere, include it here to assist in identification]	Peter J. Gurfein 300 Walnut Street San Francisco, CA 94158

Signature blocks for an incorporeal entity (LLC, Corp., Partnership, etc.) look like this:

	Example:
[defined term for the party] [name of party entity] Bank, Inc.	Lender Penultimate National
______________________________	______________________________
[name of person signing], [title]	Michael Lesseney, President

11. Exhibits and Attachments

In the typical contract, last come the exhibits and attachments. These are useful places to incorporate lengthy, detailed material that would otherwise disrupt the flow of the main contract. Examples of this sort of information include the exception schedules relating to the representations and warranties in the contract referred to above, as well as detailed lists of property involved in the transaction, *e.g.*, a list of patents and copyrights in the sale of a technology, company.

Another popular use for exhibits is to provide the form of various instruments and other documents that may be needed in the course of performance of the contract. Examples include bills of sale, assignments of contracts, deeds of trust, security agreements, and the like. By providing forms of these instruments, drafters avoid any later dispute as to whether the form selected by a party is sufficient.

12. Exemplar Considerations

A final word in this section of the chapter is reserved for exemplars, forms or prior contracts of the type one is drafting. These may be found in an attorney's files, in form books, or on the Internet. They all must be viewed with suspicion. At best, these documents were right for the prior deal in which they were used. They are all negotiated documents that need to be customized for the current transaction. Never leave in a provision that you do not understand, thinking "that looks pretty official"—figure it out and determine if the provision should be retained, deleted, or modified for this transaction. Pay particular attention to the qualifications, carve-outs, materiality thresholds and the like in the representations and warranties; they were negotiated for the prior deal and may need to be deleted or modified for the current transaction.

D. Collaborative or Contentious Drafting

Transactional drafting and lawyering is different than litigating. Litigation requires minimal collaboration and cooperation with opposing counsel. One drafts one's complaint, motion, or other pleading and files and serves it. The other side responds. One replies. Oral argument is held, with counsel often staking out positions as far apart as possible in order to maximize the chance of an acceptable compromise decision by the judge. Indeed, the contentious nature of litigation, despite appeals from the bench and bar to maintain civility and professionalism, is one factor that motivates many to pursue a transactional practice. This is not to say that transactional practice is not contentious and, at times, filled with antagonism between opposing counsel. Rather, because there is seldom a third party decision maker for the parties to curry favor with and appeal to in order to resolve their disputes, they must resolve those disputes themselves or the transaction will not be finalized, and the lawyers will be blamed for killing the deal. As a result, it is necessary for counsel on both sides of the table to be able to give and take comments and revisions to their draft documents in a constructive, collaborative fashion.

The first level of comments that the transactional drafter is likely to receive are those from inside her own firm and from her client. These comments are meant to improve the document and make it more accommodating to your client's position. They are constructive comments and the drafter should welcome them as input from a new set of eyes, from a different, perhaps more experienced, perspective. Of these comments and edits, adopt those that actually improve the document and even those that do no harm. If there are others that you disagree with, omit them with explanation to the source of the comments. This is especially true with regard to comments from the client. The only wrong reaction to a comment from a client is to ignore it. If you disagree, explain yourself to your client and bring them along. It is also possible that the client has a concern that is not addressed in the document and the client was trying to address it. If that is the case, determine what the concern was and decide how to address it effectively if appropriate.

The next level of comments is the potentially contentious part, review by opposing counsel. When transmitting the documents to opposing counsel, invite them to provide specific line edits using black lining or Microsoft Word's "track changes" and "comments" features rather than composing a response letter detailing changes that are desired, sometimes in vague terms. The goal is to force opposing counsel to be as specific as possible to avoid any ambiguity or possibility of argument over different interpretations of the comments and reactions.

When comments from opposing counsel are received, make or accept all of them that are beneficial to the deal as a whole. As to matters of style that do not impact your client's rights or benefits, consider making them out of courtesy to the other side; on the other hand, if you are in a negotiating dynamic where opposing counsel is using these sorts of small, inconsequential suggestions to attempt to dominate you, you may need to push back and inform them that the requested changes are not necessary, are inconsequential, and appear to pertain to matters of style that are not consistent with your firm's style for transactional documentation.

As to comments or changes that are detrimental to your client's position, examine them carefully. Are they valid requests that deserve consideration, like a request that the materiality threshold of "of more than $50,000" be added to an otherwise clean representation and warranty that there are no outstanding claims against the company that is being sold? Is this the sort of qualification to the representation and warranty that is acceptable to your client, or would it be better to respond by striking the requested materiality threshold and suggesting a carve-out of "except as disclosed on schedule x" to the otherwise clean representation and warranty? This is the sort of back and forth that is to be expected in the negotiation of transactional documents.

Finally, other comments and requested changes may address wholly new matters that are valid points for future negotiation. Consult with your client and respond appropriately, probably always asking for something in return. It is unwise to acquiesce to such a request without obtaining something in return unless your client has everything it could ever want out of the deal. The other side should have to give you something to get the benefit that it desires.

E. Contract Guidelines

Most problems in transactional documents can be traced to one or more of three things:

(1) Blurring distinctions between types of contract provisions and using the wrong one for the purpose to be achieved;

(2) Provisions that attempt to accomplish too much; and

(3) Word choice and punctuation problems.

All of these are quite basic and can be prevented by focusing on a set of fundamentals that, if adhered to, will produce better, well drafted transactional documents.

1. General Rules of Organization

(a) General provisions before specific ones.

(b) Important, central provisions before others.

(c) Rules before exceptions.

(d) What (duty, condition, etc.) before how.

(e) Separate provisions for each concept.

(f) Technical, boilerplate, housekeeping, and miscellaneous provisions grouped together at the end, before the signature blocks.

2. Titles

Is the title to the document generic, *e.g.*, "Lease," "Stock Pledge Agreement," and the like? Does it include the names of the parties and the date, *e.g.*, "by and between Kelson Corp. and Jeffery Davis dated as of June 24, 2010."

3. Introductory Paragraph

Does the introductory paragraph introduce the parties, provide a defined term for each of them, specify their capacities under the agreement, and, if needed, include the date of the agreement?

4. Recitals

Are the recitals sufficient to provide the context of the transaction for the unfamiliar reader, especially a later decision maker, like a judge? Are there fundamental concepts or items that can be the subject of defined terms if they are discussed in the recitals? Do the recitals provide reference and descriptions of other documents and agreements that are relevant to this transaction but not strictly a part of it?

5. Definitions

When using defined terms, take great care. Overly broad or narrow definitions can create ambiguity or unintentionally reallocate benefits and burdens under a contract. Three key principles apply to defined terms:

a. Do not define terms that are used in the ordinary sense of the word.
b. Do not define terms in a way that is contrary to its ordinary meaning.
c. Do define terms to narrow or broaden the scope of the term as used in its ordinary sense, e.g. "Trademark" includes "Service Mark" and "Certification Mark."

Once you have used a term as a defined term, it is best to eliminate all other uses of that term to avoid confusion. Resist the urge to include obligations within defined terms—*e.g.*, The "Financial Statements," which Little Co. will deliver to Big Co. within 10 days of the Effective Date of this Agreement shall include .... Use affirmative covenants in the main body of the document for those obligations and limit the definition of the term to the merely descriptive.

6. Covenants

Are the covenants—the promises, the parties' duties—contained in provisions clearly labeled and structured as covenants? Are they phrased in the active voice, using the verb "shall", and do they fully state which party is to do what to or for whom, when? (When creating a privilege or a right, rather than a duty, the same rules apply, but "may" should be used rather than "shall.")

Is there a consequence specified for a failure of the party to perform its covenant in a timely manner? This is especially important as, especially with more minor covenants, reasonably foreseeable damages from a failure to perform may be difficult to prove with certainty. Take the opportunity when drafting to put some teeth into your covenants by specifying the consequences that will attend a failure to perform.

7. Conditions

Are the conditions—the events that must occur before a duty becomes ripe or is discharged or modified—explicitly set out and labeled as conditions? Have the parties thought through and provided for each of the fundamental assumptions underlying their deal to be a condition to the deal itself? Are consequences for a failure of a condition to be satisfied explicitly stated? Do not rely upon events of default and remedies provisions alone to address failures in performance or changes in fundamental underlying events.

Conditions are the best contractual mechanism to address events that are both under or outside of the parties' control. But, if addressing actions that are under a party's control, use a pre-closing covenant to require them to take the action, in addition to a condition.

Finally, are the conditions workable?

8. Representations and Warranties

Are the representations and warranties made as of a particular date, generally the date of the signing of the agreement? Does the agreement require a bring-down or re-issuance of the representations and warranties as of the closing date as a condition to closing in a delayed closing deal? Are there appropriate qualifications to the representations and warranties such as materiality thresholds, carve outs, or exceptions listed on schedules? Do the representations and warranties terminate on particular dates or upon the happening of certain events or do they survive closing. Make termination or survival of representations and warranties explicit so that there is no need to turn to case law to answer this question.

9. Termination

Give some thought to termination of the agreement. Think through how it can and should terminate if necessary. Possible mechanisms for termination are termination by agreement, termination if there is no closing by a date certain, termination if a party is not satisfied with due diligence, termination if representations are found to be inaccurate, termination if events have occurred that will prevent the closing, and breach of a pre-closing covenant or failure of a condition precedent.

Also, what occurs upon "termination"—which is different from "breach." Are there items or information that must be returned by one party to another? Do some provisions of the contract remain in force, e.g., confidentiality provisions or a termination fee?

10. Closing Provisions

Examine the closing provisions carefully. Do they provide, as a condition to closing, for all acts and deliveries that your client expects to receive or benefit from? Are each of these acts and duties also the subject of affirmative covenants by the other side?

11. Events of Default and Remedies

Have you listed appropriate events of default, looking beyond mere nonperformance of the contact to include early warning signals that could cause insecurity or signal liability non-performance? Are appropriate notice provisions included so that, when it is time to give notice and declare a default, there is no doubt exactly how to do that? Are appropriate remedies in place? Will your client be in a position to regain its property, especially confidential information and trade secrets? Is there proper support for the other side's obligations, such as collateral, guaranties, letters of credit, and the like? Is it clear whether the remedies are cumulative or must be elected as an exclusive remedy? Is it clear whether to resort to state or federal contract, tort, or other causes of action is permitted?

12. Boilerplate

Review boilerplate carefully as it is often overlooked. Specific attention should be paid to severability, arbitration or other dispute resolution, and attorney's fees provisions. Do these terms, if literally applied, make sense for this transaction?

13. Signature Blocks

Silly as it sounds, is the document ready for the right party to sign it? In this era of conglomerates and affiliated groups of artificial entities whose names often only vary by a single number or word, it bears checking carefully that the right party, represented by the right officer with authority to bind the company, is listed.

14. Plain English and Clarity

Contracts should be readable. As noted earlier in the chapter, the standard to strive for is that a person of reasonable intelligence who knows nothing about the transaction can understand the deal after one reading of the contract. This is not always attainable, but it is a good aspirational goal. Examine the contract for plain, simple, direct English; use of the active voice; clear identification of who is to do what to or for whom, when. Have excess words, especially adjectives and adverbs, been eliminated?

15. Accuracy and Completeness

Is the document accurate, in the sense that it correctly expresses the transaction at issue? Is it complete, *i.e.*, does it address all possible courses of action pre-closing and during its performance? Is it exact, meaning that it is not ambiguous or unintentionally vague (intentional use of vagueness may be needed to reach agreement, but vagueness should never appear without the intent or need for it). Will this document be able to withstand hostile, critical review by a third party decision maker assisted by opposing counsel?

16. Technical

Finally, proofread the transactional document carefully. Beware, especially of those misspellings that are not caught by word processor spell checkers because they are correctly spelled wrong words. Reading the document aloud can help in this regard. Check all citations and references to other documents and laws that are incorporated into the document. Also, check internal cross-references within the document carefully. For the document to govern the parties relationship well, all these things must be correct.

Checkpoints

- Transactional documents create a record of the parties' deal and simultaneously creating mechanisms to foster agreement, encourage performance, and provide for enforcement and dispute resolution.
- Transactional documents have a distinct structure like other forms of legal drafting, and that structure should be followed and employed to produce practical, precise contracts and instruments.
- Transactional documents represent the documentation of the terms of a parties' relationship, and are drafted to reflect the stage of relationship to which they relate.
- Stages of the parties' relationship include:
  - o The first meeting of the parties;
  - o Reaching a preliminary agreement on fundamental matters, such as price and method of payment;

Checkpoints *continued*

- o Preparation of interim transactional documents such as term sheets and letters of intent and initial due diligence;
- o Preparation of the final binding transactional documents and final due diligence;
- o Closing;
- o A Post-closing adjustment period which may involve post-closing covenants or conditions; and
- o Later litigation, which hopefully does not occur.

- Keeping these stages in mind will help drafters to ensure they prepare the proper sort of documents and the proper time.
- The same organizational rules that apply to other forms of legal drafting apply with equal force to transactional documents. Including:
    - o place general provisions before specific ones;
    - o place important provisions before lesser ones;
    - o state rules before exceptions;
    - o use separate sections/subsections for each concept; and
    - o include meaningful headings for each section.
- Contractual precision requires accuracy, completeness, and exactitude.
- Exactitude, which refers to an absence of ambiguity and unintentional vagueness.
- Ambiguity occurs when a word or phrase is capable of more than one specific meaning.
- Vagueness is the lack of clarity — where the specific meaning is unclear.
- Vagueness is often used in transactional documents when the parties are unable to agree on a provision governing what is thought to be a rare or unexpected event.
- Vagueness should not be used unintentionally or inadvertently.
- Much can be accomplished in producing practical, precise documents by focusing on using the active voice and uniformly using the word "shall" for duties and "may" for rights and privileges.
- Transactional documents generally contain these components:
    - o Title;
    - o Introductory paragraph;
    - o Recitals;

Checkpoints *continued*

- o Definitions;
- o Core provisions — Consideration, Covenants, Conditions;
- o Risk allocations — Representations and Warranties;
- o Closing provisions;
- o Events of default and remedies;
- o Boilerplate;
- o Signature blocks;
- o Exhibits and attachments.
- Preparing transactional documents requires constructive, collaboration of attorneys from both sides of the deal in commenting on and revising drafts.
- Most problems in transactional documents can be traced to
  - o blurring distinctions between types or contract provisions and using the wrong one for the purpose to be achieved;
  - o provisions that attempt to accomplish too much;
  - o word choice and punctuation problems.

Chapter 9

Legislation and Regulations

Roadmap

- Drafting legislation is similar to drafting contracts and transactional documents, but the audience is broader as legislation defines the relationship between the government and the governed versus the relationship between private parties.
- The suggested format for legislation, based on the federal model, is to divide bills and codes into titles, chapters, subchapters, then sections, subsections or paragraphs, clauses, and sub-clauses.
- Legislation generally may contain a heading, a title, an enacting clause, a short title, a statement of purpose or findings, definitions, substantive provisions, enforcement provisions, amending provisions, savings clauses, transitional provisions, an effective date, and a severability or nonseverability clause.
- Many of the organizational rules and guidelines applicable to transactional documents apply to legislation.

A. Purpose, Audience, and Goals of Legislation

Drafting legislation (as used here, this includes regulations) is very similar to drafting contracts and transactional documents, except that the audience is broader. Instead of defining a relationship between, typically, less than ten entities as is the case with contracts, the legislative and regulatory drafter is defining a relationship between the government and the entire population or a particular subset of the governed. This, combined with the fact that the impetus for legislation is often a so-called "special interest group," but will affect persons beyond this group, makes legislative and regulatory drafting perhaps the most challenging from of legal drafting. The drafter must balance the need to achieve the special interest goals that give rise to the project while limiting the reach of the law so that it does not unnecessarily encompass and inhibit other groups who will seek to either block the legislation or subvert its purpose, hijacking the effort along the way.

It is useful here to make some observations about the phenomenon known as "agency capture" and related dynamics. One of the best strategies for an industry or interest group that is or is likely to be the target of legislation or regulation is *not* to oppose that trend once it is clear that legislative regulation is inevitable. Rather, the better course at that juncture may be for the industry or interest group to strongly support the process, advancing its own legislation and regulation and even the creation of an agency to provide oversight. In doing so, the affected group can draft legislation and regulations that are not too burdensome and that contain exceptions, appeals, and other mechanisms to allow the affected group to grind down the efforts of those that would seek to affect it behaving though the legislative and regulatory process. At the far end of this strategy is what is called "agency capture"—where an interest group infiltrate's an agency's leadership and technical staff with its own expert representatives and also telegraphs the availability of industry or interest group future employment opportunities to agency officials and employees, who may then be more apt to be lenient or forgiving of misconduct as a means of carrying favor with their prospective employers and benefactors. In carrying out this strategy, as well as in seeking to oppose it, a sense of proportion and balance is essential to preserve what political scientists would term "legitimacy"—once that quality is lost, "reform" is the next step, often reversing the balance of power between the regulated and the regulators, with unpredictable results for all concerned. These dynamics often lie behind the legislative process and should not be ignored by the legislative drafter.

The challenge of serving as a legislative drafter is that of working with one or more legislators to produce, often starting from scratch, a legally sound yet practical legislative solution to a real world problem. Far from being a mere scrivener, the legislative drafter uses the legal knowledge and analytical skills honed in law school along with creativity and common sense to achieve this goal.

B. Suggested Format

This book follows the accepted form for federal statutes in terms of formats and nomenclature for their parts. Under that system, the first divisional unit of a statute is generally the "section," which is numbered with an Arabic numeral.

Sections may be divided into subsections, if the division is a complete sentence and a standalone idea unto itself, which are designated by lower case letters in parentheses: (a), (b), (c), etc. So:

Section 44. (a) General. This is the main idea expressed in the statute.

(1) This is sub idea one;

(A) Which has two parts, this one and

(B) This one.

(2) This is sub idea two.

(3) This is sub idea three.

If the section is divided into statements that are not complete sentences but, rather, phrases or clauses, they are called "paragraphs" and are designated with Arabic numerals in parentheses: (1), (2), (3), etc. (Ignore the fact that these "paragraphs" are not paragraphs of English grammar and style—it is just a name for them). So:

Section 45. This section is about something that consists of:

(1) the first idea;

(2) the second idea; and

(3) the third idea.

The next division of the statute is typically called a "clause" (they need not be clauses in the sense used in discussions of English grammar and style), designated with a lower case roman (or "romanette") numbers in parentheses: (i), (ii), (iii), etc. These are followed by sub-clauses, designated with upper case roman numbers in parenthesis: (I), (II), (III), etc.

When statutes are passed as bills that cover many, many different topics, as is the case in so-called omnibus bills or Christmas-tree legislation, they may be divided into titles, chapters, and subchapters, grouping similar topics together, all above the section level.

C. Legislative and Regulatory Components

1. Types of Legislative Documents

Legislative documents include bills, resolutions, amendments, and other documents that are prepared to be considered and voted upon by a legislature, like Congress. Bills are the documents in which a statute is proposed for enactment, including bills that amend existing statutes. An amendment is a document that proposes a change to a bill once it has been proposed. A statute is the final result of the legislative process (or, at the administrative agency level, a rule or regulation is the result—this book focuses on legislation rather than administrative rule making, but the two are substantially identical in terms of drafting).

2. The Contents of a Statute

Not all statutes contain all of the parts discussed below, but most will be present in most statutes.

a. Heading

The heading of a bill contains information regarding before what legislative body and session the bill is presented, the date of its introduction, and the legislators that introduced the bill. For example:

111th Congress, 1st Session **H. R. 1942**

To amend title 11, and for other purposes.

IN THE HOUSE OF REPRESENTATIVES
APRIL 2, 2009

Mr. NADLER of New York (for himself and Mr. COHEN) introduced the following bill; which

was referred to the Committee on the Judiciary

---

b. Title

The title of the bill is generally formal and may be long and serves to both describe the legislation's purpose and identify the statutes, if any, that are to be affected by it. For example:

A BILL

To amend title 11, and for other purposes.

c. Enacting Clause

The title is followed by the enacting clause, generally words that are specifically required either by a constitution or by a previously enacted statute. In Congress, the mandated language is: "Be it enacted by the Senate and House of Representatives of the United States of America in Congress assembled." 1 U.S.C. § 101. Without an enacting clause, the document is not a bill.

d. *Short Title*

Because the full title of the bill can be very long, it is useful to have a short title for ease of reference and discussion. For example, H.R. 1942, used as an example above, in its section 1 provides that:

> This Act may be cited as "Business Reorganization and Job Preservation Act of 2009."

There usually is a bit of politics playing into the short title of the bill, and one should not take it on faith that the description is either accurate or complete.

e. *Statement of Purpose or Findings*

In general, statements of purpose or findings are not needed if the operative provisions of the bill are well drafted. The resulting statute will speak for itself and having potentially conflicting statements of purpose will only provide fodder for later disputes and litigation. That said, however, if the bill is a broad, comprehensive enactment that covers new ground, an overview of the legislature's findings, including specific facts that identify the problems to be addressed by the bill, its basis in public policy, or instructions as to how broadly or narrowly it is to be construed may be appropriate.

f. *Definitions*

The definitions section of a bill is similar to the definitions section of a contract or other transactional document, and is subject to the same considerations. A definitions section may not be needed at all, especially if there are very few defined terms or if they are used in isolation. If that is the case, including the definitions in the section of the legislation to which it relates may make the most sense.

While defined terms can make a bill very precise, they must be used carefully to avoid causing the confusion that overly broad or narrow definitions can create. The three key defined term principles are:

a. Do not define a term that is used in the ordinary sense of the word.
b. Do not define a term in a way that is contrary to its ordinary meaning.
c. Do define a term to broaden or narrow the scope of the term as used in its ordinary sense, *e.g.*, "tax" does not include a special assessment for public improvements.

Once a term has been defined, eliminate all other uses of that term to avoid confusion. Additionally, do not use definitions to state substantive law as that hides the substance of the bill from all but the most careful readers.

The legislative or regulatory drafter should be aware of things that are necessarily incorporated into the statute that is being drafted even though they are not physically present in the draft. These are the definitions and rules of construction that may have been adopted by the legislative body and are applicable to all enactments. Examples of such provisions can be found in Title 1 of the United States Code and include the rules that, unless the context requires otherwise, in all Acts of Congress, the singular includes the plural and the plural includes the singular, the masculine includes the feminine, the present tense includes the future tense, and the words "person" and "whoever" include corporations, companies, associations, firms, partnerships, societies, and joint stock companies as well as individuals. 1 U.S.C. § 1 (to refer to human beings, the term "individual" should be used; to include both persons and governmental agencies, use "entity"); see also 1 U.S.C § 2 ("county" includes "parish" or any other equivalent subdivision of a state or territory); 1 U.S.C. § 3 ("vessel" includes all means of water transportation); 1 U.S.C. § 4 ("vehicle" includes all means of land transportation); 1 U.S.C. § 5 ("company" or "association" includes successors and assigns of the company or association); 1 U.S.C. § 7 ("marriage" means a legal union between one man and one woman as husband and wife; "spouse" means a person of the opposite sex that is a husband or wife); 1 U.S.C. § 8 ("person," "human being," "child," and "individual" include infant homo sapiens that is born alive at any stage of development).

g. Principal Substantive Provisions

The principal substantive provisions of a bill identify a class of persons and gives or imposes upon them particular rights, duties, powers, or privileges. The substance of the bill should be organized according to three general principles within each group or subdivision (section, subsection, phrase, clause, or subclause):

1. Assume the reader will read the provisions in the order they appear. As a result, do not put one provision before another that is necessary to understand it. In other words, put the context before the details.
2. Provisions should be arranged in declining order of importance, with general rules before special ones or exceptions.
3. Group provisions dealing with the same subject matter together.

Note that headings may be used to make these provisions more clear by providing sign-posts along the way for the reader. Generally, headings are not used at the level of the clause or sub-clause.

h. Enforcement Provisions

Enforcement provisions contain the consequences that attach to following, not following, qualifying or not qualifying under the substantive provisions. The three primary types of enforcement are criminal, civil, and administrative. These provisions require drafters to know about the existing criminal, civil, and administrative process so that they can take advantage of enforcement provisions that may already be in place—perjury or making a false statement in a government application, for example—that can apply to the substance at hand. Duplicating existing law is at best a waste of time and at worst creates the possible implication that the other law has been repealed or somehow impaired.

In the case of a criminal substantive provision, it may simply be enough to state which member of the executive branch law enforcement administration has standing and jurisdiction to enforce the provision. Typically, this will incorporate without even the need for reference a host of procedures and processes that can be used by the selected office or officer to enforce the law.

In the case of civil penalties, the attorney general's office or its delegate is the usual enforcer, although it is also possible to create a private right of action, which can be encouraged by enhancing damages that are available and providing for the recovery of a successful claimant's attorney's fees. For administrative penalties, delegation of enforcement to the proper administrative agency, after ensuring that enforcement of the substantive provision is within its organic jurisdiction, is usually sufficient.

i. Amending Provisions

Bills that directly amend an existing statute may be subject to specific rules in the particular legislature that govern whether or not so-called "spot amendments" will be permitted. Turning back to H.R. 1942, discussed above, for an example of spot amendments:

> Title 11 of the United States Code is amended—
>
> (1) by amending section 365(d)(4) to read as follows:
>
> > "(4) Notwithstanding paragraphs (1) and (2), in a case under any chapter of this title, if the trustee does not assume or reject an unexpired lease of nonresidential real property under which the debtor is the lessee within 60 days after the date of the order for relief, or within such additional time as the court, for cause,

within such 60-day period, fixes, then such lease is deemed rejected, and the trustee shall immediately surrender such nonresidential real property to the lessor."

(2) in section 366—

(A) in subsection (a) by striking "subsections (b) and (c)" and inserting "subsection (b)", and

(B) by striking subsection (c),

(3) in section 503(b)—

(A) in paragraph (7) by adding "and" at the end,

(B) in paragraph (8) by striking "; and" and inserting a period, and

(C) by striking paragraph (9).

The alternative to spot amending like this is to repeal the original statute and to simultaneously pass an amended and restated version of the statute incorporating the desired changes.

A final consideration when amending a statute is what effect the amendment will have on the enumeration of sections, subsections, etc. If more of these enumerated divisions are added or deleted than is deleted or added, the overall numbering scheme may be affected for the whole statute. While it is possible to simply renumber the entire statute, this is not desirable, especially when the statute has been the subject extensive case law or other legal commentary which would then suffer from inaccurate citations to the divisions of the statute. If possible, strive to add as much as is taken away or move to a lower divisional level where the addition of new material will not affect prior references to the statute in these other materials.

j. Savings Clauses, Transitional Provisions, and Effective Dates

Savings and transitional provisions are an attempt to minimize disruption that can accompany a change in law. A savings clause exempts conduct or relationships that occurred before or on the effective date of the new statute. Grandfather clauses—which are provisions in licensing or permitting statutes that automatically grant a license or a permit to a person engaged in an occupation or business prior to its regulation—are one type of savings clause. Another type, common in criminal law, provides that former law will continue to apply to past conduct and relationships and the new law applies to conduct and relationships happening or formed after its effective date. Finally, perhaps the most common form of transition provision is the effective date provision, which can delay implementation of a law for some period, even years in the future, to allow people to adjust and prepare for its impact.

k. Severability or Nonseverability Clause

Severability or non-severability clauses are a proactive attempt to plan for the fate of the statute should part of it be determined to be invalid, generally in a later court case. The question of severability is actually one for the court invalidating a portion of the statute, which involves two issues: (1) can the remainder of the statute be applied without the invalid portion, and (b) would the legislature have passed the remainder of the statute without the invalid portion? If both questions are answered in the affirmative, the invalid portion is found to be severable and the rest of the statute stands. Inserting a severability or nonseverability clause into a bill is a means of attempting to address the second issue. It is not automatically enforceable but is some evidence of the legislature's intent.

D. Legislative and Regulatory Drafting Guidelines

Most problems in legislative documents, like those in transactional documents between private parties, can be traced to one or more of three things:

(1) Blurring distinctions between types of provisions;

(2) Provisions that attempt to accomplish too much; and

(3) Word choice and punctuation problems.

All of these are quite basic and can be prevented by focusing on a set of fundamentals that, if adhered to, will produce better, well drafted contracts and other transactional documents. Other guidelines for drafting legislation follow.

1. General Rules of Organization

The general rules for organization of legislative documents, such as a bill, are similar to those that underlie all quality legal drafting:

- General provisions before specific ones.
- Important, central provisions before others.
- Rules before exceptions.
- What before how.

- Separate provisions for substance and enforcement.
- Technical, housekeeping, and transitional provisions at the end of the bill.

2. Defined Terms

Legislative drafters should use defined terms carefully to avoid creating ambiguity. Five key principles apply to defined terms:

- Do not define terms that are used in the ordinary sense of the word.
- Do not define terms in a way that is contrary to its ordinary meaning.
- Do define terms to broaden or narrow the scope of the term as used in its ordinary sense.
- Once you have used a term as a defined term, eliminate all other uses of that term to avoid confusion.
- Do not include substantive obligations within defined terms; those provisions belong in separate, substantive sections of the bill.

3. Plain English and Clarity

Good legislation is clear and readable. As with contracts and transactional documents, aim to produce a document that a person of reasonable intelligence who knows nothing about the matter can understand after one reading. Examine the document for plain, simple, direct English; use of the active voice; clear identification of who is entitled to what based upon what qualifications, what is prohibited, what is permitted, what is required.

Have excess words, especially adjectives and adverbs been eliminated? They are an invitation for a court to interpret them so as to give them effect and meaning. If that is not intended, they should be deleted.

Examine the legislative document for ambiguity and eliminate any suggestion of multiple meanings. Ambiguity, if found, is an invitation for a court to conduct a wide ranging examination of legislative history and to indulge its own sense of what meaning is plain, or not. The result of this sort of activity is unpredictable, and certainty and predictability should be the goal of legislation.

Checkpoints

- Drafting legislation is similar to drafting contracts and transactional documents, but the audience is broader as legislation defines the relationship between the government and the governed, versus the parties to the agreement.
- The suggested format for legislation, based on the federal model, is to divide bills and codes into titles, chapters, subchapters, then sections, subsections or paragraphs, clauses, and sub-clauses.
- Legislative documents include bills, resolutions, amendments and other documents that are considered and voted upon by a legislature.
- Legislation generally may contain:
  - a heading;
  - a title;
  - an enacting clause;
  - a short title;
  - a statement of purpose or findings;
  - definitions;
  - substantive provisions;
  - enforcement provisions;
  - amending provisions;
  - savings clauses;
  - transitional provisions;
  - an effective date; and
  - a severability or nonseverability clause.
- Many of the organizational rules and guidelines applicable to transactional documents apply to legislation, including: general provisions before specific ones; important, central provisions before others; rules before exceptions; what before how; separate provisions for substance and enforcement; and technical, housekeeping and enforcement provisions and the end of the bill.
- Most problems in legislative documents can be traced to blurring distinctions between types of provisions, provisions that attempt too much, or word choice and punctuation.

Chapter 10

Drafting for the Record

Roadmap

- All legal drafting is drafting for the record — creating a history that can be pointed to and relied upon to justify future actions and decisions.
- Legal drafters are well served by keeping in mind that everything they draft will be part of the record and may be used in proceedings far removed from the activities for which the document is originally prepared. This should caution restraint in characterizations, superlatives, insults, and uncivil communication, among other things.

A. Making a Record

Writing of all types, but primarily financial accounting and legal writing, makes civilization possible. The birth of banking and financing has been traced to Mesopotamia in as early as 3000 B.C., when stone tablets showing markings of account for deposits of grain. Thse writings made it possible to bank deposits of current bounty to protect against future need and to earn a return on capital. The code of Hammurabi in approximately 1760 B.C. Babylon has been identified with the first stable, widely distributed body of law. These developments underlie civilization as we know it: a certain flexible constancy of law, norms, and values across generations and regions and the ability to claim rights in later periods based upon actions and events recorded in the current period. It is often this relative social stability across generations and time that the other, perhaps finer, attributes of civilization could develop such as art, literature, religion, government bureaucracy, and science. Before that, all was oral tradition, subject to memory lapse and elimination of those with knowledge, which resulted in the need to recreate all knowledge, all traditions, every few generations — generations that were much shorter than they are today in much of the world.

By creating a record, accounting and legal writing go a long way toward curing civilization's problem of 100% turnover in the workforce every generation. They allow a record to be left of transactions, agreements, legislation, and decisions that, if properly prepared, allows the next generation of accountants, lawyers, and bureaucrats to take over largely intact when the preceding generation is no longer available. This, at bottom, is why it is critical in legal drafting to show your work—all your work, including the record of considerations analyzed and then rejected. The point, at bottom, is to create the record that will survive and be accepted as true, and be relied upon in the future.

It is often observed that "history is written by the winners." Usually this statement is made to suggest *post hoc* revisionary rewrites and selective document retention and destruction by dominant cultures and small groups. What that view ignores is the other interpretation of the phrase: The winners are the ones that wrote the best history. In other words, those that made the best record.

Law, of which legal drafting is the common denominator, is and always has been a process of creative storytelling, of providing a narrative to support and defend outcomes, either those in the past or those that are desired. The substantive laws fall on a continuum from rules with elements to standards based upon seemingly endless non-exclusive lists of factors to be considered or balanced. These laws provide a more or less flexible set of norms within which the storytelling may tell a convincing story. It is not true to say that the storyteller makes no choice. Rather, every choice made by the storyteller effects how the story will progress and eventually end.

The storyteller may determine to *show*, more than *tell*—to *lead* you to a conclusion rather than *drive* you there—but this is a choice. Competent storytellers always have their thumb on the scale, influencing the audience's perception.

At every step in a lawyer's professional activities, a record is being made and this is increasingly the case in a world of e-mail, instant messaging, and the like. We advocate making sure that you, as a lawyer involved, participate fully and effectively in the record making process.

- As a private attorney, the record may begin with a client retention agreement setting out the scope of representation and terms of compensation and reimbursement. This record may come in handy should that attorney-client relationship deteriorate and accusations fly. The same goes for letters documenting advice or materials sent to the client, as well as time and billing records.

- When dealing with opposing counsel, document all agreements scrupulously and fairly with a copy to your client to fulfill your duty to keep the client informed. The same goes for demand letters.

- Internal firm memoranda allow an associate or assisting attorney to make a record of more than the factual and legal research that supports a course of action that is ultimately pursued. Build a record that speaks for itself as to your competence and diligence in exploring a full range of options and theories as well as any decision by a client or supervising attorney to assume the risk of a road not taken, a theory not pursued. Timesheets, for hourly billers, also provide an opportunity to record the substance and time spent pursuing various matters. Remember, you may not be present or permitted to speak in your own defense when accusations fly later, whether because of rules of evidence or intra-firm social pressures or customs.
- Motion papers and briefs at the trial court or administrative agency level make a record of the arguments made and evidence produced to support them. They define the scope of all later appellate review and should be viewed as counsel's chance to make a full and complete presentation of all relevant facts and law. Do not fall into the trap sprung on so many pro se litigants who take a stab at a single argument or two in the trial court, expecting to be able to expand and include further arguments later, on appeal. Those attempts fail. You must preserve arguments and evidence for appeal.
- Appellate briefs present the case below and the facts and law that are urged to support affirmance or reversal. They are based upon the record created below and designated on appeal. In prosecuting an appeal, counsel hope to show in their briefs that the court below committed error that rises above the level of the applicable standard of review and was not harmless error. Counsel defending the appeal hopes to show the opposite.
- Contracts and transactional documents memorialize a deal and its details. Optimally, they record, in their recitals, conditions, covenants, representations, and warranties, all the assumptions and understandings of the parties regarding the transaction. By completely stating these matters, they provide their own rules for a later court to enforce without resorting to default rules of law or a judge's personal interpretation of how important some provision, standing naked and alone, was to the parties at the time of contracting and whether or not it should be strictly enforced.
- Legislation and regulations and the histories of their enactment comprise the legislative record. Properly drafted, they reflect what the legislature determined was a problem that needed addressing and how the legislature determined to address the problem. These documents are pro-

> duced in less than perfect circumstances, being, for the most part, compilations of the original proposal and amendments authored separately and inserted sometimes in great haste. The legislative record and the statutes it produces is comparatively chaotic and comprised of the results of layering on the opinions and positions of a large number of people. This stands in contrast to the hopefully more focused product of transactions and litigation, where there are generally fewer persons involved to muddy the water and more time to clarify things.

All these forms of legal drafting build upon each other. Each is making up part of the record and also recording determinations based upon the record already created. Keep this in mind. Be explicit. Watch your use of adjectives and adverbs. Be as complete as needed to serve your interests and act within the scope of your professional responsibilities. The complaint that history is written by the winners is that of the losers. The winners know they won because they created and preserved in usable form the best history and told the best story.

B. Metadata

Technology has only expanded what can be discovered and included in the record. With the almost universal use of word processors and document markup software in the legal profession, no chapter on writing for the record would be complete without a mention of metadata: the electronic record of revisions and comments previously embedded in an electronic text file even after those changes and comments have been accepted or rejected by document reviewers. The danger is that, as draft documents are circulated among parties and counsel whose interests in a matter are adverse, the metadata provides a telling record of the discussions and mental impressions of those involved. For example, a comment to a price provision in a contact of $1,000,000 that says "We can go to $1.5 mm, but let's see if they bite on this" is rather telling if transmitted to the other side and decoded. The same goes for draft pleadings, joint submissions, and stipulations. Bottom line: you, your firm, your client, and all affiliated parties and clients need to establish a rigorous protocol for document control and transmission to protect metadata from leaking. Take no solace from bar association pronouncements that using the other side's metadata would be unethical. Once the cat is out of the bag, there is no way to put it back in. The recent general history of bar ethics opinions in areas of developing technology that allows information to leak has been to engage in denial by pronouncing such leaks unusable for a period only to later acknowledge a duty on the part of the attorney to maintain confidentiality. Examples include faxes, cell phones, and e-mail. Be ahead of the curve, protect and strip your metadata now, whether you are required to or not.

C. Do Not Take Solace in Privileges

The evidence codes of various jurisdictions feature privilege rules covering the attorney-client privilege, the work-product privilege, and the like. This is not the place to review their substance, which varies from jurisdiction to jurisdiction, except to note that they are subject to many exceptions—*e.g.* allegations of crime or fraud—and are generally waivable by the client—*i.e.*, the one that may be claiming the advice-of-counsel defense to charges of wrongdoing at a future date.

These privileges are far more brittle and scant than your typical evidence or civil procedure course would suggest. The best advice is not to rely upon these privileges to prevent use of items for the record. If the privilege applies, that is convenient in terms of narrowing the scope of issues and evidence at issue in a dispute, but that is all. The potential record should contain nothing that would need to be kept out should a dispute arise. Do nothing to potentially create a record that you or your client cannot stand upon without needing to depend upon privileges

Checkpoints

- All legal drafting is drafting for the record — creating a history that can be pointed to and relied upon to justify future actions and decisions.
- Legal drafters are well served by keeping in mind that everything they draft will be part of the record and may be used in proceedings far removed from the activities for which the document is originally prepared. Thus:

  o Be explicit.

  o Watch your use of adjectives and adverbs;

  o Be as complete as needed to serve your interests and act within the scope of your professional responsibilities;

  o Use restraint in characterizations, superlatives, insults, and uncivil communication, among other things.
- Metadata — those comments and records of inserts, deletions, and edits to a document that are retained by word processing programs — is also part of the record, if you let it slip out with your work product. Understand and be prepared to scrub your documents clean of in-house information before sending them out into the world.
- Do not take solace in the attorney-client or work product privilege. Both are easily waived, especially by the client, especially in this age of rapid fire, informal, electronic communication. Aim to produce a record that you and your client can stand on even if all privileges are stripped and all documents are produced for examination.

Mastering Legal Analysis and Drafting Master Checkpoints

Legal Analysis

- ❏ Legal analysis is a process that entails a combination of isolating and examining individual components of the law, and fitting them together and explaining them as a cohesive whole.
- ❏ A law can be a statement of:
  - o What is required in particular circumstances;
  - o What is permitted in particular circumstances;
  - o What is forbidden in particular circumstances;
  - o What legally results in particular circumstances;
  - o What is considered in determining if a result occurs or whether a law applies.
- ❏ Statements of law may involve:
  - o Elements — things that are required in order for a result to occur, and/or
  - o Factors — things that are considered when deciding whether a result occurs.
- ❏ Statutes are the primary source of law today. Tools for analyzing and interpreting statutes include: tabulation; the statute's context within a larger statutory scheme; case law analysis; the plain meaning rule; legislative history; similar statutes in the same or different jurisdictions; the canons of construction; and law review articles and scholarly commentary.
- ❏ While statutes are the primary source of the law, cases are the primary source of interpretation, explanation, application, and determination of the validity of the law. Read cases strategically, focusing on the issues you need to address and the law and facts that relate to them.

❑ In legal analysis you will need to distill the legal principles from multiple cases and explain what they are and how they relate to each other, and apply those principles to the facts of your client's situation and predict or advocate the outcome.

❑ Organize and present you legal analysis using the IRAC (Issue, Rule/Law, Application/Analysis, Conclusion) or CRAC (Conclusion, Rule/Law, Application/Analysis, Conclusion) formats. These formats organize and deliver information in a way that is thorough, comprehensive, and easy for the reader to understand.

Legal Drafting, Generally

❑ The key to good legal drafting is ensuring that the audience can easily understand and follow it. The three key strategies to organizing legal drafting are:

- o establish the context before discussing the details;
- o place familiar information before new information and show how new information emerges from or relates to familiar information;
- o make the structure explicit.

❑ The well-written and organized paragraph is the building block of all good writing, legal or otherwise. Paragraphs have three essential requirements:

- o Paragraphs begin with a topic or transitional sentence that identifies the point, main idea or subject of the paragraph.
- o Every sentence in the paragraph must relate to the topic or transitional sentence.
- o Every sentence in the paragraph must relate to the sentences around it. This is accomplished by arranging the sentences in a logical sequence, and by using transition words that signal how the sentences relate, e.g., similarly, moreover, however.

❑ Sentences in legal drafting should be clear, direct, and concise, and quick and easy to understand. Some tools for accomplishing this:

- o Make the subject concrete and put the action in the predicate. Where possible, always make your subject a person or entity that can act rather than a concept.
- o Stamp out narration—eliminate words or sentences that narrate the process of your analysis, *e.g.*, "Guidance is found in several cases."

- o Avoid nominalizations—unbury your verbs, *e.g.*, write "We represented Ms. Jones" rather than "We provided representation to Ms. Jones."
- o Use plain language—avoid legalese and words that might not be quickly and easily understood by the average reader.
- o Use fewer words—no more than necessary to clearly and accurately deliver the information or convey your point.
- o Avoid intrusive phrases or clauses—do not interrupt the main point of your sentences. Subjects should go close to verbs and verbs close to objects.
- o Chose the right word—the one that is correct and most accurate.
- o Put yourself in the position of the distracted, unfamiliar reader and check if any of your sentences are too long or not easy to follow. Ideally sentences should be between three quarters of a line and two and a half lines.
- o Use the past tense for events that have already occurred.
- o Keep it as simple as possible.

❑ Legal drafting is a multi step process involving:

- o Organizing your materials into an outline.
- o Writing the first draft.
- o Revising and rewriting.
- o Editing.
- o Proofreading.

Citation and Quotation

❑ Citations in legal documents are used to identify and attribute all the sources used by drafters in preparing the document and to show readers where to find those sources.

❑ Quotations are used when communicating the exact words of the original source. These words should be accompanied by a citation. Quotations should be used sparingly.

❑ Citations to legal authority are used to support all statements, explanations, and illustrations of the law and to identify the sources from which they come so that readers can look up those sources for themselves.

- ❑ Citations to factual authority—documents and evidence in the record or attached as exhibits—are used to support statements of procedural history and statements of fact in MPAs, trial briefs, and appellate briefs.
- ❑ Whenever you use a source's exact words you must put quotation marks around those words.
- ❑ Your legal drafting and analysis will be judged in part by the quality and correctness of your citation form.

Letters

- ❑ Letters are used in the legal profession to inform, persuade, create a legal consequence, or to make a request or demand.
- ❑ Keep in mind that letters are not just intended for their recipients to read; they may become exhibits to later motions or briefs.
- ❑ Confirming letters confirm an event, appointment, agreement, and the like. They should be as concise and accurate as possible, sticking to the facts.
- ❑ A demand letter is sent to the opposing counsel or party, and requests or demands that the recipient do or stop doing something. Its purpose may be to persuade or to make a record, or both.
- ❑ A transmittal or enclosure letter is used when sending a document or series of documents to the recipient. Its main purpose is to explain what those documents are. The biggest risk with transmittal letters is giving them short shrift.

Research Memoranda

- ❑ Research memoranda are used to make a record of your legal reasoning and predictions and to show that they are well supported by research and analysis. The goals in drafting a research memo are to:
    - o solve a problem,
    - o be thorough, and
    - o be concise.
- ❑ The basic formats for traditional office memoranda include (1) an introduction—either questions presented and short answers, or an executive summary, (2) a statement of facts, (3) discussion section containing law and analysis (application of the law to the facts), and (4) a conclusion.

❑ Each issue and sub-issue in the memo is addressed using the IRAC format.

I: Identify the issue or sub-issue in a point heading

R: Then set out, explain and illustrate the applicable laws/rules (favorable and not), going from broad to narrow, general to specific. Provide pin citations to supporting legal authority for each law, each explanation, and each illustration.

A: Begin each application/analysis section with a topic sentence containing your overall conclusion on the issue or sub-issue, with a pin cite to legal authority supporting it.

❑ Then tell why and show how that you conclusion is sounds and well supported:

o Tell by making assertions, supported by legal authority, that the client's facts meet or fail to meet the various rules, tests, standards, requirements set forth in the rule/law section, or by making assertions supported by legal authority, that relevant factors are or are not present in your client's facts.

o Show by comparing and/or contrasting the facts of your client's case with the facts of cases used in the rule/law section.

o Assess both the strengths and weaknesses of the client's case, either in the main application/analysis or through assessing counter arguments.

C: A separate conclusion after the application may be necessary if the analysis is complex, close, or contains several counter arguments. Otherwise, you may omit it because the topic sentence of the application section contains your conclusion on the issue of sub-issue.

MPAs and Trial Briefs

❑ The purpose of an MPA or trial brief is to persuade the court to take or not take the action requested. The audience is a judge, law clerk, or court attorney. One thing they all have in common: a heavy work load—a large number of cases, only one of which is yours. Make the court want to rule in your favor and make it easy for the court to do so.

❑ You must first know exactly what relief you are seeking or opposing; drafting a proposed order is one way to accomplish this end.

❑ MPAs and briefs are comprised of a caption, a preliminary statement, a statement of facts, a discussion or argument section, and a conclusion. Each portion has its distinct purpose.

❑ The preliminary statement sets the context and provides a road map for the MPA or brief. It is similar to an executive summary in an office memo, except that it advocates a position rather predicts a result.

❑ Drafting the statement of facts is a matter of accurate storytelling. Your goal is to tell a compelling, concise, and accurate story that will make the court want to rule your way and give it enough information to do so.

❑ The statement of facts develops and reinforces you message and sets up the analysis in the discussion section.

❑ The statement of facts must include all legally material facts, both favorable and unfavorable.

❑ Emphasize favorable facts by:

- o placing them at the beginning of a section, paragraph or sentence, or at the end of these with a solid build up, and
- o describing them using the active voice, concrete subjects, and active predicates.

❑ Minimize unfavorable facts by:

- o placing them at the in the middle of the narrative or the middle of paragraphs and sentences, and
- o describing them in words that are bland and general—as long as they are accurate.

❑ The statement of facts should be free of conclusions and argument, and must contain any fact referred to in the discussion section.

❑ Any fact set out in the statement of facts must be accompanied by a citation to the trial court record or to an attached exhibit.

❑ The purpose of the discussion or argument section in a MPA or trial brief is to persuade the court to rule your way. Think of this section as one of "discussion" rather than "argument"—that implies that you are explaining the state of the law as it is, versus arguing your version of it. You should be showing the court how to rule in your favor and why it should so.

❑ Every independent ground on which you base your request becomes a main section in the discussion. Ideally the section with the strongest most persuasive points and arguments goes first, the next strongest second, and so on.

❑ In drafting the discussion section of an MPA or trial brief, remember to:

o Keep it simple, and

o Stick to your theory, theme or pitch—the essential message you want to deliver.

❑ The discussion section is composed of CRACs (Conclusion, Rule/Law, Application/Analysis, Conclusion). Each main argument without subsections is addressed using a CRAC, and each subsection within a main argument gets its own CRAC.

❑ The conclusion section of an MPA or brief in the trial court is a simple, short restatement of what you are asking the court to do. Typically one does not restate the reasons for doing so in any degree of detail.

Appellate Briefs

❑ The purpose of an appellate brief is to persuade a court to reverse or affirm a judgment or order below. An appellate brief should not attempt to retry the case below.

❑ The audience for the appellate brief will be an intermediate appellate court or a court of last resort. Both these courts include more than one decision maker (judges or justices) and you will need to persuade a majority of them to reverse or affirm.

❑ An appellate brief should show:

o that there was or was not error below—that the decision below was incorrect or correct under the applicable standard of review; and

o that the error requires reversal because the error was not harmless or does not require reversal because the error was or was not harmless error.

❑ An overarching goal in drafting an appellate brief is for the court to adopt it in large part as the court's opinion.

❑ The standard of review is the filter through which the decision below is evaluated.

❑ The four basic standard of review are:

o De Novo (the decision below must merely be wrong).

o Clearly Erroneous (the decision below must very wrong).

o Substantial Evidence (the decision below must very wrong).

o Abuse of Discretion (the decision below must very, very wrong).

❑ If the applicable standard of review is not satisfied, the decision or action below will be upheld.

❑ If the appellant successfully convinces the court there was error below, the court then determines if the error requires reversal of the judgment or order below. This is the harmless error analysis.

❑ An appellate brief is comprised of separate components, usually prescribed by local rules of procedure. Typical components include a statement of issues on appeal; tables of contents and authorities; statement of the case; statement of facts; summary of the argument; discussion or argument with headings and subheadings; and a conclusion.

❑ The statement of issues on appeal should specifically identify the alleged error(s) or lack of error(s) below. We recommend using the whether/when format.

❑ The statement of the case should set out the nature of the case, the relevant procedural history of the case and should also contain the essential reasons why the decisions below should be reversed or affirmed. The statement of the case is the drafter's first opportunity to deliver their message. Accurate citations to the record for each fact or document are essential.

❑ The statement of facts should tell an accurate story that will make the court want to adopt your legal positions and that gives it enough information to be able to do so.

❑ The purpose of the discussion or argument section is to show the court how to rule in your client's favor and why it should do so. This involves making your points as clearly as possible, which usually means organizing complex information so that readers can understand it as easily as possible. Envision the opinion you would like the court to issue and draft it like that.

❑ Persuading the appellate court involves showing that your positions are (1) sound and well supported by authority, and (2) the better choice.

❑ Showing the court that your arguments are sound and well supported requires thorough and sophisticated knowledge of the law and authorities and how they affect the facts in the record.

❑ Showing that your positions and arguments are the better choice involves:

  o exposing and exploiting the weaknesses of the other side's arguments, and

  o using policy arguments.

❑ Policy arguments are concrete but larger reasons why the court should adopt a tenable legal position. They show the court that your position advances a particular goal and/or the other side's position will undermine this goal or cause harm.

❑ Each separate issue on appeal becomes a main section in the discussion section of both the appellant's and the appellee's brief. Often the issue of whether the error is reversible or harmless is addressed in its own section at the end of the brief.

❑ The discussion section should begin with any threshold issues, *e.g.*, standing to sue or appeal or whether there is appellate jurisdiction.

❑ After any threshold issue, the discussion section usually begins with the drafter's strongest argument for reversing or affirming the decision below, and so on.

❑ The structure of the discussion section is based on the CRAC (Conclusion, Rule/Law, Application/Analysis, Conclusion) format and is comprised of a series of CRACs. With some issues on appeal the focus will be on the rule/law portion, *e.g.*, if the issue is which law applies, or whether a particular law is valid. On the other hand, other issues on appeal may be factually intensive, such as whether a factual finding is clearly erroneous.

❑ Make time to print and proofread your appellate brief separately before filing it or turning it in.

Transactional Documents

❑ Transactional documents create a record of the parties' deal and simultaneously create mechanisms to foster agreement, encourage performance, and provide for enforcement and dispute resolution.

❑ Transactional documents have a distinct structure like other forms of legal drafting, and that structure should be followed and employed to produce practical, precise contracts and instruments.

❑ The same organizational rules that apply to other forms of legal drafting apply with equal force to transactional documents. Including:

- o place general provisions before specific ones;
- o place important provisions before lesser ones;
- o state rules before exceptions;
- o use separate sections/subsections for each concept; and
- o include meaningful headings for each section.

❑ Contractual precision requires accuracy, completeness, and exactitude.

❑ Exactitude, which refers to an absence of ambiguity and unintentional vagueness.

❑ Ambiguity occurs when a word or phrase is capable of more than one specific meaning.

❑ Vagueness is the lack of clarity—where the specific meaning is unclear.

❑ Vagueness is often used in transactional documents when the parties are unable to agree on a provision governing what is thought to be a rare or unexpected event.

❑ Vagueness should not be used unintentionally or inadvertently.

❑ Much can be accomplished in producing practical, precise documents by focusing on using the active voice and uniformly using the word "shall" for duties and "may" for rights and privileges.

❑ Transactional documents generally contain these components:

- o Title;
- o Introductory paragraph;
- o Recitals;

- o Definitions;
- o Core provisions—Consideration, Covenants, Conditions;
- o Risk allocations—Representations and Warranties;
- o Closing provisions;
- o Events of default and remedies;
- o Boilerplate;
- o Signature blocks;
- o Exhibits and attachments.

❑ Most problems in transactional documents can be traced to

- o blurring distinctions between types or contract provisions and using the wrong one for the purpose to be achieved;
- o provisions that attempt to accomplish too much;
- o word choice and punctuation problems.

Legislation and Regulations

❑ Drafting legislation is similar to drafting contracts and transactional documents, but the audience is broader because legislation defines the relationship between the government and the governed, versus the parties to the agreement.

❑ The suggested format for legislation, based on the federal model, is to divide bills and codes into titles, chapters, subchapters, then sections, subsections or paragraphs, clauses, and sub-clauses.

❑ Legislation generally may contain:

- o a heading;
- o a title;
- o an enacting clause;
- o a short title;
- o a statement of purpose or findings;
- o definitions;
- o substantive provisions;

- o enforcement provisions;
- o amending provisions;
- o savings clauses;
- o transitional provisions;
- o an effective date; and
- o a severability or nonseverability clause.

❑ Many of the organizational rules and guidelines applicable to transactional documents apply to legislation, including: general provisions before specific ones; important, central provisions before others; rules before exceptions; what before how; separate provisions for substance and enforcement; and technical, housekeeping and enforcement provisions and the end of the bill.

Writing for the Record

❑ All legal drafting is drafting for the record—creating a history that can be pointed to and relied upon to justify future actions and decisions.

❑ Legal drafters are well served by keeping in mind that everything they draft will be part of the record and may be used in proceedings far removed from the activities for which the document is originally prepared. Thus:

- o Be explicit.
- o Watch your use of adjectives and adverbs;
- o Be as complete as needed to serve your interests and act within the scope of your professional responsibilities;
- o Use restraint in characterizations, superlatives, insults, and uncivil communication, among other things.

Index